£3-

£e

,2| 50

CRAFTING COMPETITIVENESS

CRAFTING COMPETITIVENESS

Developing Leaders in the Shadow Pyramid

Albert A. Vicere
Associate Dean for Executive Education and
Professor of Business Administration
The Pennsylvania State University

Robert M. Fulmer
W. Brook George Professor of Business Administration
College of William & Mary

CAPSTONE

First published 1996
Reprinted 1997
Capstone Publishing Limited
Oxford Centre for Innovation
Mill Street
Oxford OX2 0JX
United Kingdom

British Library Cataloguing in Publication Data
A CIP catalogue record for this book is available from the British Library

ISBN 1-900961 03-2

Typeset in 11/14 Plantin by
Archetype, Stow-on-the-Wold
Printed and bound by
T.J. Press Ltd, Padstow, Cornwall

This book is printed on acid-free paper

In recognition of their tremendous inspiration,
not to mention their incredible patience,
this book is dedicated to

Nancy, Jana, and Marisa Vicere

and

Pat Fulmer and our children

That's a brilliant idea. But how could it possibly work in my organization?

How often do you think as you read a business book that if only you could ask the author a simple question you could transform your organization?

Capstone is creating a unique partnership between authors and readers, delivering for the first time in business book publishing a genuine after-sales service for book buyers. Simply visit Capstone's home page on **http://www.bookshop.co.uk/capstone/** to leave your question (with details of date and place of purchase of a copy of *Crafting Competitiveness*) and Al Vicere and Bob Fulmer will try to answer it. The authors travel and consult extensively so we do not promise 24-hour turnaround. But that one question answered might just jump start your company and your career.

Capstone is more than a publisher. It is an electronic clearing house for pioneering business thinking, putting the creators of new business ideas in touch with the people who use them.

CONTENTS

EXECUTIVE SUMMARY

Blend globalization, change and opportunity with leadership and learning, and what do you get? Our research demonstrates emphatically that the answer is *competitive advantage*. And in this book we describe how benchmark companies are addressing the challenge of crafting competitive advantage through investment in strategic leadership development.

We believe that this book is essential reading for any executive who is concerned with the future development of his or her organization. Through models, frameworks, assessments and a multitude of examples, we provide a powerful framework for designing leadership development processes that *make a significant difference to both individual and organizational performance*. The result is a compelling and provocative picture of the current state of leadership and its likely future direction. Trends and issues we discuss are:

- Corporations are turning "internal" to meet their future leadership development needs. *But do they know what action is needed and do they have the ability to deliver that action effectively and quickly?*
- Corporations are sure that courses on change management, leadership and process and performance management are needed *now* to help them adjust to the demands of a changing world. *But do they know what their leadership development needs will be in the future?*
- Universities are being asked to use their research to help organizations define and address emerging opportunities. *But how will they respond to the fact that the demand is less for basic*

research and more for outcome-oriented applications – for processes that drive change and transformation?

- Consulting firms are demonstrating that they too have the ability to do research and help clients create their future. *But how will they fare in this extremely competitive environment?*
- Corporations increasingly demand education that is tied to the work environment and they are growing more and more convinced that the action learning model is a powerful framework for leveraging investments in executive education and leadership development. *But how will they deal with the danger that leadership development can become too insular if focused only within one particular organization and only on its current competitive environment?*
- Key supply/demand partnerships are being established among users and providers of executive education. *But who will be the winners and losers if competitive advantage goes to those providers willing and able to develop innovative relationships?*

We attempt to answer these questions by profiling the strategic context for leadership development and by showing organizations how to

- design world-class leadership development initiatives
- assess development methodologies
- select effective providers, and
- assess the impact of leadership development programs.

Our models, examples, advice and analysis provide perspectives and tools to help organizations meet the challenge of crafting competitiveness through strategic leadership development.

PREFACE

In today's changing environment, traditional processes for educating and developing leadership talent are in a state of flux – so much so, that a new vocabulary is emerging. There is little interest in the old mainstay *management development*. Managers today are often viewed as bureaucrats whose major function is to create complexity and promote the status quo. *Executive education* is a more desirable term, but in today's flatter, more networked organizations, there is less demand for executives, who are often seen as aloof and removed from the realities of the competitive marketplace. Even the word "education" seems to connote the esoteric contemplation of academic issues, a process at odds with the fast pace of today's business environment. The new imperative is *leadership development*, capitalizing on processes for identifying and developing exceptional people capable of moving organizations into the 21st century.

Although developing tomorrow's leaders is a critical concern for most organizations, equally important is the need to create new structures and processes that will enable the organization to compete effectively in a fast-paced global economy. Rather than viewing these two concerns as separate challenges, benchmark organizations from around the world have begun to combine them in an expanded developmental focus we call *strategic leadership development*. This focus blends traditional executive education activities with management, leadership, and organizational development techniques to create hands-on, real-time "learning laboratories" within organizations that facilitate continuous learning, continuous knowledge creation, and organizational competitiveness.

This book focuses on the challenge of strategic leadership development – what it is, how it has and is evolving, and how it is being addressed through both traditional techniques and methodologies as well as emerging practices that are revolutionizing traditional views of executive education/leadership development.

The ideas discussed in this book are based on our years of experience as consultants, professors, executive educators, and, in Bob's case, corporate HRD executive. Many of the examples reflect our first-hand experiences with consulting clients. But we have not relied on personal experiences alone. Throughout our careers, we have conducted extensive research on executive learning and leadership development. In addition, we recently completed a ten-year trend study of the field,[1] and an additional comprehensive study that included a thorough review of the literature on executive education and leadership development along with the collection of interview or survey data from 78 executives from 47 companies, 48 consultants, and 52 university leaders from 35 business schools throughout the world.[2] We have drawn from all of this information and experience to create the perspectives outlined in this book.

Setting the Stage

We have observed that, for years, executive education/leadership development was a *Field of Dreams* – if you built a program, participants would come.[3] During that time, university business schools seemingly had a lock on the leading-edge thinking in just about every field a business person needed to understand. As a result, business schools owned the market. Now corporate sponsors look at executive education/leadership development initiatives as much as tools for strategic organizational development as tools for individual development. This shift in perspectives has created a wave of change in the competitive dynamics of the field, change that has put university business schools on the defensive and has opened the door to a myriad of alternative providers including corporate "customers" themselves. All of these providers are in search of better, more powerful ways to use leadership development as a tool to craft competitiveness in a changing world.

We have written this book to challenge both suppliers and consumers of leadership development initiatives to rethink their approaches to the process. We blend practical theory with an abundance of relevant models and detailed examples to provide a thorough, and hopefully insightful, perspective on the field. That perspective is based on our observation of a number of general trends that we believe are changing the very nature of the field. Some of these trends are listed below.

- Corporations today are increasingly interested in leadership development experiences that are linked to experience and the work environment. They are growing more convinced that the action learning model, described later in this book, is a powerful framework both for leveraging investment in leadership development and for establishing methods for calculating a return on that investment. Yet, there is a danger that leadership development processes could become very limiting if focused only on a single organization and only on that organization's current business challenges.

- Corporations today seem to prefer custom, or at least customized, leadership development programs to help them adapt to a changing marketplace as opposed to traditional open-enrollment programs and seminars. However, they often are not sure what type of experience they need and they often question their ability to internally develop and deliver those experiences in an effective, timely manner. The demand for process consulting services from the top providers of leadership development is growing, creating new opportunities for providers willing to share both their content expertise and their process expertise with the corporate community.

- The operative word in leadership development today is *partnering* – partnering with corporate sponsors to develop process and content solutions, and partnering with providers to help meet aggressive delivery schedules and volumes. As within the business environment in general, partnerships and alliances seem to be a key to the future development of the field. Competitive advantage will go to those organizations that are willing and able

to develop innovative partnerships among both providers and
users.

- Universities can utilize their research capabilities to help organizations define and address future strategies for executive/leader-
ship development. In fact, many corporations are actively
requesting this kind of assistance. The dramatic growth of
corporate/university research consortia in recent years suggests
that universities may be slowly learning to blend academic
interests in basic research with corporate needs for rapid
research-based solutions to real-world problems. These consortia are benchmark examples of educational partnerships in
leadership development. At the same time, consulting firms have
learned that there is a huge market for applied research in the
field, and have begun to respond with their own research
initiatives, consortia, and publications, challenging the traditional knowledge-creation role of universities.

- As they explore new developmental techniques and new relationships with providers to address overwhelming demands for
change and restructuring, corporations must not forget the need
to continuously build their talent pool of high-potential key
managers. In the same vein, they must be sure leadership
development initiatives are tightly linked to human resource
management practices like selection, appraisal, and compensation if they are to leverage their investment in leadership
development and facilitate organizational change. They must
continue the search for best practices and innovative techniques.
And, they must find ways to measure the impact of executive
education and leadership development initiatives – both from an
organizational and an individual perspective.

- Finally, all of these changes and more seem to be occurring in
an environment where the demand for strategic leadership
development is expanding at a dramatic rate. We believe that
demand will continue to grow, but it will be less for traditional
programs and more for a new type of *process*. This process will
be much more focused on the marketplace, driven by applied
research, rooted in partnerships, and measured by contributions
to the growth and success of corporate sponsors and individual
participants. These new processes are the foundation for what

we describe throughout this book as a new paradigm for strategic leadership development. This "new paradigm" presents significant challenges to organizations, but offers enormous opportunity as well.

Organization of the Book

Our objective in writing this book was to prepare both a solid conceptual analysis of the field, as well as a handbook for operating effectively within it. We begin with an introduction to give an overview of the context for strategic leadership development. In it we discuss several critical ideas that are fundamental to our thinking, including the nature of strategic leadership and the concept of a learning organization. These two ideas are then combined to present a basic model of a "new paradigm" for strategic leadership development – the way benchmark organizations are using leadership development techniques to facilitate both individual growth and organizational competitiveness. This introduction draws on our detailed investigation of the state-of-the-practice of executive education/leadership development which is reproduced in the Appendix. Our analysis, based on comprehensive research findings, portrays a field in the process of fundamental change. This sets the stage for our discussion. The book is then divided into three sections.

Assessing the challenge of strategic leadership development is the focus of the three chapters that make up Section I. In Chapter 1, we expand our discussion of the new paradigm for executive education and leadership development, tracing its evolution from the exclusive, individualistic process still in place in many organizations, to a more vibrant, flexible, learning-oriented process being used by benchmark organizations to lead fundamental change and craft organizational competitiveness. In Chapter 2, we relate leadership development to organizational life-cycles. In the process, we describe how strategic leadership development can and does contribute to the ongoing revitalization of a firm. The examination of a new strategic context for leadership development is the focus of Chapter 3. In that chapter, we discuss the nature of current restructuring efforts and the role strategic leadership development can play in facilitating change and enhancing organizational performance.

While the three chapters comprising Section I outline the *challenge* of strategic leadership development, the five chapters of Section II outline the *process* in some detail. A description of that process from a systems perspective is the focus of Chapter 4. In it, we create a systems model for strategic leadership development, and present a framework for crafting strategic leadership development initiatives from a systems perspective. The methods and techniques for strategic leadership development are examined in Chapter 5. Several frameworks are introduced to help readers select from among the many options available to design and deliver the most powerful initiatives. Chapter 6 addresses the question of internal vs. external executive education and leadership development programs. Through case study analyses of university-based general management and company-specific programs, we attempt to define the strengths and weaknesses of each approach and guidelines for their use. Processes for selecting and managing providers for executive education and leadership development are presented in Chapter 7, along with a discussion of the potential future role of universities in the field. The always challenging subject of evaluation is addressed in Chapter 8. Techniques are presented for ensuring the integrity of executive education and leadership development initiatives, as well as the generation of adequate returns on corporate investments in those activities.

The third and final section of the book is devoted to a discussion of the future. In Chapter 9, we present five examples of new paradigm approaches to strategic leadership development and an opportunity for organizations to benchmark against them. In Chapter 10, we summarize the book through a framework we call the *Seven Ps,* the seven core elements of strategic leadership development. We discuss their evolution over time and, based on the ideas described throughout the book, present our predictions of where they are heading in the future. We close with a checklist for ensuring the future effectiveness of strategic leadership development initiatives in your own organization.

Acknowledgements

There are many people who have helped make this book possible. First, we want to thank the many companies that have given us an opportunity to work with them and study their processes, especially Allied-Signal, Allstate Insurance, the American Red Cross, ARAMARK, AT&T, Bertelsmann Entertainment Group, British Petroleum, Carpenter Technology, Conrail, Daimler-Benz, General Electric, Hoechst Celanese, IBM, Johnson & Johnson, Motorola, and Westinghouse.

We also wish to thank a number of other organizations for sharing their ideas and experiences with us, especially the Business Consortium® (Miami University and the University of Cincinnati), the Center for Creative Leadership, the Center for Executive Development, the Columbia University Office of Executive Education, Indiana University, the International Consortium for Executive Development Research, UNICON – the International University Consortium for Executive Education, Kielty Goldsmith & Co., the MIT Center for Organizational Learning, the MIT Office of Executive Education, Penn State Executive Programs, the Penn State Institute for the Study of Organizational Effectiveness, and the Smeal College of Business at Penn State.

A number of individual colleagues also contributed greatly to our work. Although we could list dozens of names, we would like to especially acknowledge Gini Freeman Tucker, Maria Taylor, and Joe Cavinato at Penn State; Victoria Guthrie at the Center For Creative Leadership; Bernie Wetzel at Westinghouse; Keizo Kawata at Fujitsu; Doug Ready at the International Consortium For Executive Development Research; Ken Graham at the University of Texas; Don Kuhn at UNICON; Roger Fine, Al Anderson, Jerry Kells, Myron Goff and Inaki Bastarrika at Johnson & Johnson; Garland Bolejack, Anita Schendelman and Ron Meeks at Hoechst Celanese; Joe Isenstein at Bertelsmann Entertainment Group; Dan Burnham, Ron McGurn and Don Redlinger at Allied-Signal; Roberto Artavis and Edwardo Montiel of INCAE; Dean William E. Fulmer at George Mason University; Val Markos of BellSouth Corp.; Maurice Saias of Institut D'Administration des Enterprises Aix-en-Provence; Jay Lorsch, Leonard Schlesinger, Chris Argyris, Earl Sasser and John Kotter at the Harvard Business School; Kirby Warren and Maryann Hedda at Columbia University; Deepack "Dick" Sethi at AT&T; and Jack Goodwin at the University of Richmond.

Finally, we want to thank Debby Bennett for coordinating the production of the manuscript and Beckie Pasipanski for keeping the process moving. We couldn't have done it without them.

Endnotes

1   Vicere, A.A., M. Taylor, and V. Freeman, "Executive Education in Major Corporations: A Ten-Year Study." *Journal of Management Development*, **13** (1), 1994, pp. 4–22.

2   Fulmer, R.M. and Vicere, A.A., *Executive Education and Leadership Development: The State of the Practice*, Penn State, PA: Penn State Institute for the Study of Organizational Effectiveness, March 1995.

3   Vicere, A.A., "The Market for University-Based Executive Education Programs," *Executive Directions*, **2** (1) Jan./Feb. 1995.

INTRODUCTION

A NEW WORLD FOR STRATEGIC
LEADERSHIP DEVELOPMENT

Imagine you are gazing into a crystal ball. The blurred image gives you a hazy profile of the 21st-century leader – the characteristics, attitudes, perspectives and skills that will ensure top management effectiveness in the years ahead. Such insight would be invaluable, wouldn't it? We believe you can develop this profile right now, not by gazing into a crystal ball but by observing the changes and developments taking place in the business environment. If you look hard enough, and if you're open and honest enough to acknowledge the trends, an exciting new world of strategic leadership development awaits you.[1]

The concept of a new world is a very appropriate analogy for our discussion of strategic leadership development. Just as great explorers like Magellan and Columbus set out on journeys through uncharted waters, so too are leading-edge leadership development strategists embarking upon a challenging, uncharted journey into the future. There are lessons we can learn from the great explorers. You will recall Columbus set out to find an alternative route to distant but familiar lands where untold opportunities awaited him. What he found, however, was something far more profound. He actually stumbled upon a "New World," one that would reshape virtually every existing aspect of society, culture and knowledge – an *unexpected* source of untold opportunity.

Interestingly, Columbus embarked on his voyage amidst dire warnings that his objective was unreasonable and perhaps even insane. The conventional wisdom of the day was summarized in a quote from the Talevera Commission in 1491: "The mission Columbus has proposed is folly. Among the many reasons that might be cited as to the folly of his enterprise is the well known fact that the Atlantic Ocean is infinite and therefore impossible to traverse."[2] While some may wish that King Ferdinand and Queen Isabella had listened to their advisors, all would admit that the vision exhibited by Columbus literally changed the world.

What can we learn from Columbus' experiences? Perhaps most importantly, that the objective of developing strategic leaders may be our goal, but our pathway to achieving that goal is taking us through the uncharted and probably stormy waters of the future. The traditional leadership development objectives of identifying potential, appraising effectiveness, and developing competencies are still appropriate and achievable, but will most likely be met through the discovery of a "new world" of techniques and processes that are developing. This book is intended to help you identify some of those changes, and to guide you on your journey through the new world of strategic leadership development.

What Is Strategic Leadership?

Just about everyone agrees that strategic leadership is related to "vision." However, very few experts have provided a tangible definition of just what it really means. Some time ago, one of us heard a terrific definition of vision from James Ross, formerly CEO of Cable & Wireless in the UK: "Seeing is auditing life. Vision is interpreting life so that others may see it." Given that definition, we can address the nature of strategic leadership.

Let's go back to our New World analogy. As the chief executive of the voyage, Columbus had a vision; that of finding a new, possibly faster and more economical course to familiar lands. He had a global perspective, one that said the world was round, the ocean navigable, and that opportunity awaited the adventurous person who sailed to the west. He made use of the leading technology of the day, primitive as it now seems, and he built alliances with governments, business people, and crew members to stake his venture. Having made all the seemingly correct moves, Columbus set out on his voyage. He didn't sail the ships, his crew did, but Columbus kept them focused and directed. He also kept watch on the horizon, searching for opportunities but staying his course. When the course seemed to be taking his crew nowhere, he kept them from jumping ship. And when the horizon finally became clear, he directed the ships to a landing.

This is where vision came into play. We are sure it didn't take too long for Columbus to figure out that he had landed in the wrong place. He had a great plan and the plan took him somewhere, but it wasn't where he wanted to go. However, Columbus still saw opportunity and he convinced his crew, his sponsors, and eventually even many of our ancestors that the New World had untold possibilities.

We believe that above all else, like Columbus, strategic leaders must have an acute sense of vision – an ability to set broad, lofty goals and steer a course toward them, but with the insight and flexibility to adjust both the course and the goals as the horizon becomes clearer. They must be able to communicate the goals and the course to well-educated, technically skilled colleagues on whose skill achieving the goals depends. And, they must develop the internal and external alliances and supporting communication and reward structures that will ensure the appropriate resources are brought to bear on achieving the organization's strategic objective.

The moment you step from independence to interdependence, you step into a leadership role

Stephen Covey

As companies struggle to maintain focus in today's tempestuous business environment, greater attention is being given to strategic leadership development as a tool for promoting organizational change and transformation. The benchmark companies mentioned throughout this book have for some time realized the potential of strategic leadership development as a tool for crafting competitive advantage. They have helped establish a new form of leadership development that is focused not only on individual development but also on the overall competitiveness and strategic effectiveness of a firm. This new vision for strategic

4 • Crafting Competitiveness

leadership development is rooted in the framework for creating a *learning organization*, an organization that is able to channel the energy of environmental change into a force for organizational growth and development.[3]

The Tool Kit of a Learning Organization[4]

A central idea for a learning organization is the distinction between "single-loop" and "double-loop" learning, as defined by Chris Argyris and Donald Schon. According to their thesis, when organizational learning involves detecting and correcting "errors" (performance gaps) in a way that means an "organization [can] carry on its present policies or achieve its present policies or achieve its present objectives, then that error-detection-and-correction process is single-loop learning . . . Double-loop learning occurs when error is detected and corrected in ways that involve the modification of an organization's underlying norms, policies, and objectives."[5]

In a manufacturing company, for example, changes in business conditions lead to adjustments in production rates, changes in material orders, and the hiring and firing of workers. This constant learning that occurs within an organization is what Argyris and Schon would call "single-loop learning." On the other hand, learning that leads to worthwhile changes in the organization of the manufacturing company and its ability to perceive its environment is double-loop learning. This approach to learning requires decision makers to challenge long-held assumptions and modes of operating. So, the manufacturing company in our example could decide that to deal with constantly fluctuating demand it might engage in strategic alliances, identify new geographic markets, or utilize new technology rather than simply react to customer orders. It is not until companies adopt such new ways of looking at their environment that they are likely to practice double-loop learning. We believe that effectively organized strategic leadership development efforts can help companies evolve toward this new way of thinking.

In addition to the single-loop/double-loop distinction, researchers have identified a number of theoretical categories of organizational learning. One of the following types of learning scenario is probably the norm at this time in your organization.[6]

1. Maintenance learning Maintenance learning discovers better ways of doing what a business already knows how to do. It encourages doing things the best way without asking whether they are the right things to do. It is single-loop learning. Maintenance learning quite often misses important clues about a changing environment or emerging challenges. The search for "best practices" is at the heart of maintenance learning in that it focuses on "catching up" with the best of contemporary practice. To the extent that it is committed to preserving the status quo, maintenance learning offers little challenge to an organization's existing strategy and operations. It is therefore likely to miss emerging business opportunities, even those that could leverage existing strategy. The implications of emerging environmental change, or even news that should set alarm bells ringing such as the appearance of new competitors or changes in customers' buying habits, are likely to be downplayed. The focus of maintenance learning is short term, so it is not surprising that crises eventually overtake organizations where it is the dominant learning focus.

When 200 executives, from 12 countries, were asked for examples of specific learning approaches used by their organizations, their responses provided us with the list of techniques in Figure I.1. From this list, it is clear that most organizational learning is maintenance in nature. As an exercise, you could use this exhibit as an audit of learning techniques used by your own organization, then turn to Figure I.4 at the end of this introduction and compare your answers with those of the members of the Presidents Association of the American Management Association.[7]

2. Shock learning In the event of a crisis, organizations undergo shock learning. At best, this is reactive. At worst, shock responses aggravate the problems they are attempting to solve. Learning that takes place under the stress of a crisis is unlikely to adequately address the long-term consequences of present actions. Some managers have made careers out of managing turnaround operations. They are able to quickly perceive opportunity and adopt a creative strategy to seize it. However, while individual crisis managers may understand the likely impact of their decisions, research has shown that under intense levels of stress most individuals fail to exercise creativity. Rather, they fall back on ways of doing business that have always worked in the past.[8]

Figure I.1 How Organizations Learn: Techniques

Technique	Type A/B/C/D	Extent of Use	Importance
Statistical process control			
Task forces			
Best practices/benchmarking			
Employee suggestion scheme			
Outside management develoment programs			
Joint venture/alliances			
Internal management development programs			
Customer surveys or interviews			
Total quality/Baldrige programs			
"Work-out programs" (participative efforts to streamline work flow)			
External advisory groups			
Self-directed work teams			
Process re-engineering			
Decentralized strategic planning process			
Transferring successes within the company			
Information technology (groupware, etc.)			
Delphi technique			
Scenarios			
Content analysis			
Impact analysis			

Key: A = low participation, present-oriented; B = high participation, present-oriented; C = low participation, future-oriented; D = high participation, future-oriented.
Rate each technique from 1 to 5: 1 = used little/not important; 5 = used widely/very important.

3. Anticipatory learning This type of learning addresses both the long-term consequences of present actions and the best ways to deal with a future environment. Effective anticipatory learning is:

- *Participatory* – Anticipatory learning is unlikely to take place when there is an assumption that one party or group has all the answers that they must then communicate to a less-informed constituency. Participatory learning demands that everyone in an organization be given an opportunity to analyze information, explore alternatives, and reach a true consensus on critical challenges.
- *Future oriented* – as this implies, anticipatory learning focuses on what is likely or possible in the future. It looks to where the action will be rather than where it was or is. It considers the possible future consequences of actions taken today. Future-oriented learning may also look backward from the anticipated future; exploring the actions required today and in the near term to reach an envisioned future.

How Organizations Really Learn

We have framed these three classifications into the following four learning modes or operating styles that organizations adopt over time (Figure I.2).

1. Because I Say So In an organization that operates in the *Because I Say So* learning mode, an authority figure orders something to be done (or avoided), and all managers and employees then take their cues from the authority figure's dictum. This is the essence of maintenance learning, and in many instances is highly appropriate. For example, when Ed Hennesey arrived to take over as CEO of Allied-Signal in 1980, his first impression was that the corporate staff was tremendously bloated. He told his subordinates that they had to cut $20 million from operating overhead within six months. It wasn't a debatable issue, and the organization accomplished the objective and learned from the process.

	Present focus	Future focus
High participation	**As You Like It** (High participation, present orientated)	**Inventing the Future** (High participation, future focused
Low participation	**Because I Say So** (Low participation, present orientated)	**Change Master** (Low participation, future focused)

Figure I.2 How Organizations Learn

2. As You Like It   This type of learning occurs when individuals and groups are left to their own devices to achieve pre-set targets or objectives. *As You Like It* learning can be observed in decentralized operations where performance is measured quarterly according to growth objectives, return on investment, or some other quantifiable measure. As long as operating executives meet their operating target, the way they get there is often left to the creativity of the executive team. Mike Dingman, who led the Signal companies into a merger with Allied and later coordinated the spin-off of more than 30 unrelated operating companies in the Henley Group, is viewed by Wall Street as a master of *As You like It* leadership. He managed to let his operating managers have their own way, yet he effectively coordinated their efforts into overall corporate growth.

3. Change Masters   Some CEOs lead their organizations by setting goals and demanding that managers learn the new ways of thinking and doing business needed to accomplish them. When Jack Welch became CEO of General Electric he insisted that every business be number one or number two in its market. If it wasn't, he expected the division to prepare a plan either to become the market leader or exit the business. Welch established the goal of having all businesses be market leaders without asking for widespread participation. The pursuit of his goal, however, instigated a wave of learning throughout GE. Such leaders (Rosabeth Moss Kanter calls them "change masters") achieve organizational renewal by articulating their vision of what needs to happen and communicating it effectively to people who are willing to learn how to make it happen.[9] These leaders tend to capture the energy of this willingness to learn through strategically focused leadership and organizational development initiatives.

4. Inventing the Future In the fourth mode, *Inventing the Future*, a group of motivated individuals work together, not just to forecast, but to create a future to which they can commit themselves.

> *I worry about the dangers of complacency and short-term thinking. I want our thinking to be focused on the challenge of creating our future.*
>
> Ralph Larsen, Chairman and CEO,
> Johnson & Johnson

In 1992, Ralph Larsen was planning a three-year executive learning effort for the top 700 executives at Johnson & Johnson, the world's largest healthcare company. Such change initiatives are often given an innovative name, and their theme is usually proclaimed in advance. Contrary to expectations, Larsen declined to articulate an agenda for this conference. Instead, he outlined the importance of thinking about the future along with the dangers of trading on past successes. He refused to give more specific directions for this strategic initiative and asked a steering committee of key executives to work for several months to come up with a plan. Their experiences were supplemented with information from interviews involving almost 100 of their colleagues.

The theme they arrived at was *Creating Our Future*, and the program that evolved from their work included electronic meetings (exercises that use computer software to enable every individual to participate in large group discussions), discussion of a company case "J&J 2002", and a comprehensive strategic exercise for creating a future which included Delphi forecasting along with content analysis and impact analysis. (This initiative is discussed in more detail in the Appendix.)

In talking with senior executives around the world we were struck by how few of the strategic leadership development initiatives they mentioned were anticipatory in nature. Rather than focusing on long-term issues, as did Johnson & Johnson, most companies target their leadership development initiatives at important, but short-term *maintenance learning* targets. The frameworks and techniques discussed in this book are intended to help organizations design strategic leadership development initiatives from an anticipatory perspective, as tools for building highly competitive learning organizations.

Charting a Course for the Future[10]

All members of your organization must develop an enhanced ability to learn from and through experiences, both their own and those of colleagues, customers and competitors, if you are to create a learning organization. Although far from a revolutionary notion, the growing emphasis on learning as a potential element of corporate competitiveness has provided the impetus for revolutionary changes in how organizations are managing and utilizing strategic leadership development initiatives to facilitate learning and to craft competitiveness. The core elements of these changes are shown in Figure I.3.

	Old	New
Who?	few	many–all
What?	check-marks	lifelong development
Where?	classroom	workplace, classroom, the world
When	infrequent	ongoing
How?	programs	process
Why?	rites of passage	competitiveness

Figure I.3 New Paradigm For Executive Development

Who? Traditionally, leadership development efforts were reserved for an elite few individuals who had been identified as having high potential for advancement within the organization. This process helped companies create a small pool of executives from which senior managers could be drawn. In contrast, strategic leadership development in learning organizations is all-inclusive, involving managers at all levels in the process of continuous learning and team development. Through these processes, organizations are kept vital, flexible, and open to opportunities in the competitive environment.

What? In the past, the leadership development process for most organizations consisted of a series of check-marks on a manager's file indicating that he or she had completed a predetermined rite of passage into the next level of management. Today, strategic leadership development is a process of lifelong learning for managers at all levels, involving training, education, experiential assignments, team building, and enculturation. These processes are designed not only to facilitate individual development, but also to help leaders to implement strategy cultivating managerial talents and organizational values essential to long-term competitive effectiveness.

Where? The main venue for traditional leadership development has been the classroom, where individual managers were exposed to issues and perspectives in general management. Today, the venues for strategic leadership development are still the classroom, but also the workplace and even the world. The action learning model of executive development, in which managers learn by doing, is moving to the forefront of leadership development, as companies attempt to promote learning and personal growth by encouraging executives to solve real-world problems on a real-time basis.

When? For executives in most companies traditional development opportunities were few and far between. Attending an external executive education program, for example, was often a once-in-a-lifetime event. Strategic leadership development is a continuous, ongoing process that fosters an ingrained ability to continuously learn, innovate, and improve.

How? Leadership development has often been viewed as a series of relatively discrete programs, including classroom activities, rotational assignments, and perhaps some form of performance feedback. Individual managers were frequently left to their own devices to integrate these loosely coordinated activities into a personal developmental plan. For learning-oriented organizations, strategic leadership development is an ongoing process designed not only to influence individual talent but also to define and cultivate organizational values and culture. This systems view of leadership development enables an organization to tap into the energy and experience base of all managers, to build a *hard-to-replicate* form of human resource-based competitive advantage.

Why? Traditionally, leadership development activities have been seen as rites of passage – stripes earned perhaps for achievement, but often for long-term organizational membership. The new, learning-oriented perspective takes advantage of the real value of leadership development by utilizing it as a force for building organizational capability, the ability to maintain both flexibility and focus in a complex, changing environment. This type of organizational capability cannot be developed through management edicts, analytical techniques, or quick-fix programs. Rather, it requires a new perspective toward leadership and organizational development that realizes the contribution of continuous learning to an organization's competitive advantage.

Strategic Leadership Development as a Force for Competitiveness

In today's environment, the secret to long-term competitiveness is the ability of an organization to continuously learn, evolve, and grow, to exhibit the kind of visionary leadership discussed at the beginning of this chapter. Strategic leadership development can be a key driving force for building and sustaining this essential capability. We believe that to harness the potential of leadership development as a force for building organizational capability and influencing competitive advantage, organizations must adapt their leadership development efforts to the new, learning-oriented paradigm outlined in this chapter. Making that shift in perspective requires commitment to the following basic assumptions, assumptions that are the foundation of the ideas discussed in this book.

> (1) *To compete in an era where speed, flexibility and quality are essential to competitiveness, management processes must evolve from a focus on control to a focus on interpretation.*

Management by control is focused on techniques and analyses that extrapolate from the past into the future. Those processes do little to help leaders deal with rapid, unpredictable change. interpretation helps leaders to observe proactively to respond to changes.

(2) *Long-term corporate effectiveness is generated not by the development of a strategic plan, but through the commitment to strategic intent.*[11] The learning organization is committed to the long term and develops an overarching objective that drives continuous learning.

Examples like GE's commitment to global market leadership and British Airway's commitment to becoming the "World's Favorite Airline" demonstrate how strategic intent can ingrain as a core organizational value the desire for continuous improvement, innovation and learning. In a learning organization, strategic leadership development efforts become the vehicle for communicating those values, cultivating the talents and building the networks that translate them into action.

(3) *The core purpose of strategic leadership development is not to build a small pool of successors to senior management, but to cultivate and refine the managerial talents needed to move the organization towards its strategic objectives.*

Through long-term vision and an enhanced ability to anticipate and interpret environmental change, the learning organization is better able to identify the core talents and capabilities necessary to gain competitive advantage in the marketplace. Strategic leadership development becomes the operative force that helps develop and refine these talents while continuously reinforcing the organization's strategic intent.

(4) *Strategic leadership development is a process for cultivating both the individual and collective talents of the organization.* In today's business environment, competitiveness is most likely to be achieved by groups of talented individuals working together to address real organizational problems and issues.

The learning organization focuses leadership development efforts on this type of teamwork. Leadership development is used not only to round

Figure I.4 How Organizations Learn: Techniques and Their Use

Technique	Type A/B/C/D	Extent of Use	Importance
Statistical process control	A/B	3	3.5
Task forces	B/D	3.7	3.9
Best practices/benchmarking	C/D	2.7	3.4
Employee suggestion scheme	A/B	2.8	3.2
Outside management develoment programs	C/D	2.9	3.3
Joint venture/alliances	C/D	3	3.5
Internal management development programs	B/D	3.4	3.9
Customer surveys or interviews	B/C	3.3	4.1
Total quality/Baldrige programs	B/D	2.6	2.9
"Work-out programs" (participative efforts to streamline work flow)	A/B	2.7	3.1
External advisory groups	A/C	2.7	3.1
Self-directed work teams	B	3.1	3.4
Process re-engineering	B/D	3.1	3.6
Decentralized strategic planning process	D	3	3.3
Transferring successes within the company	A/B	2.9	3.5
Information technology (groupware, etc.)	A/C	3.5	3.8
Delphi technique	C	1.8	2.2
Scenarios	C/D	2.5	2.9
Content analysis	A/C	2.6	2.7
Impact analysis	C	2.7	3.3

Key: A = low participation, present-oriented; B = high participation, present-oriented;
C = low participion, future-oriented; D = high participion, future-oriented.
Rate each technique from 1 to 5: 1 = used little/not important; 5 = used widely/very
important.

out and fill in individual managers, but also to communicate and clarify strategic intent, promote teamwork and the development of internal networks, and solve real-world problems on a real-time basis. In this mode, strategic leadership development becomes a core mechanism for communicating and implementing strategy in addition to being a tool for promoting individual development.

We are living in a new world of opportunity for leadership development. That new world involves more than traditional, often loosely coordinated efforts in executive selection, succession planning, job rotation, and training. It involves the charting of a course, a strategy to combine all of these elements into an integrated process designed to guide managers at all levels from the start of their careers towards a new world of competitive advantage and success through anticipatory learning. We hope this book will help you to chart that course for yourself and your organization.

Bon voyage!

Endnotes

1 Adapted from Vicere, A.A. "The 21st Century Executive," *Executive Development*, 3, (1), 1990.

2 This statement was attributed to Fray Hernando de Talevera, head of the Talevera Commission, in 1486.

3 See Senge, P., *The Fifth Discipline*, Doubleday & Company, 1994; Wick, C and L. Leon, *The Learning Edge*, New York, Doubleday & Company, 1993; McGill, M. and J. Slocum, *The Smarter Organization*, New York, Wiley & Sons, 1994.

4 Adapted from Fulmer, R.M. "A Model for Changing the Way Organizations Learn," *Planning Review*, May–June, Vol. 22, No. 3, 1994.

5 Argyris C. and D. Schon, *Organizational Learning: A Theory–Action Perspective*, Addison-Wesley, Reading, MA, 1978.

6 See Botkin, J. *et al.*, *No Limits to Learning*, Club of Rome, 1979. For more details, see Fulmer, R.M. "Anticipatory Learning For the 21st Century," *Journal of Management Development* (special edition), 12, 6, 1993.

7 Robert M. Fulmer and Marshall Sashkin, "How Do Organizations Really Learn?" Manuscript Draft, AMA Briefing, 1996.

8 Sullivan, S. E. and R. S. Bhagat, "Organization Stress, Job Satisfaction and

Job Performance, *Journal of Management*, Vol. 18, pp. 353-374 (1992) and S. J. Motawidlo *et al.* "Occupational Consequences for Job Performance," *Journal of Applied Psychology*, 71, pp. 618-629 (1986). See also Judith Bardwick, *Danger in the Comfort Zone*, American Management Association, New York, 1991.

9 See Kanter, R.M., *Change Masters*, Simon & Schuster, NY, 1985.

10 This section is based on Vicere, A.A. "The Changing Paradigm for Executive Development," *Journal of Management Development*, 10 (3), 1991, pp. 44-47.

11 See Hamel, G. and C. K. Prahalad, *Competing for the Future*, Harvard Business School Press, September, 1994.

SECTION I

THE CHALLENGE

1

TOWARD A NEW PARADIGM

Although Robin Williams is not always a great source of philosophical insight, he captures the challenge of leadership development in the film, *Dead Poets Society*. As a young instructor in a stuffy prep school, Williams has each of his students stand on the teacher's desk to "see the room from another angle." Rather more intellectually, William James observed, "The mark of real genius is simply the facility to see the world in unhabitual ways." One of our favorite existential philosophers, Yogi Berra, may have summed it up best when he said, "It is amazing what you can see by just looking." Especially, we would add, if you look from a different perspective.

Decision-makers have traditionally learned from experience. Corporations have indicated to us that generally they have relied on experience to provide as much as 80 percent of the necessary learning for those whose careers will move to senior levels. Education and training have provided about 10 percent of the preparation, and coaching and mentoring have accounted for the rest. These figures show how critically important it is to provide meaningful career developmental assignments for managers.

The purpose of leadership development, then, is *not* to create programs. At the very least, leadership development should broaden the horizons of participants so they can see and understand different realities or alternative courses of action. At its best, it should inspire and enable leaders to progressively higher levels of achievement. As shown in Plato's classic *Allegory of The Cave,* one of the demands of leadership is to persuade individuals and organizations that have accepted limited approximations of reality, like flickering shadows on a cave wall, to see greater potentialities for themselves and their world. Instead of separate "roles and goals," corporations, higher education institutions, faculty members, and consultants involved in leadership development share a common objective. That objective is to develop (not train or teach) transformational leaders of learning organizations.[1] Yet, the ability of a corporation and its leaders to learn is often hampered by the "traditional paradigm" for leadership development. This chapter describes the traditional paradigm, and goes on to discuss today's challenges to this way of thinking.

The Traditional Paradigm Defined[2]

Over the years, we have conducted extensive research and worked with dozens of companies to assess leadership development needs and determine the most effective ways to address them. During this time, we have noticed a remarkable consistency in organizations' perceptions of how the leadership development process *should* operate. This pattern of perceptions is so widespread that it can only be described as the *traditional* paradigm for leadership development.

The traditional paradigm is based on several key assumptions:

- Age is a valid indicator of an individual's stage of development.
- An individual's formal education prior to employment is an adequate base for a 40-year career.
- Leadership development efforts should be focused primarily on candidates for senior management. However, once candidates reach senior management positions, further training and education is unnecessary.
- Senior officers only are responsible for developing and communicating the corporation's missions, goals, and visions.
- Training and education programs should be developed course by course, based on specific current needs within the business.

This traditional outlook has as its focal point the leader as an individual. Organizations that subscribe to the traditional paradigm tend to have a somewhat regimented leadership development process in which high-potential managers are identified at an early age and moved through a relatively standard sequence of developmental experiences that includes job rotation, training, and further education. This cultivation of talent, skills, and experience is expected to lead to the achievement of senior management status by a select group of carefully nurtured individuals.

Typical of this traditional paradigm is a tendency to discuss leadership development in terms of candidates' ages and/or years of business experience. For most companies, then, the leadership development process can be broken down into four distinct phases, as shown in Figure 1.1. Each of these phases accounts for approximately one quarter, or ten years, of an individual's traditional 40-year career span. Furthermore, a consistent array of developmental techniques seems to be associated with each of these four phases. For the most part, these techniques are employed to help confirm an individual's executive potential and to refine individual capabilities during a career phase.

> The traditional leadership development process itself is frequently described as a pyramid, with decreasing numbers of managers participating in the process at each phase. Movement from one phase to the next is based on the premise that an individual has *already been identified and selected* as a person with high potential for increased managerial responsibilities.

The Traditional Process

Phase one of the traditional leadership development process begins when individuals are selected carefully from "good" colleges and hired into positions generally recognized as "breeding grounds" for future managers. (For instance, at Procter & Gamble these positions were traditionally in brand management; at Johnson & Johnson and IBM they were typically in sales; at General Motors and Nissan they were usually in finance.) Most often in their twenties, these individuals are exposed to leadership development activities that include initiation into or orientation to the company, technical or specialized training, evaluation/

Figure 1.1 Executive Development: "Traditional Process"

Developmental phase	Age	Characterization	Traditional development activities
One "learning the ropes"	Mid-20s–early 30s	Individual contributor	• selection • initiation • further technical education • evaluation • coaching • project management • rotation – functions/divisions • supervisory experience • identification of potential

Two
 	
"rotational assignments"
	Early 30s–early 40s	Promotable mid-career	• budget responsibility
			• manage others in larger units
			• rotational assignments across:
			  • business environments (growth, mature, etc.)
			  • line/staff units
			  • divisions
			  • functions
			  • countries/cultures
			• coaching
			• evaluation
			• limited external developmental experiences

Three "becoming a general manager"	Early 40s–early 50s	Experienced mid-career	• move to senior functional positions • external executive education experiences • leap to general management positions • some rotation still appropriate • manager of managers – developing a CEO perspective • executive education in-depth if senior leadership potential
Four "foundation for the future"	Early 50s and beyond	Senior leader, statesman	• occasional briefing sessions • external representative to society and other businesses (directorships, etc.)

identification of their future potential, and some exposure to top management through focused project assignments and related developmental opportunities.

Those individuals identified as having high potential during this first stage are then advanced to phase two. Now in their thirties, these managers traditionally are exposed to rotational assignments, increased levels of management responsibility, and further attempts to confirm their potential.

Those who emerge successfully from this stage move on to phase three. Having advanced to their early forties or fifties, these managers typically are viewed as prime prospects for general management positions. They are likely to be given increased levels of management responsibility and very likely to be involved in both internal and external executive education programs. During this stage, they are carefully groomed for general management responsibilities.

Those who eventually become general managers are observed for their effectiveness and perhaps exposed to additional executive education programs. If successful, they advance to phase four of the process and move into senior leadership positions at some point in their fifties. At this stage of a leader's career, he or she traditionally is viewed as having "arrived" at full executive potential with little need for further leadership development attention other than occasional briefings on topical issues or perhaps participation as a director of an external organization.

> Generally, the traditional model portrays what was, until recently, the *standard pattern of leadership development* across most of the organizations we observed.

Training *vs.* Education

Within the traditional model, there appears to be some confusion with regard to the differences between training and education. The goal of training is to develop specific skill sets where performance can be measured. For example, a new employee is trained to work the cash register, then serves customers by ringing up sales. Their performance can be tested, monitored, and verified. Training in particular skill sets also is essential for middle and senior managers. Corporate officers take training courses that build skills in effective oral presentations, in dealing with hostile securities analysts or reporters, or in "coaching" so that employees can be empowered rather than ordered about. Again, in some manner, their learning can be monitored and progress verified.

Education, on the other hand, tends to focus on conceptual thinking:

the ability to think in terms of relative emphases and priorities among conflicting objectives and criteria; relative tendencies and probabilities, rather than certainties; and rough correlations and patterns among elements rather than clear-cut cause and effect relationships.[3] Educational programs tend not to be designed to teach specific skills, but rather to promote a higher level of leadership thinking. By encouraging a greater openness to, and awareness of, differing perspectives and ideas, education can build greater flexibility into an organization's decision-making processes.

From the end of World War II through the mid-1970s, most corporations were engaged in *training*. The focus was on addressing gaps in job-related skills as perceived by key managers within the organization. These needs were met one course at a time. The vast array of individual course titles still to be found in a course catalogue from the American Management Association would serve as an example of management training in the larger traditional context.

During this era, *education* was limited to a select handful of pre-identified future senior leaders and was delivered primarily by business schools. According to a 1988 report issued by the American Assembly of Collegiate Schools of Business, Harvard and Stanford controlled one third of the total general management education market.[4] This type of executive education typically stressed the use of cases and acted essentially as a tour of the significant functional areas of a corporation, a "mini MBA." Traditionally, exposure to executive education would occur once in a lifetime for a given corporate executive. With fewer than 15 percent of all corporate executives then holding business administration degrees, leadership development relied more heavily on experience than on the study of business. But that has all changed. A global survey of 1508 executives predicted that 78 percent of all CEOs would have a graduate degree in business by the year 2000.[5] The value of traditional general management executive education programs becomes less significant as a larger percentage of managers already hold business degrees.

An Emerging New Perspective

The exclusive, individualistic focus of the traditional era was acceptable in a stable business environment, but today's profound and rapid environmental changes make many of the assumptions underlying this traditional viewpoint obsolete.[6] As a result, a new paradigm for leadership development is being framed. Four critical drivers of this emerging perspective are discussed below. They include changing views on the role of age and career longevity in the leadership development process, as well as new perspectives on who should be involved in leadership development efforts and what directions those efforts should take.

Age

In an era of decreasing management layers, age can no longer be considered a valid indicator of an individual's stage of development. Today the determining factors must be his or her expertise and experience base. Downsizing and reorganization efforts have pushed decision-making responsibility downward in organizations and, as a result of this, authority and autonomy are often delegated to individuals at much earlier career stages. These individuals tend to be bright, well-educated, ambitious specialists who bring high levels of technical, financial, marketing, and other types of functional expertise to their organizations as members of various project teams.[7] As noted by Katzenbach and Smith in their book *The Wisdom of Teams*,

> **"** *teams – real teams, not just groups that management calls "teams" – should be the basic unit of performance for most organizations... In any situation requiring the real-time combination of multiple skills, experiences, and judgements, a team inevitably gets better results than a collection of individuals operating within confined roles and responsibilities... The record of team performance speaks for itself.*[8] **"**

The authors go on to cite example after example of organizations like GE, Motorola, Kodak, Ford, Hewlett-Packard and others that now use teams as the basic building blocks of their organizational structure. The ability of these companies to move faster, more efficiently, and more aggressively in the marketplace is undisputed. But teams require new skill sets for both team leaders and team members, all of whom must have a much deeper understanding of the workings of the organization and the marketplace than in the past. If they are to fulfill their responsibilities, these individuals must receive earlier and broader orientations to general management issues than would have been necessary under the traditional approach to leadership development.

> *It was no longer enough for our managers to learn about new concepts from business schools or other companies. It was essential that they understand and challenge the company's policies and strategies.*
>
> Ken Graham, former VP HR Planning
> Allstate Insurance

For example, in the mid–1980s, Allstate Insurance Company eliminated the zone offices that separated each region from corporate headquarters. As a result, regional vice presidents suddenly found themselves with multifunctional responsibilities, and a direct reporting relationship to the home office, far earlier in their careers than traditional Allstate executives. Many had been prepared for careers as functional specialists and had had little exposure to the generalist perspective required in their new roles.

This situation caused Allstate to rethink its corporate approach to leadership development. The firm decided to give greater attention to promoting a general-management orientation among managers at all levels of the company. These efforts focused on building depth across the entire management team – not the kind of technical depth for which a specialist is originally hired, but *business depth*, a working knowledge of the insurance business and a vision of the entire organization as an operating entity comprised of interconnected, often interdependent, parts. Allstate's objective was not simply to use leadership development to facilitate business depth within individual managers. Rather, it was to evolve a distinct form of competitive advantage in their industry by creating well-prepared, well-informed teams of managers at all levels who were committed to growing and to developing an aggressive, strategically focused company.

In organizations with fewer management levels and greater demands for specialized knowledge, some leaders may never achieve what we have traditionally called "management status."[9] This is especially true in industries that rely heavily on research, scientific, or technical expertise. In this era of specialized talent, multifunctional project teams, and networked organizations, it is crucial that team members, whether managers or not, are helped to develop an early appreciation of the business as a whole in addition to a network of contacts throughout the firm. Without this exposure, the broad-based, team-oriented perspective required in today's organizations is difficult, if not impossible, to cultivate.[10]

For example, 3M Corporation is widely recognized for its ability to sustain an innovative culture by sharing information, by the cross-pollination of ideas, and by tolerating risk-taking. Similarly, General Electric (GE) encourages its research and technical experts to develop ideas and then market them throughout the company. As a result, the *Wall Street Journal* reported, "GE is turning around the equation of US business. Instead of pushing marketers to come up with ideas and then asking scientists to make them work, the company gives researchers wide berth to imagine and invent – and then shop the invention around GE's divisions."[11] This form of cross-pollination helps GE blend the expertise of its managers and technologists to more effectively manage the transfer of technology from laboratory to market, a critical success factor for competitiveness in the 1990s.

Longevity

Traditional approaches to leadership development were based on the notion that an individual's formal education prior to employment would provide him or her with an adequate base for a 40-year career within an organization. Today, however, restructuring efforts, coupled with continuous environmental and technological change, are making people jobless at all organizational levels. Unsurprisingly, then, John Kotter has cited one of his "new rules" for success as: "Never stop trying to grow; lifelong learning is increasingly necessary for success."[12] Thomas Stewart, in a recent *Fortune* article, footnoted Kotter's rule:

> " *In biblical times, a talent was a unit of money. These days ... learning is the coin of the realm. Treat your wealth of knowledge as the wise servants did in the parable of the talents: invest it and make it grow. If you bury it, as the fearful servant did, you'll lose it.*[13] "

'Intellectual capital' is becoming one of the few real sources of competitive advantage today, both for individuals and organizations. Stan Davis and Jim Botkin described tomorrow's successful business as:

> " one that leverages the economic value of knowledge. It is always figuring out how to define, acquire, develop, apply, measure, grow, use, multiply, protect, transfer, sell, profit by, and celebrate the company's know-how. And it may be know-how about developing new products, about serving customers, about any number of things.[14] "

This emerging focus on knowledge creation requires that leadership development efforts begin to focus as much on continuous learning and networking across the entire organization as they do on the identification and development of high-potential management talent. For example, General Electric has long understood the importance of leadership development to both individual and organizational effectiveness. Their expansive commitment to leadership development processes like "work out" (see Chapter 10 and the Appendix) is sufficient testimony to the strategic importance the organization attaches to it. The mission statement for GE's Crotonville education and development center underscores the critical role leadership development plays in the company:

> " [Crotonville's] mission is to leverage GE's global competitiveness as an instrument of cultural change, by improving business acumen, leadership abilities and organizational effectiveness of General Electric professionals. "

Noel Tichy, a former director at Crotonville, refers to the operation as "a staging ground for corporate revolution."[15] He credits GE's leadership development efforts with being a major force for positive evolution and change throughout the company. He also emphasized the critical importance of GE Chairman Jack Welch's commitment to making the process a force for competitiveness. Dave Ulrich added that to fully utilize leadership development as a tool to facilitate competitiveness, "top managers, particularly the CEO, are involved... [It requires] top management ownership, visibility and commitment."[16] When top management assumes ownership for building the organization's talent base, leadership development often becomes a major catalyst for knowledge creation and organizational development. We will discuss several examples of this idea in Chapter 3.

Focus

One of the major problems in today's competitive business environment is that organizations are facing a lack of "bench strength." Due to reorganization and rightsizing efforts, they simply do not have ready replacements available to fill vacant management positions. At the same time, with fewer management positions available, the notion of a "promotion every two years" is a thing of the past for incumbent talent. These perplexing developments have challenged the traditional belief that leadership development efforts should focus primarily on candidates for senior management. Finding and developing tomorrow's CEO is clearly important, but that person will need a team of well-educated, competent, dedicated managers in middle-level positions to bring strategic visions to reality.

"It is the worst of times for middle managers ... either jobs are vanishing in mergers, takeovers, and restructuring, or management vogues are radically altering their traditional roles."[17] So said Kenneth Labich in a *Fortune* article. Without the luxury of excess organizational layers and the resulting stockpiles of management and professional talent, today's organizations must work to keep all their sources of knowledge and intellectual capital committed and involved. They must also learn to cultivate the abilities of these individuals to function in teams, make decisions, and convey the lessons learnt form their experience to newly developing talent within the company. GE Chairman Jack Welch noted: "As for middle managers, they can be the stronghold of the organization. But their jobs have to be redefined. They have to see their roles as a combination of teacher, cheerleader, and liberator, not controller."[18]

- Leadership development planners today must acknowledge that middle managers have options.
- They can play a key role in the organization's future development.
- They can be part of a flexible, project-oriented talent pool that enables the organization to move in a swift, agile manner.
- They can improve and enhance the job they currently hold.
- They can act as intellectual resources for senior managers who develop and implement policies and strategies.

- They can serve as instructors, coaches, mentors, and role models for technical specialists and newer managers.
- They can function as external scanners for environmental trends, opportunities, and challenges that are identified more easily by seasoned managers than by novices.

However, these benefits can accrue only if middle managers are encouraged to maintain their vigor and intensity. Horizontal moves, rotational assignments, knowledge updates, and other developmental experiences must be coordinated for these individuals. The value and importance of their efforts must become an acknowledged part of the corporate culture. Without these experiences, their potential for individual boredom, withdrawal, and disaffection could spell disaster for the organization.

This focus on the continuous, ongoing development of talent at all levels is a core element of a learning organization.[19] As we noted in the introduction, a learning organization is a company that engenders within itself the capacity to change, the ability to anticipate, embrace, and capitalize on events and opportunities in the business environment. Nonaka has called this built-in capacity "middle-up-down management."[20] He noted middle managers working in multifunctional teams are best positioned to integrate information from top managers and line workers in the development of new products, processes, and perspectives. As such, he points out that it is "middle management's role to create and realize verifiable business concepts for the creative solution of contradictions and gaps between the ideal and the actual."

In a case discussion of the highly successful Honda Motor Company (a company with a distinct middle-up-down culture), Nonaka showed the kind of competitive leverage that can be gained when organizational development efforts adopt this middle-focused perspective toward developing strategic and competitive effectiveness. In that example, through the use of a focused, committed team of top-notch managers, designers, and engineers, Honda was able to create a revolutionary new product, the Honda City, that helped the company set a new standard for small car design in Japan.

Perspective

One of the most dramatic recent shifts in organizational culture is the way managers are changing their view of what leadership *really is*.

Traditionally, leadership was seen as the province of senior officers. For the most part, only the top women and men in the organization were expected to deal with the public, interface with the political environment, facilitate joint-venture relationships, plan on a global basis, or explain corporate policies and directions to subordinates. That is no longer the case. In streamlined, more flexible, "shadow pyramid" organizations (see Chapter 3), these skills and abilities must be shared at all levels of the firm. Failure to cultivate an understanding of that role early in an individual's career can leave a company dangerously vulnerable to external influences. As Raymond Miles noted: "In the newer, flatter, and leaner firms, management jobs are fewer, more demanding and, for the most part, more satisfying ... instead of being in charge of a division or department, the top executive of production, design or supply components is a general manager running a complete business itself. His or her staff must also share a broader vision."[21]

Traditional approaches to leadership development left the tasks of developing and communicating corporate missions, goals, and visions to senior officers. In a highly competitive environment, characterized by growing reliance on the network or project organization form, these capabilities must be developed throughout the organization. Driving this strategic focus down to lower levels of the organization requires greater emphasis on communication and team-building efforts. As a result, the skills-oriented training programs that were the backbone of internal management education and development efforts at phases one and two of the traditional model are now being supplemented by leadership development efforts geared to facilitating deeper understanding of corporate strategic issues across the organization. These company-specific leadership development programs, formerly reserved for managers at phases three and four of the traditional model, are fast becoming a core element of organizational efforts to facilitate change and development.[22] This shift is a key factor in the dramatic growth of "customized" leadership development programs (see the Appendix).

For example, Allstate determined that in order to quickly and effectively implement their reorganization and facilitate competitiveness, managers at all levels needed to be actively involved in policy-level discussions of corporate objectives and directions. Through an ongoing series of internal leadership development programs, Allstate managers, directors, and officers discuss not only their firm's current policies but also the strategic "whys" behind the policies. These programs help open channels of communication within Allstate, helping management to understand and commit to key policy decisions and organizational changes.

Similarly, in 1976 the US Congress enacted legislation to form the Consolidated Rail Corporation (Conrail), a company comprised of a number of bankrupt railroads serving the Northeast and Midwest sections of the country. Early on, Conrail senior management realized that the key to the company's viability was to move away from a traditional railroad culture toward a new, strategic vision of a market-driven transportation company.

One effort to enact this vision involved establishing a leadership development program targeted at the company's middle managers. The purpose of this two-week general management program was to enhance the management capabilities of participants by strengthening their abilities to work *as a team*, to understand, communicate, and implement this new, marketing-oriented strategy. The positive contribution of this effort to Conrail's impressive record of performance improvement is reflected in this comment from a past program participant:

> " *Now I can more knowledgeably talk about why our corporate structure has changed with time... I can build into my conversations an 'advertisement' for the importance of a market orientation for Conrail.* "

The New Paradigm Context

Our analysis shows that although many organizations have within their grasp the elements for a successful, forward-looking leadership development effort, most make little effort to focus these elements to build overall organizational competitiveness. For a few notable companies, however, leadership development has become more than just a vehicle for individual development. For them it has become a mechanism for cultivating the collective managerial talents, perspectives, and capabilities that will help propel the organization into the future. The exceptional companies that share this strategic, organization-oriented approach to leadership development also have a remarkably consistent view of how the process should work. Their's is the *new* paradigm for leadership development.

As we mentioned in the introduction, this new paradigm has as its fundamental purpose the utilization of leadership development as a force for *overall organization development*, as a tool to develop knowledge and intellectual capital, shape organizational culture, create commitment to strategic directions, promote teamwork, facilitate a broader understanding of the organization, and cultivate an environment for continuous improvement and innovation. One of the greatest challenges facing organizations today is how to retool and reinvigorate organizational cultures after sustained periods of retrenchment, reorganization, and turmoil. New paradigm companies are turning to leadership development processes to help refocus the organization and enhance competitive effectiveness.[23]

Instilling a Learning Orientation

To harness the potential of leadership development as a force for building competitive advantage, organizations are adapting their leadership development efforts to the new, learning-oriented paradigm. The basic operational requirement of this new approach to leadership development is commitment to a strategy that includes:

- early and ongoing cross-functional, project, and action-learning assignments designed to build business depth;
- early and ongoing education and training in interpersonal skills and strategic management, coupled with opportunities for coaching and mentoring that help cultivate and hone leadership capabilities;
- early and ongoing opportunities for external executive education designed to refresh perspectives and challenge basic operating assumptions;
- early, ongoing, and regular performance appraisals and feedback, coupled with regular briefings on the organization and its culture and strategy designed to facilitate communications, commitment, and organizational development;
- opportunities to serve as a coach/mentor to teach others about the organization and its business.

Individually, each element is far from new. *Together, however, they form the major elements of a leadership development process that can help foster overall organizational development and a renewed sense of competitiveness.* All of these activities help maintain the open, broad-based management perspective necessary for competitiveness in today's business environment. Throughout this book, we present frameworks that bring these elements together into a powerful force for crafting competitiveness.

Adapting to the New Paradigm

The experiences of organizations like GE, Conrail, Allstate, and the many others we will discuss are helping us learn how to harness the potential of leadership development as a force for change. Their experiences suggest that to be effective, a company's leadership development process must flow logically from its strategic agenda. The focus of the process should be on identifying and developing the talents and perspectives the company needs to achieve its long-term strategic objectives. Specific initiatives should be built around this market-oriented focus, coupling it with a strong element of competitive analysis, to help managers at *all* levels understand the respective strengths and weaknesses of the firm and what it will take to build competitive advantage in the marketplace. This understanding must then be related to the organization itself, the systems, structures, processes, goals, and relationships necessary for success in a highly competitive world. Armed with this strategy/culture/consistency focus, an organization engaged in strategic leadership development is positioned to build both competitive advantage and management depth in pursuit of organizational excellence.[24]

As leadership development practitioners step back from the traditional process and analyze their function, many are concluding there must be a better way to cultivate leadership talent. By overcoming preoccupations with individual development, age, and tenure as driving forces in the process; by refining views on middle managers and teamwork; and by viewing leadership development as a key tool for influencing organizational change and development, strategic leadership development can move beyond a process that benefits only a few individual managers toward a process that helps drive the flexibility, commitment, and competitiveness of the entire organization.

Endnotes

1 Senge, P. and R.M. Fulmer, "Simulations, Systems Thinking and Anticipatory Learning," *Journal of Management Development*, 12 (6), 1993, p. 21.

2 This section is drawn from Vicere, A. A. and K. R. Graham, "Crafting Competitiveness: Toward a New Paradigm for Executive Development," *Human Resource Planning*, 13 (4), 1990, pp. 281–295.

3 See Vicere, A. A., "University-Based Executive Education: Impacts and Implications," *Journal of Management Development*, 7 (4), 1988, pp. 5–13.

4 Porter, L. and L. McKibbon, *Management Development: Drift of Thrust into the 21st Century*, McGraw-Hill, 1988.

5 Korn, L.E., R.M. Ferry, D.C. Hambrick, and J.W. Fredrickson, *Reinventing the CEO*, Korn Ferry International, 1989, p. 85.

6 See Handy, C., *The Age of Paradox*, Harvard Business School Press, 1994.

7 Stewart, T., "Planning a Career in a World Without Managers," *Fortune*, March 20, 1995, pp. 72–80.

8 Katzenbach, J. R. and D. K. Smith, *The Wisdom of Teams*, Boston: Harvard Business School Press, 1993.

9 Ibid.

10 Ibid.; Stewart, T., 1995; op. cit.; Handy, C., 1994, op. cit.; C. Savage, *5th Generation Management*, Digital Press, 1990.

11 Naj, A.K., "GE's Latest Innovation: A Way to Move Ideas from Lab to Market," *Wall Street Journal*, June 14, 1990, p. 1.

12 Kotter, J. P., *The New Rules*, New York: Free Press, 1995, p. 5.

13 Stewart, T., 1995, op.cit.

14 Davis, S. and J. Botkin, *The Monster Under the Bed*, New York: Simon and Schuster, 1994, p. 110.

15 Tichy N. and S. Sherman, *Control Your Own Destiny or Someone Else Will*, Doubleday, 1993.

16 Ulrich, D., 1989, "Executive Development for Competitiveness." In A.A. Vicere (ed.), *Executive Education: Process, Practice and Evaluation*, Petersons, 1989.

17 Labich, K. "Making Over Middle Managers," *Fortune*, May 8, 1989, pp. 58–64.

18 Tichy N. and R. Charan, "Speed, Simplicity and Self Confidence: An Interview with Jack Welch," *Harvard Business Review*, September–October 1989, pp. 112–120.

19 See de Geus, A. "Planning As Learning," *Harvard Business Review*, March–April 1988, pp. 70–74; R. Stata, "Organizational Learning–The Key to Management Innovation," *Sloan Management Review*, Spring 1989,

pp. 59–77; W. Keichell III, "The Organization That Learns," *Fortune*, March 12, 1990, pp. 133–136; C. Wick and L.S. Leon, *The Learning Edge: How Smart Managers and Smart Companies Stay Ahead*, McGraw-Hill 1993.

20 See Nonaka, I. "Toward Middle-Up-Down Management: Accelerating Information Creation," *Sloan Management Review*, Spring 1988, pp. 9–18.

21 Miles, R. "Adapting to Technology and Competition: A New Industrial Relations System for the 21st Century," *California Management Review*, Winter 1989, pp. 9–28.

22 Fulmer R.M. and Vicere, A.A., *Executive Education and Leadership Development: The State of the Practice*, University Park, PA: Penn State Institute for the Study of Organizational Effectiveness.

23 See Vicere, A.A. "Executive Education and Strategic Imperatives: A Formula for Crafting Competitiveness," *American Journal of Management Development*, 1 (2), 1995.

24 Miles, R. and C. Snow, *Fit, Failure and the Hall of Fame*, New York: Free Press, 1994.

2

THE CYCLES OF
LEADERSHIP
DEVELOPMENT

In today's era of reorganization, revolution, and change, strategic leadership is essential to the competitiveness and development of an organization. We described in Chapter 1 how organizations are refocusing their leadership development efforts to better prepare and develop their pool of strategic leadership talent. This chapter discusses how strategically focused leadership development processes can be used to build sustainable organizational competitiveness.

A Model of the Strategic Leadership Process[1]

One very useful way to examine strategic leadership development is to look at typical patterns of leadership in the evolution of major organizations. Numerous authors have made significant contributions to the understanding of this crucial process.[2] The model portrayed in Figure 2.1 is a synthesis of the work of these authors, coupled with new insights on the role of strategic leadership in building organizational competitiveness.

This model is a simple representation of the stages of an organization's development over time from its inception through its potential demise. Time is plotted on the vertical axis. In this instance, time is signified by five developmental stages, from emergence (when an organization comes

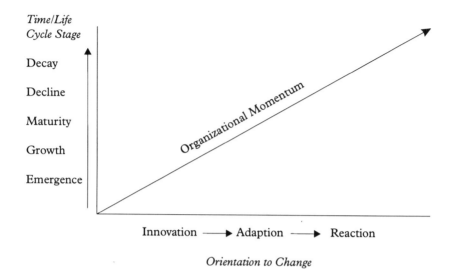

Figure 2.1 The Organizational Development Model
Source: Vicere, A. A. "The Strategic Leadership
Imperative for Executive Education," *Human Resource
Planning*, 15(1), 1992, pp. 16–31.

into existence) through the stages of growth, maturity, decline, and decay (when, effectively, an organization ceases to exist).

> *It is important to note that demise is not inevitable. Effective strategic leadership can enable an organization to avoid the consequences of decline and decay.*

The horizontal axis is a measure of orientation to change based on the concept of "adaption/innovation theory."[3] This theory holds that creative style and orientation to change can be gauged on a continuum ranging from very strong focus on adaptive creativity or a preference to work with what exists in an effort to do *better* what is currently being done, to a very strong focus on innovative creativity or a preference to give little relevance or credibility to what currently exists, and then to a tendency to do things *differently*.

To survive and prosper, an organization must be able to adjust its strategic behavior to the changing demands of its market. Adaption/innovation theory asserts that both adaptive creativity and innovative creativity are effective styles of dealing with such changes. But while innovators are focused on creating new and different organizational elements, adapters are focused on creating effective ways to implement and perfect those elements.[4] As such, the most effective organization is one that can blend the strengths of each approach in a culture that avoids the tendency to favor one to the exclusion of the other.

As organizations develop, their cultures tend to evolve from being more innovative and open to change, to being more adaptive and focused on improving what currently exists with the organization's competitive domain.[5] To a degree, this *momentum* is essential and necessary to deal with growth and success. Over time, however, an organization can become so inwardly focused that it eventually ceases to be creative at all: it no longer does things differently; it no longer improves what exists; it simply reacts to the pressures of the outside environment.

When an organization reaches this reactive stage, it is left with only three options. First, it can continue in its reactive mode and eventually cease to exist. Second, it can be acquired (or conquered) and somehow refocused through external influence. Third, it can attempt a massive restructuring of the status quo (a "revolution") in an effort to revitalize its culture, a very difficult and painful process. Again, it is important to note that this evolutionary process can be managed. An organization need not evolve to a stage of decline or decay.[6] Rather, strategic leadership development processes can be used to manage the cycles of change in an organization, enabling it to better balance the need for innovation and adaption in an effort to build organizational capability and competitiveness.[7]

Time has a way of changing our assets into liabilities.

Peter Drucker

The Stages of Strategic Leadership

The implications of the strategic leadership model can be clarified are represented in the expanded model depicted in Figure 2.2. In this model, the style of strategic leadership typical at each stage is indicated. A description of each of those styles is detailed below.[8]

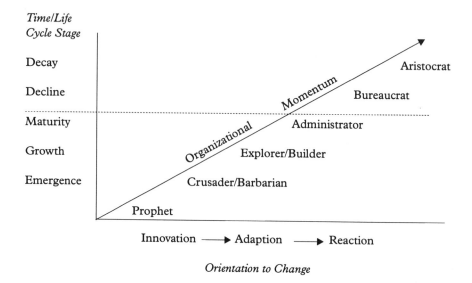

Figure 2.2 Leadership, Culture, and Organizational Development
Source: Vicere, A. A. "The Strategic Leadership
Imperative for Executive Education," *Human Resource
Planning*, 15(1), 1992, pp. 16–31.

Prophet

In the emergence stage, the style of strategic leadership necessary for organizational growth and development is best summed up as a *prophet*. A prophet is a visionary, a zealot driven by an ideal, which is typically a new and different way to deal with the world and/or some of its opportunities. Prophets lead organizations that are intense but unstable, often surviving on a day-to-day basis. Commitment to the visionary ideal is the prime reason for membership in the organization and the primary driver of motivation. Throughout history, there have been many prophets. And throughout history, many of those prophets have been ostracized, exiled, and sometimes even killed. But those that survived often were responsible for revolution and change, usually for the betterment of society. That is because prophets challenge the system, break with the status quo, and discount conventional wisdom. Real change and development is unlikely to occur without prophets.

The history of business is laced with prophets – people like Ray Kroc at McDonald's, Thomas Edison at GE, and Stephen Jobs at Apple

Computer. These individuals envisioned new worlds, created new products, and established new industries. They and their fellow prophets have been the lifeblood of technological and social change and development.

Clara Barton was the prophet who founded the American Red Cross in 1881. Barton was responsible for establishing the ideal of the Red Cross in the United States. Through her energy and relentless commitment to that ideal, she helped create one of the world's foremost humanitarian organizations. In doing so, she established a growing concern, one that demanded an expanded form of strategic leadership exemplified in the next stage of the model.

Crusader/Barbarian

If the prophet survives and is persistent, as was Clara Barton, the ideal he or she champions and the loosely structured organization that supports the ideal begin to take root. At that point, the strategic leadership focus required by the growing organization must shift from the prophet's zealous pursuit of an ideal to the relentless development of an organization capable of making that ideal a reality, the *crusader/barbarian* stage. To some, strategic leaders at this stage are crusaders, spreading the word and enhancing the survival of the ideal. For others, those leaders are barbarians who are ruthlessly transforming the ideal into a structured, regimented process. Control is the essence of strategic leadership at this stage, as leaders seek to put structure to the often chaotic zeal of the emerging organization. It also is at this stage that many would-be entrepreneurs fail as the unbridled intensity of innovative creativity and structured control of adaptive creativity collide in the formation of a viable organization.

Some prophets are able to recognize the need for different leadership skills and develop successors with the appropriate talent to take their organizations to the next level. However, many prophets falter at this stage, falling victim to the need to run their organization more like a business and less like an informal network. Stephen Jobs met such a fate at Apple, as did Clara Barton. Barton is held in the highest esteem in the history of the American Red Cross, but she was so successful in building support for the ideal that the organization outgrew her ability to lead it. With the ideal firmly in place, the growing organization needed structure and controls. Clara Barton was proficient at neither. So, in 1904 Mabel Boardman forced founder Clara Barton out of office.

Was Boardman a crusader or a barbarian? To supporters of Barton, she may have been the latter. But to supporters of the ideal of the American Red Cross, Boardman was a crusader, taking the organization to new heights of growth and achievement by adding a necessary element of structure and control to chaotic growth.

Explorer/Builder

If crusader/barbarian leaders are successful in bringing structure to the emerging organization and positioning it in the marketplace, the strategic leadership style must again shift. At this stage, organizations enter a period of "textbook management," having taken an ideal at the emergence stage and turned it into a viable organization during the crusader/barbarian stage. The term "textbook management" is used to describe the *explorer/builder* stage because it tends to be a period of opportunity and growth. The organization is past the start-up, entrepreneurial stage. It has met the need to secure investment capital and it has established a position in the marketplace. It is now at the point of development most frequently assumed by business management textbooks. Analytical management techniques are much more applicable at this stage, as demand for products and services often exceeds the organization's capacity to produce them, and external competition has yet to become a factor.

Growth is the watchword of the explorer/builder stage and strategic leaders seek to capitalize on growth by investing in business development, "perfecting" the organizational structure, hiring new people, expanding into new markets, and developing new management systems to meet the demands of growth and success. Gradually, however, if those systems begin to dominate the strategic thinking of the organization, the organization moves on to the next stage of the model.

Administrator

Growth and success bring about several crucial consequences for the organization. First, they invite competition. As outsiders see the possibilities for success in the organization's domain they attempt to enter the arena. Then, as competition heats up, the inevitable inefficiencies created by growth but hidden by seemingly boundless opportunity become apparent. Organizations that reach this stage are often described as "mature" businesses or in "mature" (slow growing) markets. The need for greater efficiency and control in a "mature market" signal a movement toward further adaption – major efforts to improve and enhance the efficiency and effectiveness of existing products, services, structures, and systems.

This call for greater control and adaption leads to the *administrator* stage. Generally, there is a tendency toward centralization in planning, budgeting, and controls during this stage. In fact, control systems and processes seem to dominate the managerial agenda as the organization seeks to gain consistency and stability. Simultaneously, leadership tends to become more impersonal as administrative systems become the driver of organizational decision making.

Administration is a two-edged sword. When asked if "administrator" is a positive or negative label, most people hesitate to answer. That is because there is a fine line separating the positive contribution to competitiveness of effective controls/administration from the negative consequences of over-organization caused by overemphasized administration.[9] This type of over-organization can propel the organization into a bureaucratic morass.

As a result, some form of corporate reinvention is called for. The "succession by clone syndrome" that often typifies organizations at this stage can be disastrous as IBM, General Motors, and Westinghouse discovered in the early 1990s. Some companies are able to navigate these treacherous waters through the recognition of the constant need to reassess strategic leadership capabilities. At Johnson & Johnson, Jim Burke balanced his external orientation, vision for global growth, and commitment to traditional corporate values with a down-to-earth, pragmatic administrator, Dave Clare, who served as his chief operating officer. Clare was less widely known than the visionary Burke, but he was a vital part of the J&J management team.

Former General Electric CEO Reginald Jones recognized, as he neared retirement in 1979, that the management skills and practices that had caused him to be named the most admired executive in America for three successive years would not be enough to lead GE into the new era of challenges it faced. Consequently, Jones launched a search for his successor that resulted in the selection of a younger, more flamboyant, leader in the person of Jack Welch, a leader not in the traditional GE mold who consciously began a process to reshape the corporation.

Bureaucrat

If the organization fails to follow the path to reinvention typified by Johnson & Johnson or GE, the efficiency focus that dominates the administrative era tends to become the strategic leadership focus of the organization. At this point, the organization crosses into the dangerous stage of *bureaucrat*. The ideals of the emergence stage have been left behind and all but forgotten. The market orientation of the explorer/builder stage has been lost to efficiency measures and controls. Strategic leaders have become bureaucrats, no longer innovatively creative, no longer adaptively creative, but reactive to the pressures of the outside environment.

A bureaucracy is easy prey to new crusaders and explorers (competitors) in the marketplace. Some leaders at this stage see these new competitors as prophets/barbarians to be shot for challenging the status quo, changing the rules of the game, and swaying marketplace commitment away from traditional ideals. This reactive posture propels organizations dominated by a bureaucratic perspective into the next stage of the model. For other leaders, however, the appearance of new competitors on the horizon is a sign that a new social order is called for within the organization, and revival and turnaround efforts are put into place in an effort to restore competitiveness and bust the emerging bureaucracy.

Revivals are often painful and difficult undertakings for organizations that have reached the bureaucracy stage. Typically, it has been quite some time since attention has been given to the ideals upon which the organization was founded. Consequently, the organization is often adrift and frequently devoid of its core competencies.[10] Furthermore, many current leaders have risen from the ranks of *successful administrators* and therefore lack the vision of prophets and the market knowledge of explorer/builders. For that reason, revivals often require crusader/barbarian leaders who are able to mount a revolution to restore focus on the ideal and reposition the organization in the marketplace.

L. Stanley Crane, former CEO of Conrail, is an example of such a revolutionary. Crane took over the top spot at Conrail in 1981. At that time, Conrail was a quasi-government-owned railroad with over 70,000 employees. During the period between 1976 and 1980, Conrail had posted losses in excess of $1.5 billion. When Crane assumed his CEO position, Conrail was losing over $1 million a day.

Formerly the president of Southern Railway, Crane was an experienced manager and a capable leader. He presided over a massive reorganization effort that included substantial divestment of unproductive assets and headcount reductions of nearly 60 percent. Crane worked with managers, union leaders, and employees to build understanding and support for these changes, changes that resulted in an operating profit of $431 million in 1986, marking six straight years of profitability for Conrail.

Crane ultimately helped transform Conrail from a hemorrhaging appendage of the government to a highly profitable transportation services company. When Elizabeth Dole, then US Secretary of Transportation, recommended that the government sell the now profitable Conrail to Norfolk Southern in 1986, Crane was able to lobby Congress and the financial community to secure a public offering of Conrail and ensure its independence and viability.[11]

It is important to reiterate that evolution into bureaucracy is not inevitable. Some corporations are able to recognize the need for significant cultural and strategic change and select leaders who have the appropriate vision and strength of character to carry out this task. Stanley Crane had the vision to reinvent Conrail. Jack Welch saw that GE could not succeed with such a wide array of diverse businesses without the competitive advantages associated with market leadership.

To explore the connection between corporate culture and performance, John Kotter and Jim Heskett of the Harvard Business School collected data on a number of firms that had successfully made the transition from bureaucracy to renewed growth.[12] The common characteristics of those firms were:

- An effective leader on top
- An outsider's openness to new ideas

- An insider's power base
- A perceived need for change
- Communication of a new vision
- Motivation of a growing group of "believers"
- Adaptation to environmental change

History is written by the winners, firms that exhibit these characteristics. Organizations with long life-spans inevitably have been able to predict the need to change and have had the courage to make changes happen.

Aristocrat

Sometimes revolutionary turnaround efforts, such as those we have discussed above, do not occur. If a bureaucracy is strong enough, and if it has become too entrenched in the organization, a senior leader can become an *aristocrat*, removed from the realities of the organization and sheltered from the storms of change. In many ways, aristocrats are engaged in a similar struggle for survival as were the organization's founding prophets. But whereas prophets press for the survival of the ideal, aristocrats press for their personal survival, often at the expense of the organization itself. Strategic leaders at these organizations tend to suffer a sad but inevitable fate. Typically, they are purged from the organization, sometimes at the cost of the organization's very existence. Recent senior executive turnover at companies like IBM, General Motors, Digital Equipment Corporation, Westinghouse, and Morrison Knudsen are blatant examples of what can happen to an organization at this stage.

The Strategic Leadership Model in Action

Adizes[13] noted that the life-cycle stage of an organization can be gauged by observing the degree to which control systems and administrative procedures dominate an organization's decision-making process. He further suggested that over-reliance on administrative systems was a major factor in the ultimate demise of many organizations. As such, the Strategic Leadership Model depicts one of the most significant challenges facing organizations. That challenge is how to deal with the aftermath of growth and success in a turbulent environment. To meet that challenge, an organization must have the appropriate leadership capabilities in place to initiate and implement competitive change.[14]

This idea is clearly depicted in the rise and fall of the Soviet Union. Although Lenin was clearly a prophet to the Soviet Union, it was Stalin who crusaded for the ideal and created the empire. Stalin was followed by a progression of leaders who became more and more removed from the people, until society itself was on the verge of collapse. Enter a new prophet, Mikhail Gorbachev, who presented the people with new ideals and visions of a new social order. Gorbachev was unable to lead the crusade for his new ideals and was replaced by Boris Yeltsin, who is struggling to forcefully take control of the new Russia.

The Soviet example illustrates the degree of difficulty faced by an organization attempting to revitalize from the stages of decline and decay. The challenge is immense. It is imperative, therefore, to prevent the natural momentum of organizational evolution from leading the organization into bureaucracy and decay. Meeting the challenge of this imperative is the essence of strategic leadership development.

This imperative is evident in the organizational development efforts implemented by General Electric. GE was far from a declining company when CEO Jack Welch took over in 1981, but Welch believed that the seeds of bureaucracy and aristocracy were taking root throughout the organization. His focus on making GE a "boundaryless" company, his commitment to making each of GE's businesses number one or number two in world markets, and his support for employee involvement efforts such as "work-out" reflect his strategic leadership role as a prophet/crusader for a new social order at GE, one focused on an ideal and rooted in the marketplace.[15]

But the real lesson of the GE example is not the contribution made by Welch as a strategic leader. Rather it is the company's overall management of its leadership talent pool. When former CEO Reginald Jones and the GE Board of Directors selected Jack Welch, they knowingly unleashed a prophet/crusader whose management perspective was a far cry from the analytical, administrative focus that dominated GE at that time. Welch brought a renewed sense of purpose to the company, one that helped GE regain its balance between the forces for innovative creativity and the forces for adaptive control.

Under Welch, leadership development processes have continued to play a key role in the company. GE's ongoing management development and employee involvement efforts have helped to instill the new ideals of boundarylessness and competitiveness across all levels of the organization. These processes have enabled the company to identify executive talent and observe potential through action/learning projects and task force assignments.[16] In short, GE has used executive education and leadership development to build a strategic leadership talent pool and to use that pool to create dynamic tension in the organization, tension that stymies the organization's natural float toward bureaucracy.

British Petroleum's reorganization efforts in the early 1990s provide another example of the Strategic Leadership Model in action. When former CEO Robert Horton took office in 1990, he saw the need to rekindle the ideals of the organization to prevent stagnation and bureaucracy from stifling competitiveness. He initiated BP's "Project 1990," an effort to survey the company's employees, review current operations, and generate recommendations for enhancing the effectiveness of the firm.[17] Horton was influential in selecting the project head, a mid-level high-flier with a proven track record, thanks in part to BP's well-regarded high-potential management development program.

Horton gave the project head the freedom to select six other high-fliers from throughout the organization to serve on the team. Horton maintained weekly contact with the project head but empowered the team to do its own analysis and make independent recommendations. As a result, the Project 1990 team painted a candid portrait of BP as an over-controlled organization in need of radical transformation.

The Project 1990 team's final reported to a massive reorganization effort was designed to make the company more responsive to the marketplace. This reorganization included the development of BP's "egg" organization, an oval organigram that depicted the breaking down of organizational "chimneys" in the new organization, and the establishment of BP's OPEN culture, a set of behavioral ideals based on Open thinking, Personal impact, Empowerment, and Networking.[18] For BP, OPEN was an ideal designed to focus all members of the organization on the company's marketplace. Ultimately, Horton hoped that OPEN would enable the company to reach its objective of being the world's most successful oil company in the 1990s and beyond.

BP has made major progress toward these goals, but without Horton. It seems that despite the early success he achieved with the Project 1990 initiatives, Horton was unable to avoid the fate of a leader raised on the principles of traditional management. In a *Forbes Magazine* interview on the changes he instituted within BP,[19] Horton said, "Because I am blessed with a good brain, I tend to get to the right answer rather quicker and more often than most people. That will sound frightfully arrogant, but it's true." The aristocratic perspective reflected in this quote cost the once prophetic Horton his job later that year.

A final and more positive example of the model in action is shown, once again by Conrail. Conrail was established in 1976 by the US government in an effort to maintain essential rail service in the northeast manufacturing corridor of the United States. At its inception, Conrail was a conglomeration of seven bankrupt railroads, each with a long history and a distinctive culture.

As such, Conrail was unusual in beginning its organizational life as a bureaucracy. Its first CEO, Ed Jordan, worked to establish the controls, systems, and infrastructure necessary to make Conrail a viable railroad. In short, he succeeded in making Conrail a well-administered entity. Jordan was followed by L. Stanley Crane, who crusaded for the survival of Conrail as an independent company by relentlessly pursuing a drive for efficiency and effectiveness in the company's operations. Crane's tenure was capped by the public sale of Conrail in 1987 in what was the largest public offering in US history to that date.

Crane was succeeded in 1989 by Richard Sanborn who brought a new market-focused, employee-oriented ideal to Conrail. Following Sanborn's untimely death that same year, James Hagen took over the top job. Hagen has added his own version of market-focused, employee-oriented ideals to the company, enabling Conrail to continue to evolve toward progressively higher levels of performance in a highly competitive industry. Recently, David M. LeVan was appointed as Chief Executive Officer. LeVan brings financial and operating experience back to the top of the company, along with a strong market orientation gained when he served as head of strategic planning under Stanley Crane, Dick Sanborn, and Jim Hagen.

Conrail is clearly a story of the right strategic leader being selected at the right time in the organization's development.[20] But it is more than that. Like GE and BP, Conrail has made a massive effort to use leadership development to drive its remarkable turnaround and transformation. Conrail senior and upper middle managers operate in a well-oiled network that engages influential managers in the active analysis and implementation of key organizational decisions.[21] Conrail middle managers are brought into the loop in an intensive leadership development program that involves Conrail senior managers, including Hagen, LeVan, and other key leaders as instructors.[22] Finally Conrail has brought this strategic leadership thrust to the supervisory level through additional development efforts.

Since 1983, Conrail has used leadership development to communicate and to build commitment to a strategic leadership focus that has helped fuel one of the business world's most stunning turnarounds. In so doing, Conrail has created a strategic talent pool from which it can draw effective, proven leaders capable of meeting the challenge of change and competition as the company and its market evolves and develops.

Lessons Learned

In Figure 2.3 we see strategic leadership portrayed as a cyclical process in which an organization is engaged in a continuous effort to identify, develop, and harmonize a cadre of strategic leaders capable of performing the roles of prophet, crusader/barbarian, explorer/builder, and administrator. By building this type of strategic leadership talent pool, an organization is better positioned to exploit the opportunities of a changing competitive environment.

This is not to suggest that an organization must actually change leaders at different stages. But it does suggest that an organization needs leaders who are able to recognize the developmental stage of the organization, the competitive demands of the marketplace, and the style of strategic leadership needed to maintain competitiveness in that environment. Some leaders will be capable of making such shifts in style and perspective; some leaders will be unable to adjust. In either case, leadership development processes should be in place to ensure that the organization maintains a pool of leadership talent that embraces each perspective and maintains a match between the strategic leadership perspective of incumbent managers and the demand of the competitive environment. This requires the development of a consistent strategy for the recruitment, selection, and development of leadership talent.

In order to do that, leadership development strategies must focus on

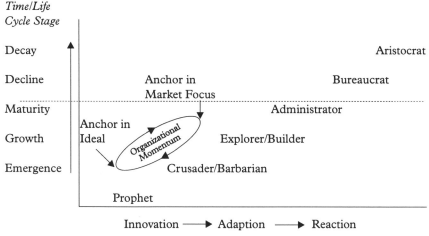

Figure 2.3 Leadership, Culture, and Organizational Development:
Anchors for Effectiveness
Source: Vicere, A. A. "The Strategic Leadership
Imperative for Executive Education," *Human Resource
Planning*, 15(1), 1992, pp. 16–31.

the evolutionary nature of strategic leadership as implied by this model. The first component of that evolution can be found in the prophet stage, in the zealous pursuit of an ideal. In studying defunct organizations, there is a tendency to find one striking commonality. As those organizations developed over time, they seemed to lose sight of their ideal, their reason for existence, their competitive essence. In short, they lost their ability to learn, change, and develop so as to achieve continually higher levels of success.

The organization development model is an excellent tool to help managers understand the nature of organizational momentum and what actions can be taken to manage the development of an organization throughout its life-cycle.

Participant,
Penn State Human Resource Management Program

We learn from the demise of the Soviet Union that when the people no longer hold dear the founding ideal, the organization lives on borrowed time. We learn from GE that an ideal (boundarylessness) can be used to drive the development, transformation, and effectiveness of an entire organization. We learn from Conrail that instilling the ideal is a time-consuming process that requires relentless commitment but can bring with it enormous results. Thus, the first anchor point necessary to the establishment of a strategic leadership talent pool is the building of commitment to an ideal, a reason for being (what Hamel and Prahalad call "strategic intent."[23]) that serves as a driver for motivation and a guide for decision making.

Commitment to an ideal, or a strategic intent, is not sufficient however. The organization also must be able to implement that ideal, to bring the ideal as close to reality as possible despite the enormity of the challenge. As the organization develops from its emergence through the explorer/builder stage, it builds a base of competitiveness by *providing value for its customers in a unique manner*. In studying defunct organizations, a second striking feature stands out. As these organizations moved through the explorer/builder stage and into the administrator stage, they tended to take market growth and acceptance for granted. Because growth had been the norm for a time, and because the market had been continually expanding, they tended to develop a sense of invincibility. This over-confidence was magnified by the adaptive focus inherent in an organization's culture at the administrator stage. As a result these organizations became rapidly and dangerously reactive, ultimately falling victim to their inability to adapt to a changing environment.

Once again, we learn from the demise of the Soviet Union that the market (in this case the people) will ultimately determine the value of the product, and will eventually make the ultimate purchase decision. We learn from GE that a strong market focus (the target of number one or two in world markets), coupled with commitment to an ideal (boundarylessness), can be an immensely powerful force for organizational development and competitiveness. We learn from Conrail that a market focus coupled with strong commitment to an ideal can lead to stunning turnarounds and exceptional corporate performance.

So, the second anchor point in the establishment of a strategic leadership talent pool must be a strong focus on the marketplace, on the value added by the organization, on the unique capabilities that make the organization competitive, and on the core competencies that are heart and soul of the organization.[24]

Implications for Strategic Leadership Development

Figure 2.3 suggests that a leadership development strategy that is anchored in an ideal or strategic intent and that also has a strong market/customer focus is more likely to create a pool of strategic leadership talent capable of dealing with the challenge of organizational change and development.[25]

Commitment to the *ideal* anchors the organization in innovation and encourages prophets to be creative and to pursue new and different ways to bring the ideal into reality. The market focus anchors the organization in the external world, encouraging explorer/builders to expand the boundaries of the organization through market development and exploit the core competencies of the organization through product and service development.

Prophets and explorer/builders are complemented by crusader/barbarians who are called upon to lead revolutions and capture new territories in this dynamic, growing organization. Administrators are called upon to enhance organizational effectiveness by designing ways to learn from experience and thereby enhance performance. The tension created by the interplay of these four perspectives serves to keep the organization vital and in a state of dynamic equilibrium between the forces for innovation (continuous undirected change) and adaption (continuous stability and constant analysis).

Can an individual leader operate across all four strategic leadership perspectives? Miller found that they seldom can, although the ability to bridge two perspectives is not uncommon.[26] Nevertheless, through leadership development processes, individual leaders can be schooled in the art of building management teams and networks that embrace all four perspectives and are therefore more effective in dealing with the challenge of change.[27] The creation of this kind of talent pool is the essence of strategic leadership development as a force for competitiveness.

The Challenge of Strategic Leadership Development

The Strategic Leadership Model presents several challenges to organizations attempting to create a strategic leadership talent pool – the kind of talent pool that enables the organization to maintain dynamic equilibrium in a changing environment. These challenges relate directly to our core recommendations.

|| *1. The organization must view management as a process of interpretation, not a process of control.*

To prevent the natural progression into bureaucracy, leadership development strategies must view management as much more than a series of analytical techniques and planning processes. Rather, management must be viewed as a process of *interpretation*. This requires a heightened sense of leadership judgment to focus the strategic directions of the organization and exploit its capabilities.

GE's use of action learning and "work-out" exemplifies the application of this idea.[28] This type of orchestrated interaction helps to focus management attention on the ideals of the organization, promote network building, and enhance market orientation. Most importantly, it helps to develop an open leadership perspective among managers through the challenge of interaction and group problem-solving, a perspective that enhances awareness of the need for dynamic tension between innovation and adaption in leadership style and organizational processes.

|| *2. Organizations must view leadership development as a tool for building commitment to strategic intent and engendering a market focus.*

GE's and Conrail's management development programs are good examples of this concept in action. These efforts help both to indoctrinate leaders in the ideals of the organization and empower them to work together to bring those ideals to reality by exploiting opportunity in the marketplace. In so doing, these exemplar companies are utilizing leadership development as a focal point for building organizational focus and competitiveness.

3. *Organizations must design leadership development strategies to create a talent pool of strategic leaders at all levels of the organization.*

A strategy that focuses on creating only a small pool of successors to top management can actually prod the firm toward bureaucracy. Instead, development strategies should focus on cultivating, across managerial ranks, the core talents, perspectives, and capabilities necessary to build long-term competitive advantage in the marketplace.

The Soviet Union focused on developing a small pool of successors to senior management. The result was a succession of clones, each farther removed from the realities of society and each more of an aristocrat than his predecessor. Effective leadership development strategies take a broad approach to talent development, and they build into development efforts the opportunity to observe performance and identify potential.

4. *Organizations must focus leadership development efforts on building both the individual and collective talents of leaders.*

Every individual leader has developmental needs that must be addressed if that leader is to reach his or her full potential. These may include skill-building, to be dealt with through training, organizational knowledge-building, to be dealt with through internal education programs, background development, to be dealt with through experiential assignments, or perspective broadening, to be dealt with through external executive education. All of these efforts are valid *tactical* interventions necessary to build a strategic leadership talent pool.

But effective leadership development strategies need to go beyond tactical interventions. The organization's ideal and strategic intent should always be the focus of the development agenda and the marketplace should always be the context. Strategic leadership development, then, is an effort to promote individual development through the creation of internal and external networks focused on building organizational effectiveness and competitiveness.

Once again, the networks, interactions, and project teams that have been described within GE and Conrail serve as examples of this concept in action. These processes show that leadership development can and should be more than narrowly focused programs in training and development. Rather, leadership development, when viewed in a strategic context, can be a core lever for organizational change and development, fostering organizational development while promoting individual development.

> 5. *Organizations must recognize leadership development as a competitive capability that assists in the development, implementation, and revitalization of organizational strategy.*

Strategic leaders use executive development as a tool to help focus the organization, build competitive capabilities, and cultivate a leadership talent pool. Welch's involvement with GE's leadership development programs and Hagen's involvement with Conrail's management network and development program both serve as testimony to this principle. Strategic leaders use leadership development as a focal point to pull an organization together and move it through the cycles of growth, revitalization, and competitiveness (see Chapter 3).

> 6. *Organizations must view leadership development as an element of strategic business development.*

Strategic leadership development is a tool to prevent the natural bureaucratization of an organization. As such, it is a driver of both strategic ideals and intent *and* of market awareness and development. In short, it is an arm of the strategic business development process.

Managers of leadership development, then, must be strategic leaders themselves. They must understand the business and the competitive environment. They must develop a perspective that views executive development as a competitive weapon to implement strategy through the creation of a strategic leadership talent pool where the dynamic tension between innovative and adaptive leadership is cultivated to promote the kind of organizational learning necessary for long-term growth and success.

> 7. *Organizations must make leadership development part of a consistent HR strategy that blends the processes of recruitment, selection, development, appraisal, and reward into an integrated system for talent pool management, rooted in the ideals of the organization and focused on the marketplace.*

Creating such a talent pool is the driving imperative for leadership development efforts.

Conclusion

In a time of reorganization, revolution, and change, strategic leadership is essential to the competitiveness and development of an organization. The Organizational Development Model provides insight into ways of meeting this challenge. At the core of this challenge is a new strategic context for leadership development, as well as an emerging systems approach to the process. These issues are discussed in Chapters 3 and 4.

Endnotes

1 This section is adapted from Vicere, A.A., "The Strategic Leadership Imperative For Executive Education," *Human Resource Planning*, **15** (1), 1992, pp. 16–31.

2 See the work of Griener, L., "Evolution and Revolution as Organizations Grow," *Harvard Business Review*, July–August, 1972, pp. 37–46. Adizes, I., *Corporate Lifecycles*, Englewood Cliffs, NJ: Prentice Hall, 1989. Miller, L., *Barbarians to Bureaucrats: Corporate Life Cycle Strategies*, New York: Fawcett Columbine, 1989.

3 Kirton, M., "Adapters and Innovators: A Description and Measure," *Journal of Applied Psychology*, **61** (5), 1976, pp. 622–629.

4 Ibid; also see Kirton, M., *Kirton Adaption-Innovation Inventory Manual*, 2nd Edition, Occupational Research Centre, Hatfield, UK, 1987.

5 Adizes, I., 1989, op. cit.

6 Ibid.

7 See Ansoff, I., *The New Corporate Strategy*, New York: John Wiley and Sons, 1988; Ulrich, D. and D. Lake, *Organizational Capability*, New York: John Wiley and Sons, 1990.

8 The "labels" given to each stage are adapted from Miller, 1989, op. cit., and Vicere, 1992, op. cit.

9 David, S. and W. Davidson, *20/20 Vision*, New York: Simon and Schuster, 1991.

10 Prahalad, C.K. and G. Hamel, "The Core Competence of the Corporation," *Harvard Business Review*, May–June, 1990, pp. 79–91.

11 Spychalski, J., "Consolidated Rail Corporation (Case Study)," Penn State Executive Programs, 1991.

12 Kotter, J. and J. Heskett, *Corporate Culture and Performance*, New York: Free Press, 1992.

13 Adizes, I., 1989, op.cit.

14 See Kotter, J. *A Force for Change*, Free Press, New York, 1990

15 See Tichy, N. and S. Sherman, *Control Your Own Destiny Or Someone Else Will*, New York: Doubleday, 1993; also, Tichy, N. "GE's Crotonville: A Staging Ground for Corporate Revolution," *Academy of Management Executive*, **3** (2), 1989, pp. 99–106.

16 Noel, J. and R. Charan, "Leadership Development at GE's Crotonville," *Human Resource Management*, **27** (4), 1988, pp. 443–447.

17 Butler, S. "Cutting Down and Reshaping the Core," *Financial Times* (London), March 20, 1990.

18 Ibid; also see Lorenz, C., "A Drama Behind Closed Doors That Paved the Way for a Corporate Metamorphosis," *Financial Times* (London), March 23, 1990.

19 Mack, T., "Eager Liars and Reluctant Liars," *Forbes Magazine*, February 17, 1992, pp. 98–101.

20 Spychalski, J., 1991, op.cit.

21 Charan, R. "How Networks Shape Organizations for Results," *Harvard Business Review*, September–October, 1991, pp. 104–114.

22 MacQueen, C. and A.A. Vicere, "Conrail's Management Program: On Track Toward Company Vision," *Personnel*, December 10–14, 1987; Vicere, A.A. "Universities as Providers of Executive Development," *Journal of Management Development*, **9** (4), 1990, pp. 23–31.

23 Hamel, G. and C. K. Prahalad, "Strategic Intent," *Harvard Business Review*, May–June, 1989, pp. 63–76.

24 Hamel, G. and C. K. Prahalad, *Competing For The Future*, Boston: Harvard Business School Press, 1994.

25 See Vicere, A.A., "Executive Education and Strategic Imperatives: A Formula for Crafting Competitiveness," *American Journal of Management Development*, **1** (2), pp. 31–36, 1995.

26 Miller, 1989, op. cit.

27 Charan, 1991, op. cit.

28 Tichy and Sherman, 1993, op. cit.

3

THE CHANGING
STRATEGIC CONTEXT

It goes by many names, among them the virtual organization, the horizontal organization, the network organization, the modular corporation, the boundaryless company.[1] By whatever name, it represents a fundamental challenge to conventional wisdom. It is today's "new" organizational form, the business world's response to the post-industrial society. And it is taking its toll on traditional approaches to strategic leadership development.

The purpose of this chapter is to discuss the nature of this new paradigm for effective organizations, how it operates, and how it relates to the evolving approaches to leadership development discussed in the two previous chapters. It is not meant to be an academic treatise on organizational theory, nor is it an endorsement of current trends in organizational structure. Rather, it is a practical look at a phenomenon that is forever reshaping the world of work, the nature of careers, and the essence of both organizational effectiveness and leadership development.

The Roots of the Challenge

The history of modern-day organizational forms can be traced back through numerous decades to the work of Adam Smith, Frederick Taylor, Max Weber, and other organizational theorists.[2] Responding to the needs and demands of the industrial revolution, these theorists created elegant frameworks for managing increasingly large and complex industrial firms in what was, by comparison to today, a relatively stable business environment. The models they created held that the key to managing the large "machine bureaucracies" created by the industrial revolution was *control* – clear lines of authority, narrow spans of control, and vertical and horizontal integration.[3] The way to establish control was to create the traditional organizational form, the hierarchical pyramid.

In the early stages of the industrial revolution, the hierarchical form of organization worked remarkably well. It helped companies like General Motors, Sears, IBM, US Steel, and others grow into large, profitable entities.[4] There is no denying that the bureaucratic form of management these companies perfected added great value to their operations – their past successes are part of business history.

As we moved through the 1970s and 1980s, however, the business environment changed. The bureaucratic, control-oriented form of organization no longer seemed to work. The economic environment had gone global, and traditional management practices, once viable and value-adding, became steadily obsolete. To complicate the situation further, the world was experiencing the onset of the information age, and the very nature of management practices, at once slow, controlling, impersonal, and directive in the bureaucratic model, had to adjust to the needs of knowledge workers who demanded more open, empowering management processes.[5] These compounding influences gave rise to a rash of restructuring efforts resulting in a frantic search for new approaches to organizational design.[6]

The New Organizational Framework

The establishment of a new framework for organizational design did not come about in a single wave. Rather, it emerged through a series of fits and starts that together constitute a fascinating and fundamental shift in management thinking. The nature of that shift is described below.

Established organizations have been challenged to rethink their competitive strategies and operational processes by increased global competition and enhanced information technology. Many once-dominant competitors seemed nearly powerless to fend off the onslaught of new competitors that did not follow traditional "rules".[7] As a result of this intensified competitive environment, many established organizations lost market share and saw dramatic declines in profit margins.

These competitive pressures forced companies to take action, perhaps the most significant of which were the extensive downsizing efforts that continue even today.

Downsizing, in itself, was a reasonable response to the competitive pressures of the emerging global economy. Many "new" competitors were much younger, much leaner, and, through better use of IT, significantly more streamlined in their organizational processes. These new competitors were often faster moving, more efficient, and more in touch with the marketplace than their "traditional" rivals. So, first-wave responses to this new competitive environment tended to involve attempts "to do more with less" by flattening organizational pyramids and incorporating new technologies, thereby gaining efficiency and improving cycle times.[8] To make these leaner, flatter, faster structures work, and to further enhance competitiveness, many organizations simultaneously embarked upon efforts to engrain total quality management (TQM) into their new management structures. TQM was seen as a way to revitalize organizational processes and thereby rekindle the competitiveness of a firm.[9]

Yet, despite the apparent logic of these first-wave downsizing efforts, despite the unrefuted importance of total quality management to global competitiveness, and despite wave after wave of continued restructuring, many organizations still were unable to reestablish their competitive position. It appeared that while fewer layers and fewer people could make a short-term contribution to an organization's bottom line, while new technologies could streamline and speed up certain processes, and while TQM could create a short-term fervor for reinventing a culture, these efforts frequently did little to help revitalize an organization's long-term competitive position in the now established global economy.[10] This realization has triggered a second wave of restructuring efforts and the emergence of a new organizational form, a form that is fundamentally changing the nature of work, of organizations, and of the practice of management.

The Emergence of a New Form

The shapes in Figure 3.1 trace the history and evolution of organizational forms. In Figure 3.1a, the traditional organizational model is symbolized as a tall pyramid. With the onset of the global competitive environment

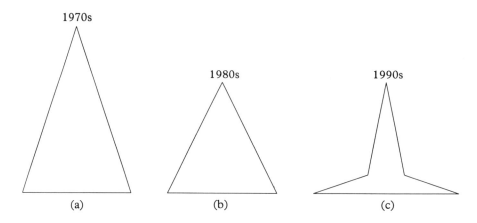

Figure 3.1 Evolution of organizational form
Source: Vicere, A.A. *The Changing Context for Leadership and Organizational Development,* Penn State University: Institute for the Study of Organizational Effectiveness, WP 95-01, 1995.

and its penchant for dynamic, unpredictable change, the traditional model became dysfunctional. The tall pyramid organizational form fell prey to first-wave downsizing and delayering efforts, resulting in the flatter organizational pyramid portrayed in Figure 3.1b.

At least theoretically, the flat pyramid held great promise. Its supporters proclaimed that in addition to being more cost effective due to the need for fewer people, it brought the customer closer to the decision-making mechanisms of the firm; it eliminated unnecessary layers of bureaucracy; it gave workers broader scope and scale of responsibilities; it sped up decision making and cycle times – all potentially positive benefits. Yet, although these benefits often would accrue to a recently downsized organization for a short while, many organizations never really regained the competitive position they sought through their restructuring efforts. This tended to result in another wave of flattening (downsizing), then another, and so on. This vicious cycle of activity left many organizations in search of a better way to address the competitive challenges of the global economy.[11]

A key explanation for the inability of the flat pyramid to deliver on renewed competitiveness is revealed in Figure 3.2. It shows a symbol referred to as an *oval of activity,* which represents all of those activities, actions, and processes in which an organization engages to accomplish

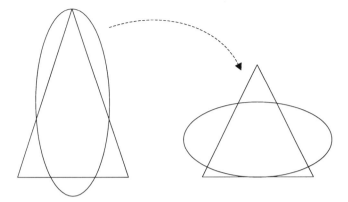

Figure 3.2 The "oval of activity"
Source: Vicere, A.A. *The Changing Context for Leadership and Organizational Development*, Penn State University: Institute for the Study of Organizational Effectiveness, WP 95-01, 1995.

its work. In the traditional tall pyramid, the oval of activity is shown to be standing on its end. In first-wave downsizing efforts, organizations simply tend to push the oval of activity on to its side. That is, they often continue to do all the things they always have done, but with fewer people. Consequently, even if the organization generates some short-term benefit from their restructuring effort, the chaos and stress it creates often trigger a different set of performance problems, leading to another round of downsizing, and so on.[12]

Until recently, most companies seemed to be caught up in this restructuring nightmare. Rather than restructuring with a purpose, they seemed to be moving through this vicious cycle of continuous shrinking with no focus on creating unique value in the marketplace, no focus on growing and developing the organization as a competitive entity. Instead of finding new ways to craft competitiveness for a changing world, they seemed committed to doing what they always had done. but with fewer people.

The Impetus for Evolution

Two of today's most provocative and influential management theorists are Gary Hamel and C.K. Prahalad. Through a compelling series of articles and a best-selling book, they have described how competitive effectiveness is related to a focused sense of purpose – a "strategic intent" coupled with a unique set of "core competencies," which together drive the development of the organization.[13] Similarly, in their current best-seller, *The Discipline of Market Leaders*, Michael Treacy and Fred Wiersema discuss an organization's need to focus on "value disciplines" to build real competitive advantage within their industry.[14] Again, the authors suggest that an unyielding sense of purpose coupled with unique sets of capabilities are the keys to organizational competitiveness. In their 1993 *Harvard Business Review* article, Goss, Pascale and Athos noted a clear and distinct "declaration" of purpose was essential if an organization was to successfully ride what they termed the "reinvention rollercoaster," the path of continuous change organizations must follow if they are to remain competitive in today's dynamic marketplace.[15]

Regardless of the label attached to the process, whether it is strategic intent, core competencies, value disciplines, declarations, or some other term, the need to define the strategic purpose of a firm and its critical capabilities is considered to be of paramount importance in current approaches to strategic management.[16] Organizations that subscribe to this logic seem to pare themselves down to a core of activities resulting in an organizational form that can be best symbolized by the drawing in Figure 3.1c. This unique symbol is the heart of a new and evolving organizational form that might best be described as the *shadow pyramid*.[17]

How the Shadow Pyramid Works

The new organizational form portrayed in Figure 3.1c is flatter, leaner, more focused, and very directed. The organization itself has been pared down to its essence. It represents only that mix of competencies, capabilities, functions, and processes that enable the organization to compete on a truly unique basis as an industry/world leader. All non-essential activities, functions, etc. have been removed from the core. Some of the removed activities have been deemed by the organization to be unnecessary, to add no value to the work of the firm, and therefore have been eliminated entirely. Many organizations have created enormous efficiencies through such efforts. Other activities, although not unique in themselves and therefore not defined as part of the core, are

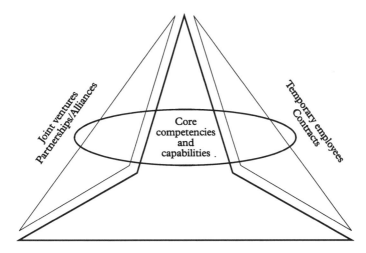

Figure 3.3 Shadow pyramid organization
Source: Vicere, A.A. *The Changing Context for Leadership and Organizational Development*, Penn State University: Institute for the Study of Organizational Effectiveness, WP 95-01, 1995.

still necessary for the effective operation of the business. For the organization to compete, it must find alternative ways to economically and effectively engage in these essential non-core activities.

It is quite common today to talk of "outsourcing" as a means of dealing with this challenge.[18] This establishment of a network of partner-suppliers of goods and services in non-core areas is often viewed as a key to building efficiency and flexibility into an organizational structure. At the same time, it can help ensure that corporate investment is being appropriately directed toward those core competencies and capabilities that enable the organization to compete on a truly world class basis. Discussions of the outsourcing phenomenon with Dr. Joseph L. Cavinato have led us to the development of the full-scale shadow pyramid model depicted in Figure 3.3.

A Symbol of Change

The fully developed shadow pyramid model (Figure 3.3) portrays the organization not as a fully vertically and horizontally integrated mono-lith, but as a lithe and nimble core of unique competencies and capabilities competing and growing not by control, but through relationships. As reflected in the model, these relationships can involve contract suppliers or temporary workers in traditional outsourcing relationships. They can also include joint ventures, partnerships, and alliances – "new" ways of stretching and leveraging the core competencies and capabilities of the firm.[19] An organization's shadow pyramid is likely to include some combination or variation of all of the above as it positions itself to compete in a dynamic business environment characterized by new organizational principles and new leadership roles. Those principles and roles are symbolized by the new oval of activity shown in Figure 3.3, an oval that does not encompass the entire organization, but rather one that links part of the core to a dynamic network of partners that enable the organization to leverage its core competencies in the marketplace.[20]

> *The shadow pyramid shows that an organization does not need its own complete structure. It can enhance its performance and expand opportunities through relationships with other well-managed organizations.*
>
> Captain, US Navy

Three Cases in Point

The following three examples, although brief, help to broadly characterize the nature of the shift toward the shadow pyramid framework and its impact on organizational strategies and processes. All three examples will be discussed in greater detail throughout the remainder of this chapter.

Carpenter Technology Corporation

Carpenter Technology Corporation, a US-based producer of specialty steel and other advanced materials, has embarked upon an ambitious plan to nearly double its business over the next few years. Building on its core expertise in steel production, metallurgy and advanced materials development, and customer service based on advanced electronic data interchange capabilities, Carpenter Technology is positioning itself as a global player in the advanced materials business. Their recent acquisition of Aceros Fortuna, a steel distributor in Mexico, along with the establishment of a joint venture with Walsin Liwah in Taiwan, have given the company a solid foothold in growing markets outside their traditional market in North America. In addition, joint ventures and acquisitions in structural ceramics development and production, as well as expansion of their European distribution network, have helped to reposition Cartech as not just another American specialty steel company, but as a serious global producer and distributor of advanced materials used in the automotive, aerospace, and chemical industries. In effect, Cartech is attempting to build a network around its core capabilities in advanced materials production and distribution to enable itself to evolve, grow, and prosper in the global economy.

ARAMARK

ARAMARK (formerly ARA Services) is a world leader in contract/managed services, including food services, facilities services, uniform rentals, and healthcare management. Purchased by its employees in a leveraged buyout ten years ago, ARAMARK is a highly successful company that is benefiting greatly from the development of the shadow pyramid. As other businesses seek to pare down to their core and gain efficiencies in their organizational structures, ARAMARK finds itself in a rapidly growing market for contract/managed services, a market in which it is a dominant player. But ARAMARK itself faced a dilemma – how to move from a collection of independently operating service provider businesses to a flexible provider of multiple services capable of assisting customers to both gain efficiency and enhance internal operations through partnerships with ARAMARK across multiple fronts. Today, ARAMARK is working to build its own internal network to help position itself as the world's premier managed services provider with a permanent position in the shadow pyramid "wings" of its customer base.

Daimler-Benz

As one of the largest conglomerates in Europe and the largest industrial company in Germany, Daimler-Benz is among Europe's crown jewel corporations. Yet Daimler-Benz, too, is adjusting to the shadow pyramid challenge. Reeling from economic pressures in Europe and throughout the world, and anticipating a dramatically different and more intensely competitive environment, Daimler-Benz has begun a corporate restructuring of its own, with a core focus – to be the world's premier transportation systems technologies company.[21] Daimler-Benz hopes to use this focus to stretch and leverage its resources by gaining greater focus and therefore greater synergies across its vast global network of operating partners, including subsidiaries like Mercedes-Benz, Freightliner, and Mercedes-Benz Credit Corporation; venture partners like Ssang Yong, SMH Corporation, and Detroit Diesel; and other relationships. In effect, Daimler-Benz is attempting to carve out a niche as a world-class competitor in transportation and mobility related technologies and is building its internal and external networks to leverage those capabilities.

Implications of a Shadow Pyramid

As these and other organizations evolve toward the shadow pyramid form, they are finding that it presents a multitude of implications both for redefining the essence of leadership and organizational effectiveness, and for reconfiguring processes for developing organizational, leadership, and individual effectiveness.[22] Some of these implications are discussed below.

Leadership and Organizational Effectiveness

The formation of a shadow pyramid is a process that requires a great deal of time, effort, and leadership. Senior leaders must lead the charge to define and clarify the organization's strategic intent and its core competencies and capabilities. They also must enable and empower the organization to build the internal and external networks that must be in place for the organization to function effectively in a relationship-based environment. Similarly, business unit leaders within corporations must work to define the core of their business unit and facilitate the network development necessary for business unit success, including appropriate links with the corporate center and other internal business units. Operating managers within business units must create the same type of focus within their own area of responsibility.

> Even individual managers and professionals, if they hope to build a successful career, must continually ask themselves what their personal core competencies are, and what they must do to build the internal and external network connections that will enable them to maximize their contributions to the organization and, therefore, their personal development.

This fundamental shift in thinking changes many of the "rules" of leadership and organizational effectiveness. Leaders no longer manage by control, they manage by relationships, trust, and communication.[23] As a result, effective leaders in a shadow pyramid must combine exceptional technical knowledge with superior influence skills to develop a unique blend of relationship-focused leadership capability. With such relationships in place, organizations no longer grow by controlling their entire supply chain. Rather, they grow by performing some portion of that supply chain very well, and by linking up with partners and providers to complete the process.[24] The most successful organizations, and the most successful leaders within them, are those that are best able to manage the "interfaces" that must be established between their core and their partner/provider network (see the "oval of activity" in Figure 3.3).

As a result, this new organizational form brings two business functions to the forefront of management thinking – logistics (supply chain management)[25] and information technology.[26] In earlier times, business schools emphasized marketing and financial capability as the essence of competitive advantage. Today, world-class capabilities in finance and marketing are simply the ante to the business game. Similarly, quality and productivity have recently been championed as the essence of competitive effectiveness. These capabilities have run their course as differentiators as well. Excellence in them is essential and expected.

In a shadow pyramid, however, logistics management and information technology become key differentiating capabilities that enable an organization to effectively manage the critical interfaces that exist within its operating network. These two functions, long viewed as peripheral areas within a business, move to the forefront of strategic thinking in an organization where internal and external relationships must be woven together into an efficient operating system.[27] The examples of ARAMARK,

Daimler-Benz, and Carpenter Technology provide testimony to the nature of this shift.

Organizational Development

Implemented effectively, a shadow pyramid can enable an organization to focus its activities and build momentum toward a strategic intent, a core sense of purpose that drives the development of the organization. In effect, it can enable the organization to stretch its aspirations, leverage its resources, and grow toward the future. This requires an organization to define not only its strategic intent and core competencies, but also demands an operational focus that drives investment in those core activities in a way that can lead to world-class competitiveness in particular technologies, functions and/or processes. This helps the organization to develop and leverage its core competencies and capabilities – its real value and uniqueness in the marketplace – through the relationships it establishes with its shadow pyramid partners.[28]

Although there is an intuitive logic to this process, it presents a host of challenges to organizations. One is the mistaken notion that mission and vision statements are surrogates for core competency identification. Defining a company's essence is not something that can or should be done superficially; defining the core is a process that requires careful consideration. As IBM Chief Executive Lou Gerstner said in 1993, "the last thing IBM needs now is a vision."[29] IBM's recent level of success is testimony to the fact that Gerstner was on to something.

In the early stages of restructuring and transformation, what IBM or any company needs is a thorough understanding of external opportunities, internal capabilities, and possibilities for developing competitive advantage. Wordsmithed vision statements not rooted in this level of strategic analysis can direct a company's focus away from the marketplace, a certain way to lose position in today's competitive environment. On the other hand, an organization that takes careful stock of its essence will be in a better position to create a form of values-based "glue" that can enable the organization to better stretch and leverage its resources,[30] a challenge IBM seems to be slowly but steadily meeting.

This may lead to the conclusion that developing a core focus is a time-consuming process, and to a degree it *is*. That is because to create such a focus, senior management must be intimately involved in an effort to define strategic intent and core competencies. They must get input, agreement, and commitment from organizational members with regard to the definition of the core and what it means to business practices and processes. And, they must help establish the internal and external networks necessary to leverage that core into a thriving, growing business. Paul Evans of INSEAD referred to this senior management responsibility as "applying glue technology."[31] The framework shown below, adapted from Evans' work, suggests how organizational glue technology offers further steps toward crafting competitive effectiveness within a shadow pyramid organization.

Organizational "Glue Technology"

1. Face-to-Face Relationships
2. Horizontal Business Interactions
3. Horizontal Project Work/Assignments
4. Establishing Vision and Values
5. Applying Vision and Values to Build Competitiveness

Establishing Face-to-Face Relationships

For most companies, developing organizational glue technology requires significant rethinking of human resource management, organizational development, and business development practices. The first step in this process involves the establishment of face-to-face relationships among the leaders of the organization. However, this relationship-building process goes well beyond the socializing aspect commonly associated with face-to-face contact. Rather, it involves a more in-depth process of helping managers across the organization get to know each other's businesses and personal capabilities as a basis for internal network building.

For example, for Daimler-Benz to truly leverage its core competencies and capabilities in mobility systems technologies, it must make significant progress in building bridges across business units that heretofore have been fully independent operations. To establish preliminary linkages Daimler-Benz is conducting a series of seminars in various regions around the world in which groups of senior managers from each region gather together to discuss issues, share experiences, and learn about each other's operation. Because of where the company is in its repositioning program, these sessions are designed to build face-to-face contacts among leaders across the organization, as well as greater understanding of the entire Daimler-Benz family of companies.

As the North American region has gone through the first round of this process, part of which is built around a discussion of the shadow pyramid model, considerable momentum has built for maintaining and enhancing the emerging North American leadership network. In this instance, however, the senior managers in the region are driving the process rather than it being a corporate initiative. In addition, two of the major North American business units have adapted part of the program to their own businesses in an attempt to define and leverage their own core. For Daimler-Benz, the glue seems to be taking hold, and spreading. The challenge for the North American region is to move to the next level. ARAMARK has done just that by creating the ARAMARK Executive Leadership Institute (ELI), an intensive organizational and individual development forum for the top 150 leaders in the company. From CEO Joe Neubauer on down, this budding leadership network has worked to redefine the future of the company and revitalize its already successful organization, putting it on a track for even greater growth and profitability in the years ahead.

As part of ELI, ARAMARK leaders participate in two educational seminars totalling eight days of classroom involvement. At the outset, participants share a brief outdoor leadership development experience to help "break the ice" and facilitate interaction. This exercise is followed with a core curriculum of classroom sessions designed to create a common vocabulary and develop frameworks for business analysis. Through the use of company-specific case studies and carefully focused discussion sessions, participants share insights on each others' business units to promote better awareness of the overall core competencies and capabilities of the firm. The out-of-classroom social interaction that takes place serves to further cement the establishment of the network. This type of activity lays the foundation for phase two of the process.

Horizontal Business Interactions

Once face-to-face relationships have been established and a common language developed, then the organization must provide opportunities for cross-business interaction to further advance the development process. That is, the organization must promote cross-organization learning through business-focused interaction of leaders from all parts of the organization. For example, the Daimler-Benz North America Leadership Program includes a session in which participants from the same business group analyze a particular business within their group, prepare a report on that business, and share that report with their fellow program participants. In this manner, working relationships are developed among program participants while knowledge of business capabilities is shared across the emerging network of leaders.

Going a step further, ARAMARK's ELI participants engage in an action learning experience called "action projects" in which they work in cross-organization teams to tackle real business issues submitted by the heads of ARAMARK business units. They do this work under one constraint – no individual can work on a project within their own business unit. In this way, ELI gives ARAMARK first-hand experience with other parts of the company. This type of interaction promotes cross-organizational awareness of capabilities and cross-business assessment of opportunities, laying the foundation for phase three of the process.

Horizontal Project Work

With growing interaction and broader understanding of the competencies and capabilities of the organization, leaders are prepared to explore on a real-time, hands-on basis opportunities to grow and expand the organization across multiple fronts. ARAMARK uses its action projects to facilitate this process. ELI participants work on their action projects, over and above their regular job responsibilities, for approximately six months. At the end of that time, they present their findings to both senior management and their business unit project sponsors. This horizontal project work ensures the glue is taking hold within the organization and simultaneously reinforces the networks, vocabulary, and business processes established in the early stages of ELI. With the glue technology now firmly in place, the organization is prepared to move on to the next phase of the process.

Clarification of Vision and Values

Once the internal operating network has been initiated, the organization is in a position both to define its core competencies and capabilities and to create a process to leverage these capabilities in the marketplace. As ELI evolved, ARAMARK's senior managers used their budding leadership network to help restate, clarify, and begin the process of communicating the company's vision, values, and competencies across its 130,000 employees. Taking advantage of the anniversary marking ten years of employee ownership, linking that occasion to the creation of a new name and corporate identity, and leveraging both those activities through the ELI internal network, ARAMARK positioned itself to enter the final phase of the process with remarkable momentum.

Use Vision and Values to Drive Business Planning

Once the strategic intent and core competencies have been defined, the organization can use them as the focal point for organizational development initiatives. For ARAMARK, the challenge is to continue its positive momentum by aligning their human resource management systems to the strategic imperatives and organizational values created through ELI. Most of its action projects were focused on analyzing ways to better manage interfaces with customers, partners, and providers, both internal and external. However, others focused on creating both organizational structures and human resource management systems (compensation, appraisal, etc.) to enable the organization to grow and prosper. ARAMARK is using the input generated by these ELI teams to develop a new leadership competency model, design a related performance appraisal process, rethink compensation systems, and refocus business metrics. In that manner, they are positioning the organization for continued growth and success.

Leadership Development

Organizational development is not the only thing affected by the shadow pyramid. It has an impact on leadership development well, including career planning processes. Note the different form the oval of activity took in Figure 3.3. This oval does not encompass the entire organization as in previous organizational models. Rather, it spans a segment of the core of the organization and segments of the wings. This drawing symbolizes the personal challenge of leadership and career development within a shadow pyramid.

> *Our business is focused on rapid, global growth. We want to retain our core competencies but reduce our costs. A shadow pyramid structure is the only way for us to succeed.*
>
> Engineering Manager, Westinghouse Electric Corporation

A leader in this new form is, in effect, a node within the core, a node from which relationships are established, developed and nurtured. As such, the battered and bruised middle managers of today's corporations, as well as aspiring managers and professionals of tomorrow, find themselves in a unique position. As organizations have pared to their core, middle level positions slowly but surely have been whittled away. As that has happened, however, those few individuals left in the middle of a shadow pyramid must take on new and critically important roles that are radically different from their former roles in the traditional model.

To succeed in this type of environment, an individual leader must be able to think and operate beyond the confines of his or her organization and job responsibilities. In short, he or she must be ready, willing and able to identify and facilitate opportunities for building relationships both within the organization and with external partners to enable the firm to compete effectively in the global business environment.[32] To do this with any degree of success, the leader must be a true expert in his or her area of responsibility, both because there is so little depth in the middle of the organization, and because the establishment of business relationships is often related to the leader's ability to link the organization's unique capabilities with the unique needs and/or capabilities of a partner. This means that leaders must not only be technical experts, they must also truly understand the business of their organization and the potential benefit of various relationships to the business. They must have a detailed understanding of the marketplace in which the organization operates in order to identify opportunities for stretching and leveraging organizational resources through relationship building. They also must be a master of influence processes capable of leading and directing people and partners over whom they have no direct authority.[33] The scale and scope of these jobs are, by comparison to the traditional model, enormous. In the shadow pyramid, mid-level managers and professionals are the true backbone of the organization. Without their commitment and involvement, the "organizational network" will simply fall apart. Developing these leadership capabilities is, therefore, a challenging task.

The establishment of the Daimler-Benz North America (DBNA) leadership network is an example of an initiative designed to challenge leaders to better understand and adjust to this new challenge. The company designed the Daimler-Benz North America Leadership Program, with the help of partner Penn State Executive Programs, to bring together the top 150 leaders from DBNA companies in groups of 25 to 30 at a time both to build an internal network and to address the leadership challenge described above. Each group is hosted by one of the DBNA business groups for a four-day session. The first day is spent learning about the host business. The next two days are spent discussing key leadership issues for the future development of the organization. The final day is spent interacting with a board member from parent company Daimler-Benz, AG who discusses key strategic issues from both a regional and a worldwide perspective. This gives North American executives an opportunity to further the development of their glue technology while promoting the development of the individual leadership skills of the participants at the same time.

Similarly, Carpenter Technology Corporation realized the critical nature of this challenge when they began to establish their own internal network. After having defined a set of strategic imperatives for business development, Cartech partnered with Penn State Executive Programs to create the Strategic Leadership Development Program. This program has been running since January of 1994 and has involved Cartech's top 120 managers. The program includes a series of five two-and-a-half-day seminars geared to both internal network building and leadership competency development. Action projects are also being used, with a focus on building the internal and external networks essential to the company's growth and to create a "practice lab" for putting newly developed leadership competencies to work. Cartech managers have visited other countries, analyzed potential partners, and reconfigured systems and processes as part of the effort. Cartech CEO Bob Cardy is intimately involved in the initiative, as are the senior officers of the company. In this manner, the new leadership capabilities being discussed within Cartech are not just topics on a syllabus, but are key strategic issues being discussed, debated, and modeled throughout the company.

Individual Development

A shadow pyramid not only demands a different kind of leader, it creates one as well. To understand this challenge better, think of a leader in the middle of a shadow pyramid. These individuals are less likely to be looking for the type of long-term employment security sought by previous generations of managers. They realize that there is much less of that in this new form. They are more likely to be concerned with finding positions that enhance their overall employability, with how a given position or assignment contributes to their personal portfolio of skills and experiences, and how their experience with an organization will contribute to their advancement within or apart from their current employer.[34]

Because of this shift in worker values, the issues of employee loyalty and motivation are critical within the shadow pyramid. The form requires a radically new definition of the employer–employee compact, one more focused on open communication, personal involvement, and personal development.[35] For some senior managers, this appears to be a welcome change. It can enable an organization to have a continuous flow of fresh ideas and. It can lead to employees becoming more intense, more interested in making their mark on the organization.[36] Yet, left unchecked, this individualistic focus can also lead to the emergence of an army of mercenaries in the middle of the organization, mercenaries more concerned with advancing themselves than with advancing the organization.

As companies become more aware of this potential problem, the need for creating some form of glue technology becomes overwhelming, bringing new approaches to human resource management and organizational development to the forefront of the organization's strategic agenda. A shadow pyramid's demand for defined core competencies and a clear strategic intent enables an organization to channel the energy of high-achieving managers and professionals in pursuit of the organization's long-term goals. In addition, the focus on network interactions and project work gives organizations enormous opportunities to truly enrich jobs and challenge capable people. Yet, none of these opportunities will be capitalized on unless the organization actively creates strategic leadership development processes, as in the examples of ARAMARK, Daimler-Benz North America and Cartech. Further, human resource management systems must be appropriately aligned to address the demands of the shadow pyramid organizational form.

Aligning Human Resource Management Systems

A full analysis of the human resource management implications of a shadow pyramid are beyond the scope of this chapter. However, a look at a few broad implications is in order. First, the sheer scale and scope of the manager's job in this new form demands an individual focus on continuous learning and an organizational focus on continuous development. However, the logistics of these developmental processes may need to change. The idea that leadership development should be focused on identifying and cultivating the individual potential only of a select group of high-potential managers must give way to the idea of combining individual development with organizational development to create competitive effectiveness.[37] In addition, the idea of removing a high-potential employee from the business core to enable that individual to participate in a longer term, off-line, formal education experience is likely to be a thing of the past. Instead, companies will endeavor to blend ongoing education with ongoing experience through the more effective use of new educational technologies and action learning experiences similar to those described within ARAMARK and Cartech.[38]

Second, the world of employee education and development, including traditional university degree programs, will be under incredible pressure to adjust to new demands for real-world, on-line, just-in-time training, education and development practices.[39] Perhaps the most visible example of this challenge is the training, education and development initiative being mounted by Motorola. The company spends over $100 million annually on these activities and claims to have proof that when implemented properly, *these investments pay off at a rate of 30 to one.* Motorola is so convinced of the value of its process and its superiority over traditional providers, that the company is working to establish its own fully-accredited Motorola University.[40]

Finally, employee benefits and reward systems will need to change, adjusting to the demands of the more fluid organizational structures and processes created by a shadow pyramid. Retirement programs and healthcare benefits will need to be portable and more the responsibility of the individual. Reward systems must be more individualized and linked to the accomplishments of networks, project teams, and other types of horizontal business groups.[41] All of these elements of the human resource management infrastructure will need to be reconsidered and redesigned to accommodate the demands of this new organizational form.

Beyond the Shadow Pyramid

If the shadow pyramid model describes the nature of organizational structure in today's environment, then what's next? Will the pendulum swing back to the traditional pyramid, or will a new model emerge? We believe that, like all good ideas in the field of management, the shadow pyramid idea will be overdone – it will be taken too far, implemented without careful consideration of its potential ramifications, used as a temporary fix for a much more significant problem. But when the dust settles, we believe the lessons learned from the shadow pyramid will change the nature of effective organizations for ever. As we learn to work in networks and through relationships in a global economy, and as we learn to use technology and information backbones to a fuller extent, the potential benefits of a shadow pyramid will be in even greater demand. Organizations will continue to evolve toward more "virtual" designs, involving dynamic networks of partners operating across many aspects of business operations (see Figure 3.4). As this new structure evolves, the skill sets deemed necessary to operate in today's shadow pyramid will become even more critical to an organization's ability to forge competitive advantage in the global marketplace.

The core leadership challenge is framed by an apparent paradox: by defining a set of boundaries around a strategic intent and a set of core competencies, an organization is in a position to become "boundaryless," to grow faster and more profitably than before by leveraging its shadow pyramid partnerships. If the profits from that growth are reinvested to keep the organization's core competencies at the leading

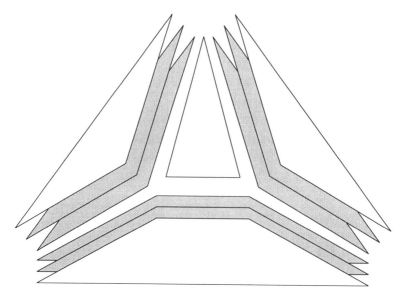

Figure 3.4 What's next? The "virtual" corporation: the core business surrounded by a dynamic network of partners operating at multiple levels

edge, the organization creates for itself a powerful cycle of continuous growth, innovation, and development around those unique capabilities that enable them to add value to their customers.

Competing in a knowledge-oriented, information-driven global economy requires leaders to give serious consideration to the shadow pyramid organizational form as they develop their companies' competitive strategies. The model, in all its simplicity, can help in the visualization of this challenge. The task at hand is to further investigate how to avoid the pitfalls and reap the benefits of the opportunities this new model presents. That task is addressed throughout the remainder of this book.

Endnotes

1 A number of books and articles have described these emerging models of organizational structure, including Handy, C. *The Age of Unreason*, Boston: HBS Press, 1990; Mills, D.Q. *Rebirth of the Corporation*, New York: Wiley, 1991; Quinn, J.B. *Intelligent Enterprise*, New York: Free Press, 1992; Stewart, T. "The search of the organization of tomorrow," *Fortune*, May 18, 1992,

pp. 91–98; Miles, R. and C. Snow, *Fit, Failure and the Hall of Fame*, New York. Free Press, 1994; Byrne, J. "The virtual organization," *Business Week*, February 8, 1993, pp. 98–102; Tully, S. "The modular corporation," *Fortune*, February 8, 1993, pp. 106–114.

2 See chapter one in Hammer, M. and J. Champy, *Reengineering the Corporation*, New York: Harper Business, 1993.

3 See chapters one and two in Nadler, D. et al., *Organizational Architecture*, San Francisco: Jossey-Bass, 1992.

4 Loomis, C. "Dinosaurs?" *Fortune*, May 3, 1993, pp. 36–42.

5 See Drucker, P. *Managing for the Future*, New York: Truman Talley Books/Dutton, 1992.

6 For discussions of the changing competitive environment and its impact on organizational design, see Nadler, 1992, op. cit.; Stewart, T. "The search for the organization of tomorrow," *Fortune*, May 18, 1992, pp. 91–98; Drucker, P. "The new society of organizations," *Harvard Business Review*, Sept/Oct, 1992, pp. 95–104; Handy, C. "Balancing corporate power: A new federalist paper," *Harvard Business Review*, Nov/Dec, 1992, pp. 59–72; Handy, 1990, op. cit.

7 Davis, S. and B. Davidson, *20/20 Vision*, New York: Simon & Schuster, 1991; Hamel, G. and C.K. Prahalad, "Corporate imagination and expeditionary marketing," *Harvard Business Review*, July/August, 1991, pp. 81–92.

8 Henkoff, R. "Getting beyond downsizing," *Fortune*, January 10, 1994, pp. 58–64.

9 Jacob, R. "TQM: More than a dying fad?," *Fortune*, October 18, 1993, pp. 66–72.

10 Hammer and Champy, 1993, op. cit.; Cascio, W., "Downsizing: What have we learned?," *Academy of Management Executive*, 7, 1, 1993, pp. 95–104; also *Best Practices in Corporate Restructuring*, Chicago, The Wyatt Company, 1993.

11 *Best Practices in Corporate Restructuring*, ibid.; Henkoff, op.cit. see also, Hamel G. and C.K. Prahalad, *Competing For the Future*, Boston: Harvard Business School Press, 1994.

12 Ulrich, D. and D. Lake *Organizational Capability*, New York: John Wiley & Sons, 1994. see also, Hamel and Prahalad, 1994, idem.

13 Hamel and Prahalad, 1990 and 1994, op.cit.

14 Treacy, M. and F. Wiersema *The Discipline of Market Leaders*, Reading, MA: Addison-Wesley, 1995.

15 Goss, T., R. Pascale, and A. Athos "The Reinvention Rollercoaster: risking the present for a powerful future," *Harvard Business Review*, Nov/Dec, 1993, pp. 97–108.

16 See Ready, D. *Champions of Change*, International Consortium for Executive Development Research and Gemini Consulting, 1994.

17 For the purposes of this book, the implications of the "shadow pyramid" are discussed from the standpoint of broad-based leadership and organizational development issues. We have elected not to discuss operational issues related to changes in the "base" of the new model, many of which are reflected in ideas like the "virtual" organization.

18 For a discussion of this shift, see Handy, 1990, op. cit.; for a discussion of outsourcing, see Tully, 1993, op. cit.; for a discussion of challenges in outsourcing, see Bettis, R., S. Bradley, and G. Hamel, Outsourcing and industrial decline, *Academy of Management Executive*, 6, 1, 1992, pp. 7–21.

19 Hamel, G. and C. K. Prahalad, 1994, op. cit.; Hamel, G. and C. K. Prahalad, "Strategic intent," *Harvard Business Review*, May/June, 1989, pp. 63–76; Prahalad, C.K. and G. Hamel, "The core competence of the corporation," *Harvard Business Review*, May/June, 1990, pp. 79–91; Stalk, G., P. Evans, and E. Shulman, "Competing on capabilities: The new rules of corporate strategy," *Harvard Business Review*, March/April, 1992, pp. 57–69.

20 Hamel, G. and C. K. Prahalad, 1994, ibid.

21 For a discussion of current developments at Daimler-Benz, see Gumbel, P. and A. Choi, "Corporate Germany revamps operations – and boosts economy," *Wall Street Journal*, April 7, 1995, p. 1.

22 Handy, 1990, op. cit.; 1992, op. cit.; Stewart, T. "How to manage in the new era," *Fortune*, January 15, 1990, pp. 58–72; Huey, J. "Managing in the midst of chaos," *Fortune*, April 5, 1993, pp. 38–48; Kiechell, W. "How we will work in the year 2000," *Fortune*, May 17, 1993, pp. 38–52.

23 See Hirschorn, L. and T. Gilmore "The new boundaries of the 'boundaryless' corporation." *Harvard Business Review*, May/June, 1992, pp. 104–115.

24 See Kanter, R.M. "Collaborative advantage," *Harvard Business Review*, July/August, 1994, pp. 96–108; Magnet, M. "The new golden rule of business," *Fortune*, February 21, 1994, pp. 60–64.

25 For a useful discussion of the changing role of logistics management, see Henkoff, R. "Delivering the goods," *Fortune*, November 28, 1994, pp. 64–78. For additional discussion of supply chain management issues, see notes on Chrysler in Tully, S., 1993, The modular corporation, op. cit. Also, see Woodruff, D. "Chrysler's Neon," *Business Week*, May 3, 1993, pp. 116–126.

26 Quinn, 1992, op. cit.; Davis and Davidson, 1991, op. cit.; Bleecker, S. "The virtual organization," *The Futurist*, March/April, 1994, pp. 9–14.

27 Savage, C. *5th Generation Management*, Bedford, MA: Digital Press, 1990.

28 Hamel, G. and C.K. Prahalad, "Strategy as stretch and leverage," *Harvard Business Review*, March/April, 1993, pp. 75–84.

29 For a discussion of IBM's revitalization efforts, see Kirkpatrick, D. "Gerstner's IBM," *Fortune*, November 15, 1993, pp. 119–126.

30 See Goss, T., R. Pascale, and A. Athos, 1993, op. cit.

31 Evans, P. "Management development as glue technology," *Human Resource Planning*, 15, 1, 1992, pp. 85–106.

32 See Stewart, T. "Planning a career in a world without managers," *Fortune*, March 20, 1995, pp. 72–80; Handy, C., *The Age of Paradox*, Boston: Harvard Business School Press, 1994; see also, Mills, 1991, op. cit.; Savage, C., 1990, op. cit.

33 See Dumaine, B. "The new non-manager managers," *Fortune*, February 22, 1993, pp. 80–84; Stewart, 1995, ibid.

34 See O'Reilly, B. "The new deal," *Fortune*, June 13, 1994, pp. 44–52.

35 O'Reilly, 1994, ibid.; Handy 1990 and 1994, op. cit.; Fierman, J. "The contingency workforce," *Fortune*, January 24, 1994, pp. 30–36; Bridges, W. "The end of the job," *Fortune*, September 19, 1994, pp. 62–74; Stewart, 1995, op. cit.

36 O'Reilly, 1994, op. cit.

37 See Vicere, A.A. and K. Graham, "Crafting competitiveness: Toward a new paradigm for executive development," in Levit, R. and C. Ghikakis, *Shared Wisdom*, New York: Human Resource Planning Society, 1994, pp. 181–201.

38 See Wick, op. cit.; also, Fulmer, R.M. and A.A. Vicere, *Executive Education and Leadership Development: The State of the Practice*, University Park, PA: Penn State Institute for the Study of Organizational Effectiveness, 1995.

39 This challenge is discussed in O'Reilly, B. "How execs learn now," *Fortune*, April 5, 1993, pp. 52–58; Wick, C. and L.S. Leon, *The Learning Edge*, New York: McGraw-Hill, 1993.

40 See Kelly, K. "Motorola: Training for the millennium," *Fortune*, March 28, 1994, pp. 158–162.

41 See Fierman, J. "The perilous new world of fair pay," *Fortune*, June 14, 1994, pp. 57–64.

SECTION II

THE PROCESS

4

DEVELOPING A
ROAD MAP

Our hypothesis is that powerful forces within the field of leadership development drive both provider and consumer behavior. Without an understanding of these forces and their origins, companies investing in leadership development will be unable to exert maximum leverage in controlling their futures.

A Road Map for Leadership Development Planning

There is a growing awareness among major corporations that executive and organizational development activities must be employed in concert with firm strategy and other human resource programs. This concept of aligning corporate activities also reflects systems thinking. In the following section, we outline an emerging role for leadership development in the strategic management process, develop a preliminary model for integrating executive development into an organization's strategic planning system, and present a case study of a firm that is committed to developing a systems approach to strategic leadership development.

A recent research report published by the International Consortium for Executive Development Research noted the following observations based on their research observations, the fundamental redefinition of purpose taking place within the field of leadership development:[1]

1   Executive education and leadership development activities are being highlighted as vital components of the strategic

development of a firm, especially with regard to the recognized need for continuous improvement and learning.

2   Organizations are focusing more on organizational development efforts than on individual development as they seek to enhance their ability to adapt to the global competitive environment.

3   In order to leverage their investment in learning, organizations are using fewer external development opportunities and are focusing instead on development activities specific to the organization and more tightly linked to the realities of the workplace.

4   Organizations are planning to increase their level of activity in leadership and organizational development efforts to help facilitate change and revitalization.

This suggests that as executive education/leadership development has matured over the past decade it has assumed a much more strategic role in the organization. Once an activity offered only to a select few individuals identified as having high potential for future senior leadership positions, leadership development has now become a major tool for revitalizing corporations and building learning-oriented competitiveness.

As a result of this change in stature and purpose, the field is undergoing a number of dramatic changes, not the least of which is a growing level of research into redefining the process. For example, in response to a dramatically changing business environment, much attention has been given to identifying the competencies and characteristics of the *21st-century leader*. This search for the leader of the future has been a dominant theme in the redefinition of leadership development practices and techniques. At the same time, some critics of contemporary leadership development practices have argued that placing too strong an emphasis on specific leadership competencies is insufficient for preparing managers and executives for enacting complex strategies in the future. By concentrating too heavily on specific competencies, organizations may find they have done a very effective job of developing *yesterday's* leaders for *tomorrow's* business environment.

This debate has led to a careful reappraisal of leadership development activities and a greater push for the development of a systems approach to the function. In this systems approach, all of the parties involved are actively engaged in the development process. The organization uses development activities to build commitment to a corporate direction and promote a learning orientation. Individuals are encouraged to take responsibility for their own learning and to encourage similar ownership among their subordinates and colleagues. Leadership development specialists are actively engaged in the development of the core strategic objectives of their organization as well as the development of their individual "clients." All of this activity is focused on enhancing the ability of all parties to engage in continuous learning.

To develop a systems perspective, organizations must endeavor to understand which developmental processes will be most effective under a variety of changing circumstances, for different levels or target groups of participants, at different stages of individual development. This will maximize the ability to promote both individual and organizational learning.

Crafting an Integrated Systemic Framework

Executive education and training is but one small component of a much more complicated set of choices that companies must make as they strive to identify and develop the critical human resources that will create their firm's superior ability to learn. One of the major challenges faced by human resource development professionals is linking leadership development objectives more closely to strategic and organizational objectives. This sounds logical and straightforward but it is actually very difficult to do. The challenge has become all the more difficult now that leadership development is more of a professional field, with its own language, specialties and specialists. There is clearly a danger that as sub-specialties grow within the field, the possibility of strategic integration could become even more remote.

The model depicted in Figure 4.1 is an attempt to illustrate the necessary linkages among those elements that can provide leverage for leadership development as a force of organizational learning and competitiveness. It depicts a view of an integrative "systems perspective" for leadership development.

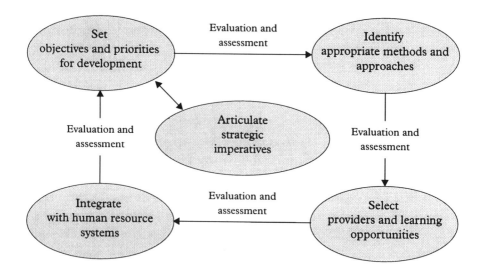

Figure 4.1 An integrated approach to Leadership Development Planning

The catalyst for this systems perspective is a focus on the organization's strategic imperatives, the core drivers of its competitive thrusts. The importance of this core focus is emphasized throughout this book. Based on these imperatives, the firm must define priority objectives for leadership development as well as target clients for developmental activities. Once these second-level objectives and priorities have been identified, the organization must then determine the appropriate methods for achieving the target objectives and select potential providers of those opportunities. Throughout the entire process, evaluation and assessment are conducted at critical points to ensure that focus and integrity are maintained, and that *expected* results are generated. This in turn ensures that the evolving leadership development process is fully integrated into the strategic and human resource management systems of the firm. This last step helps to maintain a consistent focus on strategic imperatives and priority objectives for development. In this systems framework, all elements of the leadership development system are linked together to focus on the most essential outcome of the process – the development of a sustainable focus on organizational learning and ultimately on competitiveness.

A Case in Point: Leadership Development at AT&T

One of the best examples we have found to illustrate the power of this model is the approach to strategic leadership development being taken at AT&T.[2] AT&T is known for its commitment to all forms of management, executive and leadership development. The company is currently in the process of developing a new "leadership framework" as part of its strategy to reexamine and revitalize *every* aspect of its business. The nature of that framework is summarized in Figure 4.2 and discussed below.

1. Define Strategic Imperatives   At AT&T, CEO Bob Allen recognized that dramatic shifts had occurred in the global business environment. These shifts required changes in the company's strategy, operations, and skills. Allen articulated a set of strategic imperatives for the company, which included improvements in customer focus, globalization, diversity, total quality, and innovation. He further suggested if AT&T was to compete in this fast-paced, changing environment, an across-the-board transformation of leadership style was required. This became one of the top challenges for HRD at AT&T.

AT&T believes that building depth and breadth of expertise, as well as an understanding of how to integrate both business *and* technical perspectives and capabilities, is essential for leadership development. For current and aspiring leaders, that meant moving beyond a traditional role of one who "knows all and decides," to one who has a knack for awakening knowledge and competence in others. It involved inspiring a shared purpose and being responsible for creating the climate necessary to pursue that purpose. It meant developing a process for helping leaders to learn how to act with urgency, and seize decisively upon opportunities by building partnerships with other people, business units, corporations, communities, industries, cultures, and countries. And it meant finding ways to ensure that leaders embraced and embodied what AT&T called "Our Common Bond," a statement of five major corporate values, including "respect for individuals, high standards of integrity, dedication to helping customers, innovation, and teamwork." Enabling AT&T leaders to deliver on these values became a key strategic initiative for HR in 1993 – it was called "Leadership Talent Transformation."

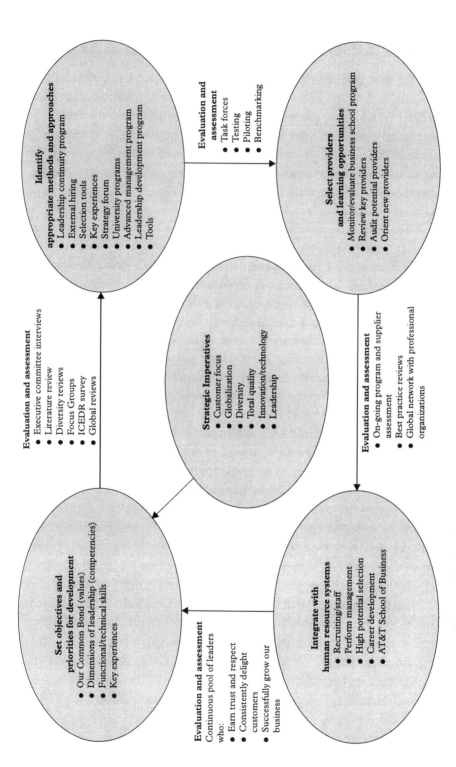

Figure 4.2 Leadership Development Planning: an integrated approach at AT&T

Evaluation and assessment
- Executive committee interviews
- Literature review
- Diversity reviews
- Focus Groups
- ICEDR survey
- Global reviews

Identify appropriate methods and approaches
- Leadership continuity program
- External hiring
- Selection tools
- Key experiences
- Strategy forum
- University programs
- Advanced management program
- Leadership development program
- Tools

Evaluation and assessment
- Task forces
- Testing
- Piloting
- Benchmarking

Select providers and learning opportunities
- Monitor/evaluate business school program
- Review key providers
- Audit potential providers
- Orient new providers

Strategic Imperatives
- Customer focus
- Globalization
- Diversity
- Total quality
- Innovation/technology
- Leadership

Evaluation and assessment
- On-going program and supplier assessment
- Best practice reviews
- Global network with professional organizations

Set objectives and priorities for development
- Our Common Bond (values)
- Dimensions of leadership (competencies)
- Functional/technical skills
- Key experiences

Evaluation and assessment
Continuous pool of leaders who:
- Earn trust and respect
- Consistently delight customers
- Successfully grow our business

Integrate with human resource systems
- Recruiting/staff
- Perform management
- High potential selection
- Career development
- AT&T School of Business

2. Set Objectives and Priorities for Development The common bond values and the strategic imperative for leadership talent transformation became the foundation of a process for setting objectives and priorities for leadership development. The common bond values were developed in more detail with specific illustrations of the kinds of behaviors that could be associated with each. This set of leadership behaviors or competencies became a starting point for discussion of what would become the AT&T "Transformational Leadership Framework." The framework outlined categories of specific functional and technical skills and behaviors associated with the new leadership focus. Each business unit then articulated specific expectations within its area, as well as key experiences for helping managers master the new leadership skill set.

3. Evaluation and Assessment Between each step in the model, evaluation and assessment is essential. For AT&T, the first step in evaluation process consisted of becoming familiar with current wisdom and practice in leadership development. Books, articles, and leadership competency frameworks from within AT&T and from other organizations were reviewed and discussed. Based on this information, the team fashioned a straw transformational leadership framework incorporating the best ideas from the diverse sources.

Next, the team tested the straw framework with focus groups of managers from numerous business unit/divisions (BU/Ds) and business functions. These groups validated much of the straw framework, but noted some missing and underemphasized concepts. They identified ambiguous phrases and generated written examples of effective and ineffective leadership behaviors for use in developing measurement tools to accompany the framework. Concurrently, interviews with management executive committee (MEC) members and other executives were conducted to gain an understanding of the driving forces affecting their business, and to ensure the framework addressed the most critical issues faced by the company.

A refined version of the framework was then shared with the cross-BU/D diversity team and line managers from 18 countries. These sources provided invaluable new perspectives that were incorporated into the framework to make it more inclusive and universally applicable. To further validate the concepts that were being developed, AT&T also participated in a global study of emerging leadership characteristics which was being sponsored by the International Consortium for Executive Development Research. Additionally, the framework was enhanced by the work of a separate "Technical Leadership Task Team."

In summary, the leadership framework was the result of a broad-based research effort which melded together input from many perspectives. The outcome was a customized set of competencies that reflected what AT&T expected of its leaders to support the successful execution of its new strategic imperatives.

4. Identify Appropriate Methods and Approaches   AT&T has a rich tradition of utilizing varied approaches to leadership and organizational development (see Chapter 6). To ensure alignment, these approaches were carefully coordinated to reinforce the new strategic imperatives being pursued in the transformational leadership initiative. Among the many coordinated approaches were new or revised efforts in the following areas:

- leadership continuity programs
- external hiring strategies
- key experiences definition
- internal development programs, including amongst others the "Strategy Forum," the "Internal Advanced Management Program" (senior management), and the "Leadership Development Program" (middle management)
- active use of external (university-based) executive programs, and
- extensive use of 360-degree feedback.

While these methods and approaches were being refined, there was a regular ongoing effort to validate their appropriateness according to best practice as well as their internal consistency or fit with the new framework and the strategic imperatives of the firm.

Our experience of re-inventing leadership development at AT&T is serving us in good stead as we face the renewed challenge of downsizing and reorganization in the new AT&T.

Deepak "Dick" Sethi, Director
AT&T Leadership Development Program

5. Select Providers and Learning Opportunities   AT&T is known for its comprehensive approach to evaluating existing leadership development programs and staying abreast of current developments in the field. This is related to the company's ongoing detailed assessment of programs based on feedback from previous AT&T participants. We will provide more details on this process in Chapter 6.

HRD staff regularly review existing providers as well as the key providers retained by other leading corporations. AT&T is active in such organizations as Executive Development Network, the International University Consortium for Executive Education (UNICON), the International Consortium For Executive Development Research (ICEDR), and many other networks. Staff members are expected to audit programs offered by potential providers, including individuals and groups that may be potential contributors to internal programs offered by the company. When a provider has been selected to work with AT&T, that provider is thoroughly oriented to the company. Every provider is expected to be familiar with both the existing culture and the extent of the changes being sought. All of these mechanisms have enabled AT&T to develop a comprehensive list of potential providers (all pre-screened) that can partner with the company in its strategic leadership development efforts.

6. Integration with Human Resource Systems   As the new leadership system began to take shape, the transformational leadership framework was used in the recruitment process. The new values and competencies were integrated in the selection process. The company's performance management system was revised to incorporate the new framework. High potential individuals were identified who seemed to possess the qualities embodied by the new framework. Career development opportunities began to shift toward the new model. The AT&T School of Business, the company's broad-based internal management education arm, incorporated the framework into its extensive catalog of offerings. Alignment was, and is, a key attribute of the integrated approach at AT&T.

For AT&T, the ultimate goal is to create an endless stream of leaders who are able to earn respect and trust within the AT&T community, consistently delight customers, and successfully grow the businesses for which they are responsible. Each of these attributes is measured by a customized internal evaluation process that gauges the perceived effectiveness of the company's leadership development process. In effect, AT&T is completely transforming its talent pool to provide leadership in the global marketplace.

Implementing a Systems Perspective

A systems perspective is essential in corporations wanting to leverage their investment in leadership development. Firms interested in building an integrated leadership development system like that of AT&T need to engage in an orchestrated effort to accomplish the following key objectives.[3]

- *Define and articulate the strategic imperatives.* These are the priorities, competencies and capabilities considered by top management to be the basis of the firm's future competitive advantage and target areas for leadership development.
- *Clarify core objectives for development based on the strategic imperatives.* This should include efforts to: define critical competencies and capabilities; engender a market focus throughout the company; build networks to leverage competencies and capabilities; enhance communication and teamwork; change organizational culture; and implement competitive strategies. In addition, the company must prioritize "clients" for development by defining which levels, functions, regions, competency areas, etc. are the most important targets for development initiatives.
- *Select methods and approaches to be used for development,* ensuring consistency with the strategic imperatives and overall learning/development objectives. This could include team and/or task force assignments, action learning projects, rotational assignments, classroom education, competency identification and development, and so on.
- *Build strategic partnerships* with a select group of leadership development providers to help gain leverage and round-out internal resources. These relationships should be reassessed periodically to ensure that they are achieving the initial objectives.

- *Link development processes with human resource practices.* To leverage the impact of leadership development efforts they must be tightly linked to the organization's human resource management infrastructure, including performance management and reward systems, recruitment and selection procedures, and succession and executive resource planning processes. This final step ensures that a learning orientation becomes ingrained within the organization's culture and operating philosophy.

Summary

A major shift in the field of leadership development is currently under way. This shift is being driven to a significant degree by the forces outlined in this chapter. Those forces suggest a move away from quick-fix education and training initiatives toward a more integrative, systems-oriented approach. As the players in leadership development change and redefine their roles and boundaries, rare opportunities to shape the future are emerging for those who understand the forces at work. We are convinced that the move toward a systems perspective will continue to exert a powerful influence on the future of leadership. Successful participants will understand this approach and will gain leverage by managing leadership development in an aligned, anticipatory manner.

In the following chapters, we will present a more detailed analysis of the core elements of this systems process along with recommendations for crafting the integrated leadership development planning systems that truly promote and enhance organizational learning and competitive effectiveness.

Endnotes

1   Much of this section is adapted from Ready, D., Vicere, A.A. and White, A., *The Role of Executive Education in Executive Resource Planning*, Lexington, MA: International Consortium for Executive Development Research (ICEDR) Working Paper, 92/3, 1992.

2   Appreciation is expressed to George Shaffer, SPHR, Leadership Development Director, Dick Sethi, Executive Education District Manager

Corporate Human Resources, and Jane L. Rifkin, Corporate Human Resources for providing information about AT&T's approach to leadership development.

3   These recommendations are drawn from Ready, Vicere and White, 1992, op. cit.

5

METHODS AND PRIORITIES

Strategic leadership development initiatives can and should be a major force for driving organizational change and crafting competitiveness. A white paper published by the International Consortium for Executive Development Research noted:

> ❝ Executive [and leadership] development must be focused strategically on both the target population and the issues that enable companies to create and sustain superior organizational capabilities. The cultivation of those capabilities is the strongest contribution that executive development professionals can make to improve firm performance and competitiveness.[1] ❞

Three issues must be addressed if leadership development initiatives are to contribute effectively to the creation of such superior organizational capabilities.

1 The initiatives must be linked to the strategic imperatives of the firm.
2 Individual and organizational development must be addressed in parallel through innovative approaches to the leadership development process.
3 A comprehensive, systems-oriented approach must be developed to create and maintain positive organizational momentum.

The systems approach involves setting priorities for leadership development based on the strategic imperatives of the firm, as well as matching appropriate methodologies with those priorities. This chapter discusses various techniques and methodologies for leadership development and presents a framework for selecting those most appropriate.

The Challenge

A recent series of studies conducted by researchers at the Smeal College of Business Administration at the Pennsylvania State University profiled the evolution of corporate executive education and leadership development initiatives over a ten-year interval.[2] Using a representative sample from the *Fortune 500, Fortune Service 500,* and *Fortune International 500* companies (surveyed in 1982, 1987, and 1992), the project produced the following list of techniques most frequently utilized for leadership development.

	1982	1987	1992
Job rotation	20%	72%	58%
In-company executive development programs	34%	47%	56%
Task forces/special projects	28%	32%	39%
External executive development programs	37%	48%	33%
On the job training	20%	28%	28%
Coaching/mentoring	37%	26%	22%
Performance feedback	48%	6%	9%
Teaching/consulting with other employees	19%	1%	5%

Job rotation was the highest rated technique in 1992, closely followed by company-specific executive education programs and task force/special project assignments. This pattern of responses was significantly different from the pattern found in the researchers' 1987 study, in which job rotation was overwhelmingly the first choice among leadership development techniques, followed by external executive education programs and internal executive education programs. The 1982 pattern differed even more, with performance feedback leading the list of favored developmental techniques.

The results of these studies reflect a shift in user perspectives toward executive education and leadership development. Work experience and company-specific educational programs have emerged as the core focus of leadership development efforts. These findings support the evolution of the "new paradigm" for leadership development disussed in the introduction. Companies that subscribe to this new paradigm are more likely to create coordinated leadership development strategies that blend job experience, educational initiatives, guided practical experiences, and targeted performance feedback into a systemic process for ongoing leadership development at all levels of the organization. This type of process is focused not only on individual development, but also the continuing development of the organization as a whole.

> *Although we find tremendous enthusiasm among companies for this new leadership development paradigm, most organizations still struggle to match individual and organizational development needs with the most appropriate developmental experiences, techniques, and methodologies.*

The "knowledge creation cycle" depicted in Figure 5.1 provides a framework for dealing with this challenge.

A Framework for Establishing Objectives

The knowledge creation cycle is a model for mapping leadership development processes. It portrays leadership development as a constantly escalating process that builds on the experience base of the leader

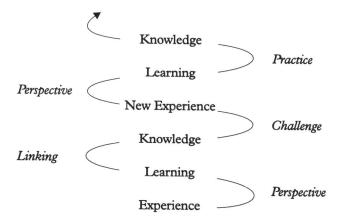

Figure 5.1 Leadership development: the knowledge creation cycle
Source: Vicere, A.A. *The Knowledge Creation Cycle: A Framework for Assessing Executive Development Techniques*, Penn State University: Institute for the Study of Organizational Effectiveness, WP 96-001, 1996.

to create an continuous cycle of both individual learning and organizational knowledge creation.[3] *Understanding the knowledge creation cycle can enable an organization to dramatically enhance its ability to learn.* We will now look at each stage of the cycle and its implications for leadership development.

> *In today's global environment, real competitive advantage is directly related to the ability of both individual leaders and their organizations to learn on a continuous basis.*
>
> Doug Ready

Experience

According to the old saying, "experience is the best teacher." This appears to be especially true when it comes to leadership. In a landmark study on the lessons of experience, Morgan McCall, Michael Lombardo, and Anne Morrison of the Center for Creative Leadership (CCL) found that leaders attributed most of their current success to past work experiences.[4] It is quite reasonable, then, for companies to pay great attention to providing high potential leaders with challenging and varied work experiences. It is through such experiences that leaders have the opportunity to learn, grow, and develop.

McCall et al. found there was no such thing as generic work experience. Rather, they found that different types of work experiences provided different opportunities for development. For example, there were different lessons to be learnt by a leader operating in a start-up situation than there were for a leader operating in a turnaround situation. Similarly, shifts from staff to line assignments, or vice versa, triggered yet more different sets of developmental opportunities. The most well-rounded leaders were often those who had experienced assignments in several dissimilar work environments. Because of their broader base of experiences, these individuals seem to be more aware of themselves and more flexible in their approach to leadership challenges.

We cannot do justice to the richness of the CCL studies on the lessons of experience in such a brief summary. Indeed, they merit a careful reading in themselves. It is clear, however, that the research strongly supports the belief that experience is the key to leadership development.

Yet, even if they are involved in diverse, learning-rich work assignments, how many leaders are actually prepared to learn from their experiences? In today's environment of constant change and time pressures, how many of them actually take time, or even have time to step back from their experiences to consider lessons learned? Very few. That is why a fundamental objective for leadership development is to provide developing leaders with both the tools and the opportunities to garner the lessons of their experiences, to gain *perspective*.

Perspective

The most commonly used techniques for helping leaders gain perspective, or learn from their experiences, are as follows.

- Classroom education
  - Internal
  - External
  - Consortium
- Feedback approaches
- Personal growth approaches
- New learning technologies
- Coaching/mentoring.

This reflects the long-standing stated goals of classroom-based leadership development programs. The classroom is a valuable and readily accessible forum for giving leaders an opportunity to prepare for and learn from their experiences. Classroom-based programs generally take the form of externally delivered programs, open-enrollment seminars; internally delivered, customized programs; or consortium programs.

In addition to classroom-based programs, feedback approaches to leadership development, primarily relying on 360-degree assessment, have been rapidly gaining in popularity. These initiatives, often delivered in a classroom, are designed to help leaders gain a better understanding of their leadership styles and their ability to influence the people around them. Personal growth programs (such as outdoor-adventure experiences) have also gained some degree of notoriety. These initiatives focus primarily on helping leaders to gain a better understanding of themselves and their aspirations. New teaching and learning technologies such as groupware and video conferencing are gaining popularity as techniques for enhancing and expanding traditional classroom-based programs. Finally, mentoring can make a major contribution to the ability of developing leaders to learn from their work experiences.

It may seem obvious to many reading through the above list that the most effective leadership development initiatives would draw from all of the above techniques and methodologies. We agree. Yet, to blend them in the most effective manner, each needs to be considered separately. For that reason, we will discuss each methodology briefly.

Classroom-Based Approaches Jay Conger recently conducted a hands-on study of a number of leadership development programs.[5] Conger or one of his associates actually participated in a number of programs in order to ascertain their potential contribution to leadership development. Conger and his colleagues conducted surveys and interviewed program participants to develop a framework for assessing the potential value and contribution of each approach. He categorized these programs into four types. Two were classroom based: "skill-building" in which complex leader behaviors are broken down into skill-sets that can then be taught to leaders; and "conceptual" approaches, focusing on presenting ideas and concepts for leaders to consider. The other two categories, "feedback approaches" and "personal growth approaches," will be discussed later in this chapter.

Skill-building approaches As noted previously, skill-building approaches to leadership development assume that leadership is comprised of practical, teachable skill-sets that can be imparted through a well-designed training experience. These types of programs have traditionally been the backbone of corporate internal leadership training initiatives. Conger noted that certain leadership skill-sets do appear to be teachable, particularly in areas like communication and motivation. This is particularly true when the skill-sets to be taught can be framed in simple models, and when the program process includes plenty of practice and opportunities for feedback. However, skill-building approaches do not seem to help with more complex skill-sets like "visioning." Furthermore, skill-based programs are often targeted on lower level managers. More senior leaders frequently, and often wrongly, are assumed to have already mastered the skills in question. Conger noted:

> ❝ *skill-building approaches should be the most effective of all because they are under the highest expectations to produce tangible results. And with some leadership skills, this can be the case. The difficulty is that many of the skills currently associated with leadership are quite complex, and a three- or five-day program offers little time to truly develop these in lasting ways. Back on the job, the workings of the organization and the manager's daily life-style may further erode his or her initial efforts to implement skills. Awareness development may be a more realistic expectation for program outcome than actual in-depth skill development.*[6] ❞

To maximize the value of skill-building approaches, then, organizations must ensure that the skills being taught and the message being delivered are well-known and accepted throughout the organization. Moreover, skill-building approaches are most likely to be effective when the training cascades down from the top of the organization.

Conceptual approaches   Conger noted that programs based on conceptual approaches to leadership development assume that leadership is a complex art that is poorly understood. Therefore, development programs should focus on creating awareness among developing leaders of the complexities of the leadership challenge. Programs such as university-based executive programs have long been designed around this model.

According to Conger, programs based on the conceptual approach are essential to understanding something as complex as leadership. They can create greater awareness and understanding of the leadership challenge if the conceptual models presented are straightforward; if they are supported by films, case studies, or exercises that illustrate concepts; and if some form of practice in applying the models is provided through simulation or other form of hands-on exercise. The weakness of the approach is that its effectiveness is almost entirely related to the motivation of the individual participants and their willingness and/or ability to apply the lessons learnt to their personal situations.

Organizations making use of such experiences must, therefore, be sure to establish objectives and expectations with participants prior to their participation. And, they must create some mechanism for bridging learning from the program back to the job. Even so, Conger noted:

> " *ideas and concepts were critically important in framing the notion of leadership in participants' minds – especially when distinctions were being made between leadership and managership, This awareness-building provided the important first step in behavior development and change. Alone, however, it is not sufficient.*[7] "

Conger's analysis of these two forms of classroom-based program outlines one of the biggest challenges facing leadership development practitioners – how do we take advantage of the strengths and overcome the weaknesses of both approaches when designing leadership development initiatives? In an attempt to deal with this challenge, much attention has been focused on program delivery modes. The three primary delivery modes for classroom approaches are external, open-enrollment programs; company-specific, customized programs; and consortium programs. Each has strengths and weaknesses.

External executive education programs   External, open-enrollment leadership development programs are one of the most commonly used leadership development techniques. Perhaps the best-known of these experiences are university-based executive education programs. These highly regarded, longer term (frequently several weeks in length), residential programs offered by major business schools around the world have long been recognized as a key element of corporate executive and leadership development strategies.[8]

Because of their longer duration, university-based programs seem to address many of the key challenges posed by Conger: they tend to be built around solid conceptual models, and they tend to involve plenty of case study applications, simulations, and other opportunities for practice. The perceived benefits of university-based executive programs, as respondents to the Penn State studies indicate, are listed below.[9]

Provide outside perspective; exposure to other viewpoints; networking	71%
Generalize specialists and broaden their vision	24%
Allow executives to reflect on, and gain insight into, career, work role, personal style and effectiveness; encourage renewal; insulate from work	23%
Expose executives to faculty experts and latest management information in a high-quality academic setting	21%
Expose executives to a variety of programs that cannot be delivered as economically or effectively in-company	8%
In-company and university programs complementary	6%
Provide rewards and contribute to self-esteem	6%
Gain specific skill or functional expertise	6%

These programs were profiled by survey participants as opportunities to provide leaders with exposure to outside viewpoints, thus enabling them to build external networks, broaden individual perspectives, and promote personal revitalization. All of these benefits seemed to be related to the *individual* development of leaders.

Company-specific programs Corporations increasingly are turning to internal, customized executive education/leadership development programs to address the critical demands of a changing corporate environment. Formerly, these programs tended to focus on skill-building. Increasingly, however, customized executive education programs, such as the GE, ARAMARK, Johnson & Johnson, and Cartech programs described earlier, are being developed to help companies adapt to the global competitive environment, and to help promote a broader conceptual understanding of the strategic directions of the sponsoring organization. Looking again at the Penn State surveys, the perceived benefits of internal programs are as shown below.[10]

Programs more specific to organization and its needs	53%
Help develop an organizational culture, bulid teams, and implement change	46%
Provide a discussion forum or idea exchange; internal networking	23%
Savings in both time and money	18%
Better control of content, faculty and participants	16%
Complementary to external programs	14%

Provide interaction with top management	12%
Better availability of resources; scheduling efficiency	2%

Specificity to the company and contribution to change management dominated the list, suggesting that internal executive education initiatives play a key role in *organizational* development efforts.

From this, it appears that external, open-enrollment programs serve a different purpose and generate different outcomes than internal, company-specific programs. External programs seem to be viewed more in the context of individual development. Internal programs seem to be viewed more in the context of organizational development. As such, both types of experience can contribute significantly to the leadership development process when used in an appropriate manner. Since the current debate over internal vs. external classroom initiatives is so intense, we will devote all of the next chapter to special case study analyses of the impact of each type of program on leadership and organizational development.

Consortium programs   A relatively new form of classroom-based leadership development is the "consortium" model. This type of classroom-based experience attempts to blend the perspective-broadening benefits of traditional open-enrollment programs like university-based programs with the specificity of company-specific programs. A group of several companies is brought together by the program sponsor and a focused curriculum designed around the specific needs of the member companies. Typically, representatives from member companies participate on a committee that oversees program design and delivery. In addition, teams of participants from member companies attend the program, enabling the discussion to be both specific to each individual organization, yet enriched by the perspectives of other teams.

Rapidly gaining in recognition and respect, the consortium format provides unique opportunities for perspective building. According to Ron Thomas and Cam Danielson, directors of the Indiana University Consortium, "The consortium model of executive education is the best of both worlds: it is a unique combination of open enrollment and custom programs that stands alone."[11] In a unique arrangement that involves a business school partnership and a number of companies, the business schools at Miami University (Ohio) and The University of

Cincinnati have combined to form the Business Consortium®. It is a cooperative venture involving the two schools and nearly a dozen Cincinnati area companies. Judy Cornett of corporate member Cinergy Corporation notes:

> " *Historically, our emerging leaders have participated in development programs throughout the United States designed primarily for the utility industry. The Business Consortium® is providing us a unique learning and partnering opportunity with a diverse business community right here at home.*
>
> *Collaboration among the membership has resulted in a learning model that allows participants to regulate and apply their own learning back in the work environment. They learn how to learn the lessons their particular job offers up each day.*
>
> *This cooperative effort is a win-win for both the business and academic communities. The initial added value of our participation has been the direct access to the bounty of expertise and experience right here in Cincinnati.*[12] "

It is clear that the consortium model holds a great deal of promise for both users and providers of executive education and leadership development. It is an emerging format that could address a major need for blending individual and organizational development in a focused manner.

In addition to classroom-based approaches to leadership development, there are several other approaches that can contribute significantly to perspective building.

Feedback approaches   Conger described "feedback approaches" as initiatives that operate under the assumption that

> *many who aspire to being an effective leader already possess in varying degrees and strengths the skills they need. The aim of the program, then, is to point out to participants their own key strengths and weaknesses so they can work to strengthen their weaker skills and can act with confidence when relying on their strengths.*[13]

Feedback-based programs tend to rely heavily on 360-degree feedback, also known as circular feedback, a process in which an individual rates him/herself on a set of leadership dimensions, and then is subsequently rated on the same dimensions by his or her boss, several peers, and several subordinates. In some instances, the ratings of customers also are obtained. The consistencies or inconsistencies across the various ratings are then used as the basis for discussions of performance, potential, and development with the individual.[14] For many organizations, 360-degree feedback is linked to competency modeling, a technique discussed later in this chapter.

Conger himself attended the Center For Creative Leadership's leadership development program, one of the most highly regarded and popular leadership development programs in the world. This one-week program makes heavy use of 360-degree assessment, other forms of testing, peer and staff feedback, and goal setting, to help individual leaders learn about their strengths as a leader, confront their weaknesses, and develop a plan of action for improvement. Although he found the program to be both stimulating and a worthwhile personal experience, he noted:

> ❝ Our results ... indicated that feedback often had less impact than we had expected. Only in a few cases did managers describe feedback as significantly enhancing their leadership skills. Factors within the individual and outside the programs played major roles in mitigating the contributions of feedback.[15] ❞

To maximize the potential contribution of the feedback approach, then, it is essential that the company manages the development context, making sure the feedback has meaning for the participant, and that resulting development plans are linked to appropriate elements of the company's human resource management infrastructure, specifically development, appraisal, and reward systems. The Westinghouse example discussed later in this chapter will further illustrate this point, as will the research on the impact of follow-up and action planning activities conducted by Keilty, Goldsmith & Co. which we discuss in Chapter 8.

Personal growth approaches   According to Conger, personal growth approaches assume that

> leaders are individuals who are deeply in touch with their gifts and passions. Therefore, only by tapping into and realizing one's passions can a person become a leader. Thus, if training can help managers get

> *in touch with their talents and sense of purpose, they will presumable*
> *have the motivation and enthusiasm to formulate inspiring visions and*
> *to motivate those who work for them.*[16]

Conger noted that the goal of personal growth approaches was to help participants understand the extent to which they have given up their personal sense of power and efficacy in their personal and professional lives. This can be achieved through outdoor adventures that involve some degree of risk, such as high ropes courses,[17] or indoor experiences that force participants to reflect on the discrepancies that exist between their personal aspirations and their current situation. Properly run, these experiences can be both eye-opening and empowering.

Conger himself attended an outdoor-adventure experience at the Pecos River Learning Center in New Mexico. There he engaged in trust walks, ropes courses, and other forms of personal challenge. His indoor experience was in ARC International's VisionQuest program. There he engaged in a highly interactive process for developing a personal vision for the future. Overall, he noted the elements of action, experience, and risk-taking introduced in these approaches tended to magnify the learning experience. Yet, he also observed that the learning seemed to be focused on areas most salient to participants at the particular point in time of their program experience. Still, he reported:

> *the power of personal growth approaches is that they directly challenge*
> *us to examine our most deeply felt emotions and most entrenched values.*
> *And if leadership is in part the emotional manifestation of one's*
> *passionate interests and aspirations, then this is where a significant*
> *portion of training must take place.*[18]

Technology-Based Learning   A further development is the use of electronic media and telecommunications in leadership development. Most organizations are currently using new technologies as supplements to traditional programs and methodologies.[19] For example, keeping participants in touch during a multi-phase leadership development program is often done through e-mail, voice-mail, videoconferencing, etc.

Programs and networks based on various forms of groupware also are appearing at a rapid rate. A recent *Forbes ASAP* article defined groupware as a tool "designed to enhance productivity by allowing users to share information ... it also allows individuals to easily customize the view of this information to suit their needs."[20] The term groupware includes technologies such as group decision support systems, teleconferencing systems, videoconferencing systems, and desktop conferencing systems. Through the use of groupware, groups or "classes" of people from various locations can be linked electronically to discuss issues, solve problems, analyze data, or simply network in a "virtual classroom."[21]

Taking advantage of this development, Westcott Communications is launching EXEN, the Executive Education Network. A number of major business schools, including Penn State, Wharton, the University of Southern California, the University of North Carolina, Wharton, SMU, Carnegie-Mellon, and the University of Massachusetts have signed on with the network to conduct executive education programs via telemedia in a "distance learning" format. Companies subscribing to the service will have the programs beamed to their remote sites where "classes" of students will interact in a classroom while attending broadcast seminars by leading faculty. All students will have direct access to each other, and electronic access to the faculty for questions and discussion during the program. EXEN is the tip of the iceberg in the movement toward delivering classroom-based "conceptual" programs via electronic media. In this distributed format, organizations have the potential to maximize the audience for programs while maintaining some degree of classroom interaction and intimacy.

On a slightly different note, LOMA, the Atlanta-based association of life insurance companies, is offering courses for member companies on topics such as, "the ABCs of Multimedia Training," and "Management Development and Multimedia Training." These types of courses are being offered by growing numbers of providers and establish the foundation for an organization to engage in interactive distance learning – training programs distributed to multiple sites through the use of multimedia technology. Federal Express has spent almost $70 million to develop an automated interactive video disk (IVD) training system, now available at over 700 company locations. The system includes self-administered tests for skill upgrades.[22] IBM has distance learning projects in multimedia, interactive learning ongoing with Cal Tech, Renssalaer Polytechnic Institute, and the State of Alabama.[23]

Despite all of this activity, technology-based learning is still "finding itself" as a tool for leadership development. Although it has enormous potential, the role technology will play in future leadership development efforts is still to be determined.

Coaching/Mentoring   A frequently mentioned, but often misunderstood technique for promoting perspective involves coaching and mentoring by bosses or more experienced colleagues.[24] Mentoring can be defined as a relationship in which a person of greater experience or expertise teaches, guides, or develops a person with less experience, helping him or her to be perform more effectively and/or to advance in the organization.

In investigating the potential role of coaching and mentoring in the leadership development process, McCall et al. noted that:

> " *Mentoring, in the sense of long-term apprentice/teacher relationships, was rare or nonexistent among these successful senior executives. Between their own rapid advancement and the movement of their bosses, they were seldom with the same person for as long as three years. What seemed to matter most was almost the opposite anyway: exposure to a variety of bosses, good and bad, who possessed exceptional qualities of various kinds.*[25] "

The researchers found that bosses were frequently mentioned as sources of significant learning for developing leaders from several perspectives. Through their observations and advice, bosses can round-out and fill-in the gaps in an individual's experience base. For example, bosses can teach some lessons that assignments alone cannot, particularly in the area of values and ethics. In addition, a boss' personal approach to the job can serve as a counterbalance to the lessons of a particular individual's experience, again reinforcing values and perspectives on leadership roles by providing a standard, good or bad, against which individuals can measure themselves.

The researchers noted that *few bosses are actually good teachers.* Yet, as with experiences, exposure to a variety of bosses can have a powerful, positive impact on an individual leader's development. Perhaps most importantly, bosses can add perspective to experience by helping developing leaders to crystallize values, both organizational and personal. This can help them tp develop a broad-based view of what leaders do, form opinions on how good and bad leaders behave, and understand and cope with organizational politics.

Some organizations like AT&T, Bell Labs, Johnson & Johnson, Federal Express, Merrill Lynch, and others have inaugurated formal mentoring programs. The Hoechst Celanese Specialty Chemicals Group has launched a program staffed by volunteers who express a willingness and have demonstrated the capability to mentor colleagues. Participants in the program report they have received useful guidance and advice with regard to performance, career advancement, visibility, and other critical developmental issues. It is also quite common for organizations to use external mentors, often consultants or well-known university professors, to provide advice and support for senior leaders facing critical issues or challenges.[26]

Summary

As we have seen, the most effective leadership development process is likely be a blend of all of the above approaches and delivery modes. Classroom programs can promote conceptual awareness of critical issues and enhance essential skill-sets. Within that mode, external programs can provide leaders with an awareness of broad-based challenges and opportunities. Internal programs can develop necessary skill-sets and facilitate understanding of the strategic directions and expectations of the company. Consortium programs might bring the best of both worlds to the leadership development process, focusing on specific developmental issues within the multiple contexts of a diverse group of sponsoring organizations. Feedback and personal growth programs can help leaders to better understand themselves, and empower them to take action to create a better future. New technologies can expand and enhance traditional approaches to training and development. Mentoring could round-out an individual's experience and fill-in gaps. Blended together, these techniques help to facilitate *learning*, the next step of the knowledge creation cycle.

Learning

Shaw and Perkins have observed that learning is, "the capacity to gain insight from one's own experience and the experience of others and to modify the way one functions according to such insight."[27] When leaders are given the opportunity to step back and see how their experiences have contributed to their growth and development, they are far more likely to learn. This type of learning is the cornerstone of individual development. Yet, more must be done if an individual leader's learning is to be turned into *knowledge*, a permanent part of that leader's intellectual repertoire as well as an integrated element of the organization's collective knowledge base. As Ikujiro Nonaka points out:

> ❝ *In an economy where the only certainty is uncertainty, the one sure source of lasting competitive advantage is knowledge. When markets shift, technologies proliferate, competitors multiply, and products become obsolete almost overnight, successful companies are those that consistently create new knowledge, disseminate it widely throughout the organization, and quickly embody it in new technologies and products.*[28] ❞

Converting learning to knowledge, both individual and organizational, demands an additional step in the leadership development process, one we will call "linking."

Linking

As we saw in Chapter 1, traditional leadership development stops at the point of individual learning. The idea of linking learning to the workplace often is ignored, with perhaps the occasional exception of performance appraisal systems or process-oriented organizational development interventions. New paradigm approaches to leadership development pay close attention to this critical step, leveraging individual learning by providing opportunities for leaders to put their new found perspective to work within the organization.

When linking opportunities are based on individuals, that person grows as a leader. However, when linking is team based, individual learning is shared throughout the team and applied to the resolution of defined organizational challenges. This type of team-based leadership development helps convert individual learning into a collective base of organizational knowledge, thereby contributing to organizational growth and development. Techniques for linking learning to the workplace include:

- Performance appraisal
- Teaching/training/facilitating
- Task force/project team assignments
- Action learning.

Performance Appraisal

With their current expenditures on leadership development in the billions of dollars, organizations should take great pains to link development to the immediate work environment. Performance appraisal processes are a readily available and powerful technique for doing so. Reporting on a recent study, Longnecker and Gioia noted:

> " *Although executive appraisal is a challenging and frequently delicate proposition, it is clear that executives benefit from systematic reviews. Appraisal has long been shown to be effective for letting people know where they stand, improving productivity, enhancing growth and development, and making training, promotion, and compensation decisions.*[29] "

Based on their research, Longnecker and Gioia listed several key myths about executive performance appraisal processes, perhaps the most important of which was that executives neither need nor want structured performance reviews. In fact, every executive that participated in their structured interview process dismissed that notion and indicated that systematic feedback in some form was crucial. Despite the critical nature of performance appraisal processes, the Penn State study of executive development trends found that reliance on performance appraisal as a leadership development technique had declined over the past decade.[30] Similarly, in a recent survey of more than 400 managers, Longnecker found only about 25 percent of the participants indicated a level of satisfaction with their organization's appraisal process.[31] Longnecker and Gioia further found that the higher a manager rises in an organization, the less likely he or she is to receive quality feedback about job performance. They noted:

> " *One of the most frequently cited concerns of neophyte and even journeyman executives was the fear of taking executive action without*

understanding that their actions were considered to be a mistake by superiors.

Making mistakes might be acceptable; not knowing they are mistakes is not. Naturally, the ambiguous executive environment breeds situations where criteria for such judgements are not easily established. And that is exactly the reason that executives want regular feedback, so that they can get on track, stay on track, or, if necessary, get back on track.[32] **"**

It is clear that performance appraisal processes can be a major tool for leadership development. It can help shape performance and link that performance to the reward and development systems of the organization. It is equally clear that performance appraisal and related performance management processes merit much deeper consideration by organizations designing strategic leadership development systems.

Teaching/Training/Facilitating

Another effective way to help developing leaders link their individual learning to the workplace is to require those leaders to teach others what they have learnt. The discipline needed to structure a lesson plan forces leaders to take stock of what they know and apply it to improve performance on the job. At the same time, by transferring the individual learning of a leader to his or her "classes," that learning is shared throughout the organization, creating powerful opportunities for organizational development.[33] For example, when Motorola made expansion into Asian markets a priority, 100 senior executives were involved in the analysis of how to move forward and were then charged with passing along the lessons of their analysis to the next 3000 managers throughout the company.[34] Clearly, this technique can be a very effective mechanism for both individual and organizational development.

Task Force and Project Assignments

Temporary assignments such as task forces and special projects provide a valuable source of linking opportunities. Although such assignments are often met with a less than enthusiastic response by those chosen to participate, they can be very effective developmental experiences.[35] The studies of the lessons of experience show that task force and project assignments give organizations a chance to expose developing leaders to different types of leadership situations, thereby enhancing their potential for development. These experiences also benefit developing leaders by helping them to realize that they cannot be an expert on everything, that there are others within the organization with complementary capabilities who are essential to both personal and organizational success. Such insights not only promote individual development, but they lay the foundation for building internal leadership networks.[36] As we saw in Chapter 3, these networks are crucial to the transfer of knowledge throughout the organization.

Action Learning

Although task force and project assignments can create a foundation for the creation and transfer of knowledge throughout an organization, action learning can help institutionalize the process. Wick and Leon noted that action learning helps make experiential learning *intentional and deliberate*.[37] According to Marsick et al., action learning involves, "learning by doing, but it is not a simulation... It is 'training' that takes the form of an actual business problem for teams of learners to solve together."[38] The authors noted that the basic characteristics of an action-learning initiative are:

- working in small groups to solve problems;
- learning how to learn and think critically;
- building skills to meet the training needs that emerge during a project;
- developing a participant's own theory of management, leadership, or employee empowerment, a theory that is tested against real-world experiences as well as established tenets.

Tracing the evolution of action learning from its roots in the UK, Louise Keys added that action learning should involve problems that are current and "live," that there should often be a set advisor present throughout the life of each team to assist in their progress, and that the client(s) – often top executives – should agree to attend an evaluation meeting and listen to the results of the teams.[39]

Team-based action learning initiatives can be a very powerful mechanism for linking learning both to the workplace and to the strategic agenda of the firm. Through action learning, an organization can convert individual learning into organizational knowledge through the hands-on resolution of real business problems. Since the projects are conducted in teams, learning is shared by all members, networking is reinforced, new perspectives are encouraged, and leadership skills are practiced. All of this takes place within the context of the organization's strategic imperatives, helping to bring those imperatives to life and give them meaning throughout the company. In addition, action learning can help resolve business issues related to the pursuit of strategic imperatives, creating an additional return on investment for the company.

The ARAMARK and Cartech examples from Chapter 3 demonstrate this power. Both organizations have developed a set of strategic imperatives that is being used to initiate change and reinvigorate the competitive nature of the company. These strategic imperatives provide the context for action learning-based development. Both organizations have created leadership development programs for their senior leaders. Both are committed to building internal networks and promoting cross-organizational interaction to leverage the resources of the firm. In addition, both companies have demonstrated the courage to use their own business issues as live case studies around which these interactions are developed. These case studies have taken the form of action learning initiatives that involve teams of leaders working together to address critical organizational opportunities within the context of the new strategic imperatives.

As a result of their use of action learning techniques, both companies have enhanced face-to-face interactions among their managers, increased understanding of and commitment to current business directions, and provided hands-on leadership development experiences. Through these interactions and experiences, each company has leveraged the commitment and involvement of its managers in setting and implementing business policy decisions. The companies themselves have become learning laboratories, with the success of current business initiatives being the test of how well the organization and its leaders have learnt their lessons.

To maximize the impact of action learning techniques, each company has devised a process whereby the lessons to be learnt are effectively developed by the program participants themselves. Although each company has developed a program, complete with faculty and content, the faculty and content are there solely to stimulate corporate leaders to rethink the effectiveness of their organization and its business processes. The formal program is a means, not an end in itself. The end is the hands-on resolution of critical business challenges by teams of leaders. This type of developmental process, complete with the tension and contention it generates, becomes a source for the continuous creation and dissemination of organizational knowledge, the next stage of the cycle.

Knowledge

As Nonaka says, "making personal knowledge available to others is the central activity of the knowledge-creating company. It takes place continually and at all levels of the organization."[40] When groups of individual leaders have had the opportunity to work together, share personal learnings, and solve real business problems, they have developed frameworks for creating new organizational knowledge. In effect, they have collectively crafted new ways of thinking, operating, and performing for the organization. This new knowledge can serve as the basis for transforming an organization's culture and operating perspective by making the organization what Stan Davis and Jim Botkin call a "learning business."[41]

Strategic leadership development initiatives are geared not only to developing individual leaders, but also to creating opportunities for leaders to share their experiences across the organization in order to grow the overall intellectual capital of the business. Through strategic leadership development processes that include team-based action learning activities, organizations are able to leverage their intellectual capital and thereby enhance organizational development.

> When team-based organizational development initiatives are tightly linked to the strategic agenda of the firm, an organization can create incredible momentum for transformation and change. The leadership development processes of the many benchmark companies discussed throughout this book are good examples of this form of knowledge creation.

Challenge

To continue the creation of new knowledge – in effect, to become a learning organization – organizations must continue to provide new challenges to leaders.[42] The key forms new experiential challenges can take are:

- Rotational assignments
- Stretch assignments
- Developmental assignments
  - start-ups
  - turnarounds
  - international
  - staff–line.

The list covers the full range of experiential opportunities suggested by McCall et al.[43] Engaging leaders in a continuous learning process that includes new experiences and new opportunities to gain perspective stimulates new individual learning, new linking opportunities, and ultimately new opportunities to create organizational knowledge. This, in turn, facilitates ongoing renewal throughout the organization.

Putting the Cycle to Work

In the previous chapter, we discussed how leadership development initiatives can be a key mechanism for revitalizing a company and crafting organizational competitiveness. By combining an understanding of the knowledge creation cycle with the focus of an organization's strategic imperatives, the stage can be set for purposeful leadership development to take place. Westinghouse Electric Corporation presents an interesting example of a company engaged in such a process.

For decades, Westinghouse has been a pillar of American industry. Although the company has seen some ups and downs over its lifetime, it has remained a well-known, well-respected business entity. Then, in 1992, disaster struck. The financial services unit of Westinghouse had moved well beyond its traditional role as an internal financing arm of

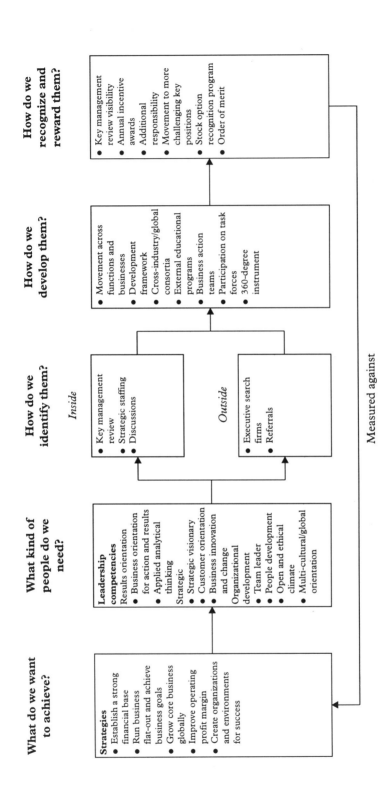

Figure 5.2 Leadership development at Westinghouse : an integrated approach

Source: Robert M. Fulmer and Ken Graham "A New Era of Management Education," *Journal of Management Development,* **12**, 1993, p.35.

the company, and had dramatically and profitably expanded its portfolio of loans, particularly in the then booming US real estate market. When that market collapsed in 1992, Westinghouse was left with billions of dollars of bad loans, a plunging stock price, and on the brink of disaster.

As a result of this chain of events, Westinghouse CEO Paul Lego resigned and was replaced by Michael H. Jordan in June of 1993. Jordan, a veteran with 19 years' experience at PepsiCo and 10 at McKinsey and Co., mounted a transformation effort aimed at repositioning Westinghouse to regain much of the luster lost during the tumultuous period that preceded him. To create an engine for this turnaround, Jordan and Westinghouse coupled a focus on strategic revitalization with a commitment to leadership development in an effort to transform the operating culture of the company. A model depicting the process they created appears in Figure 5.2.

One of Jordan's first initiatives was to define a set of five strategic imperatives for Westinghouse. These imperatives, also shown in Figure 5.2, focused on both financial stability and business growth. A leadership competency model was developed to ensure Westinghouse leaders had the necessary skills and capabilities to achieve the strategic imperatives. Assessment processes were revamped to profile the company's leadership talent pool. A set of leadership development initiatives was designed to help communicate the strategic imperatives and competencies throughout the organization and to address critical skill or perspective gaps that existed within the talent pool. These initiatives included topical workshops, executive education programs, discussion sessions with the CEO, and action learning initiatives. The entire process was reinforced by linking it to the company's performance review and compensation systems.

Although it is still far too early to say that Westinghouse is out of trouble, the company certainly has made progress. The company's leadership development initiatives have played a key role in this progress by serving as a communications medium and as a mechanism for engaging leaders in the strategic context of the firm. The example clearly illustrates the perspective of new paradigm companies discussed in the introduction. These companies see leadership development as more than programs for key individual managers. Rather, by linking leadership development to the strategic agenda of the firm, development initiatives become a key part of the strategy implementation process. This not only fosters individual development, it also encourages organizational development and transformation.

Moving Forward

Westinghouse illustrates the power of linking an organization's strategic agenda with leadership development processes. It also exposes the need to link various methodologies together to address the *why?*, *what?*, *how?*, and *who?* of strategic leadership development (see Figure 5.3).

As the model suggests, programs involving various conceptual, skill-building, feedback, or personal growth approaches seem to be most effective in addressing the *why?* and *what?* of strategic leadership development. These programs provide excellent forums for outlining challenges, presenting information, discussing and clarifying issues, and comparing ideas, practices and processes, for creating awareness of *why* individual leaders and their organizations need to change in order to perform effectively. In addition, they provide a good first-stage opportunity to discuss *what* needs to be done if an individual or an organization is to succeed, as well as *what* leaders have learned from their experiences. As discussed previously, these activities provide leaders with opportunities to gain perspective on both themselves and their organizations.

Although such programs are effective vehicles for addressing the *why?* of organizational and individual development, and although they can

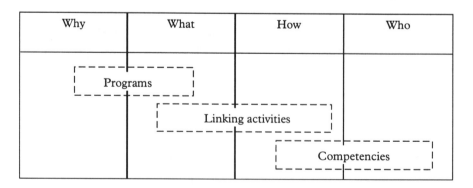

Figure 5.3 Elements of executive development
Source: Vicere, A.A., The Knowledge Creation Cycle: A Framework for Assessing Executive Development Techniques, Penn State University: Institute for the Study of Organizational Effectiveness, WP 96-001, 1996.

introduce leaders to *what* needs to be done for them and their organizations to maintain effective performance levels, transferrable learning is more likely to occur if discussions of what needs to be done are linked to actual, hands-on practice in critical thinking and problem-solving. Performance appraisal systems and action learning projects, such as those discussed in the Cartech and ARAMARK examples, are very effective vehicles for ensuring that the lessons of programs are linked to the real-world work environment. In addition, these activities also provide organizations with an opportunity to assess the *how?* of strategic leadership development by providing a forum in which particular skills, concepts, or capabilities can be applied to leadership decision making in a guided fashion, and thereby readily integrated into individual and organizational management practices.

Leadership competency models such as the one developed by Westinghouse take the process a step further by helping to clarify *how* an organization expects the leadership process to be carried out, providing even greater specificity to performance expectations. In addition, the creation of organizational competency models also addresses the question of *who* is most likely to succeed in a leadership position, contributing greatly to the appraisal and succession planning processes of the organization. This bridge to selection and appraisal helps to link the leadership development process to HR systems within the organization, giving it greater credibility, accountability, and opportunity to make an impact. In addition, analysis of the database created during competency assessment can help frame the objectives and directions of next generation leadership development programs, bringing the process full circle.

The Role of Competency Models

Competency modeling is rapidly gaining attention as a leadership development technique. Companies today are spending an enormous amount of time and money developing leadership competency models. Esque and Gilbert noted:

> " *The idea is to define a set of competencies for each job in the organization, a list of things the job holder must be able to do. These job specific competencies become the basis for hiring, developing and compensating employees within those jobs.*[44] "

To say that the development of competency frameworks is big business is an understatement. Organizations like the Center For Creative Leadership in Greensboro, North Carolina, Hay McBer in Boston, Personnel Decisions Inc. (PDI) in Minneapolis, and others do an incredible volume of business helping organizations develop competency models. These models are often translated into 360-degree assessment processes, and serve as the heart of the sponsoring company's leadership development strategy.

Competency models can be invaluable. They can help organizations profile the nature of effective leadership and effective performance. They can serve as a basis for performance assessment, appraisal, and 360-degree assessment tools. They can assist in profiling both jobs *and* potential candidates for those jobs. They can be the basis for assessing and profiling an organization's leadership talent pool, providing an ongoing needs assessment for future leadership development initiatives. All of these contributions are significant. But despite the potential benefits of competency modeling, the activity has many critics. Esque and Gilbert noted that, "the danger is that the term 'competencies' can lead people to err by focusing on behaviors instead of on accomplishments."[45] Doug Ready of the International Consortium for Executive Development Research goes even further:

> ❝ *Companies that place too great an emphasis on leadership competencies run the risk of developing a "programmatic framework" that often results in their doing a very good job of training yesterday's leaders. Companies would be well served to adopt a "competitiveness framework," which focuses on both today's and tomorrow's challenges. The process of exploring competencies should be directed toward one goal: creating competitive capabilities and a sense of preparedness for the future.*[46] ❞

Ready defined three types of competencies:

1 *Enduring* competencies related to a sense of identity and purpose within the organization
2 *Contextual* competencies related to the strategic agenda of the firm, and
3 *Process* competencies related to the ability of both the individual leader and the firm to continuously learn, improve, and grow.

Based on these classifications, Ready crafted an "International Competitive Capabilities Inventory" that blends an assessment of the strategic organizational capabilities essential for competitiveness in the global marketplace with an assessment of individual leader capabilities that are essential to the organization's ability to craft those competencies.[47]

Such a strategic approach to competency modeling can make a major contribution to the development of an organization. For example, Allen-Bradley, a highly profitable division of Rockwell International and a world leader in the design and manufacturing of automation and process controls, has used competency assessment as a tool for implementing strategic change. CEO Jodie Glore has launched the company on an ambitious growth plan driven by four key imperatives: quality, reduced cycle time, globalization, and leveraging alliances. Ready's International Competitive Capabilities Inventory is being used by Glore and Mary Eckenrod, director of human resources development, to link leadership development to the strategic imperatives of the firm through the creation of a strategic "learning plan" for the organization.[48]

Similarly, the Westinghouse competency model discussed previously is being used to define a new set of leadership behaviors. These behaviors are part of a dramatic culture change taking place within the firm. The Westinghouse competency model was developed by an internal task force to set new organizational standards for leadership performance. It now serves as the basis for the company's "key management review" process (selection and succession planning), and for portions of the appraisal process. In effect, the model is being used as an instrument of influence, linking the new strategic imperatives of the firm to the new set of performance standards for managers. As such, the framework is a powerful engine in the Westinghouse transformation process.

Despite the potential importance of competency research, Dr. Bernard Wetzel, who managed much of the Westinghouse project, reported that, "The actual 'competencies' aren't as important as the perceived relevance to the organization. After conducting considerable research into this subject for our organization, I thought that I was ready to present our conclusions to Westinghouse CEO, Mike Jordan. When his eyes began to glaze over, I paused and he began to talk about the skills he felt would be needed over the next decade. While there was considerable overlap between his suggestions and the competencies we had developed, which list do you think had more value for the organization?"[49]

The issue is whether the competency model takes on a life of its own, or whether an organization uses the model to define and craft opportunities for building competitiveness. When carefully worked into the strategic leadership development process, competency models can be a powerful tool for defining leadership roles and expectations, clarifying organizational directions and directives, and linking leadership development to other HR processes such as appraisal, succession, and compensation. Used ineffectively, competency models can be a symbol of the status quo, and anchor in past behaviors that have rapidly become bad habits in a changing marketplace.

Summary

Executive education and leadership development, when viewed from the strategic context described in this chapter, can have powerful, positive impacts on corporate performance. For that to happen, however, an organization must have a well-defined, well-aligned set of strategic imperatives that frame how it plans to build competitive advantage in the marketplace. This strategic agenda must then serve as the basis for the establishment of developmental processes that facilitate progress toward the future.

From our analysis, it appears that the leadership development demands of an organization's strategic agenda are best addressed through a balanced portfolio of methods which address both individual and organizational development. Within benchmark companies, there is a clear understanding of the role each of these methodologies plays in the leadership development process. Work experience is seen as the key driver of individual development. Programs are designed to help build perspective and outline the *why?* and *what?* of continued individual development. Linking activities such as performance appraisal and team-based action learning projects are used to provide hands-on practice, clarifying the *what?* and facilitating the *how?* of development, ultimately promoting knowledge creation and organizational development. Competency models are created to help the organization to institutionalize the *how?* as well as define and delineate *who?* – who is likely to succeed in a leadership position, how will they perform their duties, and how will the company assist them to develop to their fullest potential. Together, these elements comprise the basic tool kit for creating a strategic leadership development process.

Endnotes

1 Ready, D., A.A. Vicere and A. White, *The Role Of Executive Education in Executive Resource Planning*, Lexington, MA: International Consortium For Executive Development Research (ICEDR) Working Paper , 92/3, 1992, p. 4.

2 Vicere, A.A., M. Taylor and V. Freeman, *Executive Education In Major Corporations*, University Park, PA: Institute for the Study of Organizational Effectiveness, 1993.

3 Nonaka, I, "The Knowledge Creating Company," *Harvard Business Review*, Nov/Dec 1991, pp.96–104.

4 McCall, M., M. Lombardo, and A. Morrison, *The Lessons of Experience*, Lexington, MA: Lexington Books, 1988.

5 Conger, J., *Learning To Lead*, San Francisco: Jossey-Bass, 1992.

6 Ibid., pp. 179–180.

7 Ibid., p. 170

8 See Vicere, A.A., "University-Based Executive Education: Impacts and Implications," *Journal of Management Development*, 7, 4, 1988, pp. 5–13.

9 Vicere, Taylor and Freeman, 1993, op. cit. (Note that respondents could indicate more than one benefit.)

10 Ibid. (Note that respondents could indicate more than one benefit.)

11 Personal correspondence from Cam Danielson, Indiana University.

12 Received via personal correspondence from Bric Wheeler, Miami University, Ohio.

13 Conger, 1992, op. cit., p. xv.

14 See O'Reilly, B. 360 "Feedback Can Change Your Life," *Fortune*. October

17, 1994, pp. 93–100; also, Hoffman, R., "Ten Reasons You Should Be Using 360-Degree Feedback," April 1995, pp. 82–85.

15 Conger, 1992, op. cit., pp. 170–171.

16 Ibid, p. 156.

17 Wagner, R., T. Baldwin, and C. Roland, "Outdoor Training: Revolution Or Fad," *Training and Development Journal*, March 1991, pp. 51–56.

18 Conger, 1992, op. cit., p. 168.

19 Coyle, J. "Technology and Executive Development: The Promise and the Practice," *American Journal of Management Development*, 1, 2, 1995, pp. 37–46.

20 Rifkin, G., "A Skeptics Guide To Groupware," *Forbes ASAP*, June 5, 1995, pp. 76–97.

21 See Kirkpatrick, D., "Groupware Goes Boom," *Fortune*, December 27, 1993, pp. 99–106.

22 Davis, S. and J. Botkin, *The Monster Under the Bed*, New York: Simon and Schuster, 1994,

23 Ibid.

24 For a good overview of current perspectives on mentoring, see Applebaum, S., S. Ritchie, and B. Shapiro, "Mentoring Revisited: An Organizational Behaviour Construct," *Journal Of Management Development*, 13, 4, 1994, pp. 62–72.

25 McCall, Lombardo and Morrison, 1988, op. cit., p.12.

26 See Smith, C. "The Executive's New Coach," *Fortune*, December 27, 1993, pp. 126–134; also, Naj, A. K., "The Latest Addition To the Executive Suite Is the Psychologist's Couch," *Wall Street Journal*, August 29, 1994, p.1.

27 Shaw, R. and D. Perkins, "Teaching Organizations To Learn: The Power Of Productive Failures," in Nadler, D., et al. (eds.), *Organizational Architecture*, San Francisco: Jossey-Bass, 1992, p. 175.

28 Nonaka, 1991, op. cit., p. 96.

29 Longnecker, C. and D. Gioia, "The Executives Appraisal Paradox," *Academy of Management Executives*, 6, 2, 1992, p. 27.

30 Vicere, Taylor, and Freeman, 1993, op. cit.

31 Longnecker and Gioia, 1992, op. cit., p. 27,

32 Ibid., p. 25.

33 Ibid. See also McGill, M. and J. Slocum, *The Smarter Organization*, New York: John Wiley, 1994; also Wick, C. and L. Leon, *The Learning Edge*, New York: McGraw-Hill, 1993.

34 Miles, R., *Corporate Universities: Some Design Choices and Leading Practices*, Atlanta: Emory University, 1993.

35 McCall, Lombardo, and Morrison, 1988, op. cit., p. 32.

36 Ibid.

37 Wick and Leon, 1993, op. cit.

38 Marsick, V., L. Cederholm, E. Turner, and T. Pearson, "Action-Reflection Learning," *Training and Development*, August 1992, pp. 63–66.

39 Keys, L. "Action Learning: Executive Development Choice For the 1990s," *Journal of Management Development*, **13**, 8, 1994, pp. 50–56.

40 Nonaka, 1991, op. cit., p. 98.

41 Davis and Botkin, 1994, op. cit.

42 See McGill and Slocum, 1994, op. cit.; also Wick and Leon, 1993, op. cit.

43 McCall, Lombardo and Morrison, 1988, op. cit.

44 Esque, T and T. Gilbert, "Making Competencies Pay Off," *Training*, January 1995, p. 44.

45 Ibid., p. 44.

46 Ready, D., *Building a Competitive Capabilities Infrastructure: A New Look At Leadership Competencies*, Lexington, MA: International Consortium For Executive Development Working Paper, May 1993, p. 1.

47 Ready, D. *Champions of Change*, Lexington, MA: Gemini Consulting and The International Consortium For Executive Development Research, 1994.

48 Personal correspondence with Mary Eckenrod of Allen Bradley; see also Ready, 1995, op. cit., p. 9.

49 Wetzel T. Bernard, "The Role of Executive Educaiton in Corporate Transformation," UNICON 1996 Conference, March 19, 1996.

6

COMPANY-SPECIFIC OR EXTERNAL PROGRAMS?

One of the most hotly debated issues in leadership development today concerns the role of the classroom in leadership development. While most people would agree that classroom education and training adds an important dimension to leadership development, it is far more difficult to get agreement on when, where, and how to use classroom initiatives in the process. The growing interest in company-specific educational programs discussed throughout this book has further confused the issue, creating intense debate over the role and potential contribution to leadership development of external, open-enrollment programs like those traditionally offered by university business schools. Some critics have charged that company-specific programs provide greater benefits to the organization and are therefore more appropriate investments than external, open-enrollment programs. Others are beginning to suggest that company-specific initiatives encourages companies to spend too much time "talking to itself." This chapter addresses those charges.

The discussion is built on a central premise: programs designed for a general audience serve a different purpose and generate different outcomes than do company-specific programs. Both can contribute significantly to leadership development when they are used in an appropriate manner. This chapter will compare and contrast the objectives, process and outcomes of a traditional open-enrollment program (a four-week residential general management program offered by the Smeal College of Business Administration), a two-week general management program designed specifically for the Consolidated Rail Corporation, and a custom-designed program developed and managed by Johnson & Johnson. We will discuss the opportunities, outcomes, and potential of each type of program, and provide guidelines for deciding whether to go internal or external with a particular leadership development initiative.[1]

The Executive Management Program

The Executive Management Program (EMP) is a four-week general management program offered several times each year by the Smeal College of Business Administration on the campus of Pennsylvania State University. The EMP is typical of many multi-week general management programs offered by major business schools around the world. According to *Bricker's International Directory of University-Based Executive Programs*, the following 42 universities offered similar programs in 1996:[2]

Ashridge Management College
Banff School of Advanced
  Management
Carnegie Mellon University
Columbia University
Cornell University
Cranfield University
Dartmouth College
Duke University
Harvard University
Henley Management College
INSEAD
International Institute for
  Management Development (IMD)
International Marketing Institute
Irish Management Institute
London Business School
MacQuarie University
Massachusetts Institute of
  Technology
Monash Mt Eliza Business School
Northwestern University
Ohio State University
Pennsylvania State University

Simmons College
Smith College
Stanford University
Templeton College
University of California at
  Berkeley
University of California, Los
  Angeles
University of Hawaii
University of Houston
University of Illinois
University of Michigan
University of Minnesota
University of New Mexico
University of New South Wales
University of North Carolina at
  Chapel Hill
University of Pennsylvania
University of Pittsburgh
University of Tennessee
University of Texas at Austin
University of Virginia
University of Washington
University of Western Ontario

Launched in 1956, the EMP is attended by high-level corporate executives. Nearly 35 percent of the 30 or so executives who attend each session of the program reside outside the United States. The typical participant is 43 years old, with over 11 years of management experience. The majority of the participants are upper-middle managers, heads of functional areas in corporations, or general managers. All of them have been identified as key players in their organization's future development. To ensure integrity in maintaining this profile, each candidate's application is subject to an admissions screening process. Because interaction with a diverse group of peer managers is a key benefit of the EMP, the screening process also enables the sponsoring business school to maintain the diversity of the group in terms of companies, industries and location.

Background

As a general management program, the EMP has a strategic focus presented from the perspective of a senior corporate officer. It is designed both to challenge and broaden participants' attitudes by exposing them to the leading-edge management thinking of faculty, as well as the values and viewpoints of successful executives from different companies, cultures and industries. Through a carefully designed sequence of experiential exercises, lectures, discussions, case exercises, and business simulations, the program attempts to create an educational environment that enables executives to break out of their usual routine and develop a more comprehensive, more global orientation to management. As such, the program utilizes a number of approaches and techniques to facilitate development.[3]

Program Process

The brochure for the EMP describes it as a developmental experience. The intent is not to engage in skill-building, although there are several elements of the program, particularly in the areas of finance and accounting, that do lend themselves to skill-based development. Rather, the intent is to challenge participants' assumptions about their company, their career, and their role within their organizations. The program may be classified as one of Conger's *conceptual* approaches to leadership development.[4] To achieve their objectives, the EMP designers have developed a process they call "paying the piper", a five-step process that helps participants to maximize the value of the educational experience.[5] The *piper* process can be described as follows.

Prepare The EMP learning environment is intense, and preparation for daily sessions is critical. Participants are encouraged to devote several hours each evening to preparation of daily assignments in addition to their full-day classroom sessions and frequent evening group work. These assignments can include reading articles or case studies, completing various diagnostic instruments, or meeting with a discussion or simulation team. The EMP participants say the month-long schedule of academic activities can be grueling.

Interact Program designers note that in an EMP-type experience, participants will learn as much from each other as they do in the formal classroom sessions. Interaction with a diverse group of peers from different companies, cultures and industries provides the EMP participants with the opportunity to broaden their perspectives and increase their awareness of external issues and trends. The development of a closely knit learning community is, therefore, a paramount concern. The EMP utilizes an outdoor leadership development experience at the beginning of a session, as well as other experiential exercises, to promote interaction and involvement among participants. This part of the program's design incorporates an element of the *personal growth* approach to leadership development, but does so more from a team building perspective than a personal development perspective.

Participate The EMP coordinators report that session leaders are deliberately not called teachers, professors or instructors. Rather, they are called "faculty leaders" because their job is not to lecture the participants, but to facilitate discussion of a particular agenda to which they contribute their academic expertise. Active classroom participation is a key element of the program experience, and there are frequent small group discussions and other forms of dialogue and idea exchange. This type of process take advantage of the experience base of participants, and promotes a much higher level of networking among them.

Expand   As a general management program with a developmental focus, the EMP is designed from a futuristic perspective. It is intended to help leaders bridge between their current mind-set and a more strategic perspective of leadership. Participants are encouraged to discuss ideas among themselves and debate their applicability to organizational and leadership effectiveness in a rapidly changing, global economy. This expansion of thinking encourages a heightened sense of awareness of the leadership challenge.[6]

Reflect   The program makes extensive use of simulation and structured feedback to bring new concepts to life for participants. At least one 360-degree assessment instrument is used to provide participants with feedback on their performance as a leader. This type of experience and feedback provides fodder for what is perhaps one of the greatest benefits of attending an EMP-type experience, having a concentrated period of time away from the daily demands of the work situation. This type of "sabbatical" enables participants to take stock of their experience, capabilities, organization, and career. It can also provide an opportunity for participants to rethink their approaches to leadership and to form personal action plans for future growth and development. Participants are encouraged to make use of the resources of the university to help them in this process. Those that take advantage of this opportunity find an EMP-type experience to be a good vehicle for personal growth and perspective-building.

Program Outcomes – Participant Reactions

Most of the participants' reactions tend to focus on three particular outcomes: (1) *confidence building,* (2) *broadening/developing an external perspective,* and (3) *network building.*

Confidence Building   Most EMP graduates take a pragmatic view of their experience.

> **"** *I was looking for an opportunity to reexamine my own views on business in a controlled, structured setting with opportunities to relearn and discuss the issues.* **"**

For many participants, this opportunity for reexamination is viewed as having had a positive effect on their performance and level of confidence. They describe their heightened confidence to deal with whatever comes along. This increased self-assurance was often perceived as a major force in continued career development.

> ❝ I am confident that the knowledge, skills and contacts gained from the EMP program were a significant factor in making the move from middle management to upper corporate management. ❞

Broadening and Developing an External Perspective   Participants also discussed the impact of the EMP in terms of the development of a broadened, more externally oriented perspective.

> ❝ EMP showed me how much I have to learn... Sometimes positive effects are measured in what you are able to do for the careers of others. The program enabled me to pass much on to my employees and my children... By developing a better understanding of myself, I can manage changes in the business environment more easily... The interaction with different people from different industries and countries was exceptional in giving me a much broader view of national and international dimension of management. ❞

Networking   In a survey of corporate users of university programs, a key perceived value of experiences like the EMP was found to be the opportunities for participants to network with colleagues from other companies, industries, and cultures.[7] The EMP participants make frequent reference to this idea.

> ❝ Our group had participants from all over the world... It gave us an opportunity to understand our countries, and our businesses from the point of view of people from other countries and it added a [real] dimension to the program... We opened up our thoughts, our minds, and our hearts to each other – diverse people, different cultures. It really was impressive... Now when I'm in Europe or Asia or just about anywhere, I have a friend nearby to call on. When I need help figuring out how to deal with customers in certain industries, I have a contact who can help me out. The connections I've made are invaluable. ❞

Transfer of Learning

Although these reactions appear to be very positive, sponsoring companies must nevertheless determine the likelihood that the individual learning and personal growth they suggest *actually transfers back to the workplace*. Based on his experience with open-enrollment leadership development programs, Conger noted, "ultimately . . ., the encouragement and development of leadership skills rests with the individual's own motivation and talent and with the receptiveness of their organizations to support and coach such skills. This leaves a lot to chance."[8] It is this element of chance that may be the biggest problem with external, open-enrollment programs like the EMP. In surveys investigating the reasons why companies use external programs, opportunities to broaden participant perspectives and help them develop external networks topped the list.[9] In research which involved asking participants about the impact on their career of attending an external program, most characterized their experiences as powerful catalysts for encouraging the transition from management into leadership.[10] However, as Conger suggested, the degree to which this transition actually progresses is directly related to the effort put into the development agenda by both individual participants and their companies.

In a recent study, researchers found that of the companies they surveyed, slightly over 70 percent made it a practice to brief participants before they actually attended a program. This number was *down* from 76 percent five years previously.[11] To make matters worse, when the same researchers polled participants enrolled in the executive management program described above, *less than 30 percent* of the participants recalled having been briefed. Despite their company's view to the contrary, most said they came to the program with very little knowledge of the purpose of their attendance. With that as the case, is it any wonder that sponsoring companies are struggling to see the relevance of external programs? Only the most motivated individuals are likely to benefit personally from the experience. Furthermore, only the most fortunate organizations are likely to get a return on their investment since it appears very few had any tangible objectives for sending people to the programs, or any plans for capturing the learning and experiences of their participants.

This relates back to our previous discussion of systems thinking. If external programs are looked to as "ends" in themselves, they will have value for an individual only by chance, and value for the organization only by accident. If they are looked to as a "means" to address a particular element of the development agenda, then they have far greater potential.

> There are critical times in an individual's career, particularly when he or she is moving into a position of expanded scope and/or responsibility, when an external program can help to break the mold of an organizationally or functionally influenced mind-set by promoting a greater openness to ideas and a greater awareness of the general management perspective.[12]

At such critical points, an appropriately selected and managed external program can help broaden perspectives, boost confidence, and stimulate a deepened conceptual understanding of leadership. This has a much better chance of happening when the developmental context is managed, when participants are briefed and objectives for the experience set, when assignments are given to be completed during the program, and when participants are expected to return and share their learning and experiences with their staff and colleagues. It seems today, however, that briefing is haphazard, few participants are given assignments (less than 10 percent of the companies in the previously mentioned study reported doing so with participants they sent to university programs[13]), and even fewer are required to share their experiences. One must wonder whether a powerful source of leadership development is being squandered.

To avoid wasting these opportunities, users of external experiences would be wise to take advantage of the set guidelines for selecting and utilizing external programs developed by *Bricker's International Directory of University-Based Executive Programs*.

Guidelines for Selecting Executive Programs

Unlike investing in real estate – where the three most important criteria are said to be location, location and location – making the right choice about executive education relies on careful investigation of a variety of factors. Location does happen to be among them: weighing the relative advantages of programs offered nearby, in other parts of the country, or around the world. But scouting sites is only one step. Whether you're looking to send one executive or many, you want to receive a high return on the investment. That means narrowing the field to programs that can accommodate individual learning needs, meet your expectations for quality, and are aligned with your organization's management philosophy and strategic goals.

These guidelines highlight several key factors in making the right choice. In general, the more thorough the selection process, the better the opportunity for getting the performance results you want.

Learning Objectives

- *Identify critical business issues* that need to be addressed through an executive program, both organizational goals and those of immediate concern and directly relevant to individual executives.
- *Clarify both personal and organizational expectations,* including whether the primary objective is to build skills, enhance subject matter knowledge, or initiate a change in mind-set.
- *Match the program to the executive's learning style,* for example, one with an experiential component for an executive who responds better to hands-on activities rather than pure lecture or case discussions.

Faculty

- *Assess the level and nature of the faculty's business experience,* including the type and size of companies they've worked with and in what capacity.
- *Find out whether the faculty has experience teaching executives* as compared to strictly undergraduate or graduate-level business students.
- *Compare the faculty's management orientation to that of your*

organization by reviewing faculty publication, bios, and other background information.

- *Observe the faculty* in action if possible by visiting classes, attending speaking engagements, or viewing videotaped presentations.
- *Determine the availability of faculty* for consulting or coaching participants on individual issues.

Content

- *Ask for a detailed program schedule* – not just an overview of topics addressed – to see how time is allocated.
- *Get a sense of how the subject matter will be approached* by speaking to the program director; different programs often treat the same content in different ways.
- *Gauge how much exposure participants will have to state-of-the-art management practices and theories,* for example, by reviewing a syllabus or bibliography to see how recent the teaching and study materials are.
- *Consider the level, nature, and relevance of assignments,* including in-class exercises, individual homework assignments, group projects, and any pre-program preparatory work.
- *Check on any high-tech aspects of the program,* for example, to assure a comfort level for executives unaccustomed to working with computers or, conversely, access to up-to-date tools for the technologically adept.
- *Evaluate activities that involve individual psychological assessments and/or counseling* to discover whether they will be conducted by qualified professionals and are suitable for particular executives.

Participant Mix

- *Find out whether the program attracts largely a regional, domestic, or international participant base,* especially if your organization is looking to foster a cross-border or cross-cultural perspective.
- *Consider the industry representation* to assess the relative advantages of having an executive interact with others from the same industry or from a broad industry mix.
- *Determine the average age,* experience, and career level of typical

program participants and other such factors relevant to productive peer group exchange.

Teaching Methodologies

- *Gauge the level and nature of interaction between faculty and participants* that is facilitated by the program format, including opportunities for informal exchange outside the classroom.
- *Evaluate the type and variety of teaching methods and technologies used,* which may include case studies (ask how current they are); lectures by faculty and outside experts; directed discussion; role plays; performance feedback tools; group projects, individual exercises; participant presentations and reports; games and business simulations; self-assessment/diagnostic instruments; and instructional or interactive videos. A variety of methods can be important, especially in long programs, to enhance learning and ward off boredom.
- *Determine the opportunities participants will have to implement or practice the skills they learn* both in class and back at work, for example, action learning activities focused on current business issues of participants and their organizations, or action plans outlining specific steps participants intend to take after the program's over to apply what they have learned.
- *Assess the value of outdoor or other physical learning activities* with regard to whether they are appropriate for individual executives and transferrable to the business environment. Also be sure such activities are supervised by individuals with proper qualifications/credentials and pass muster with your organization's legal department regarding insurance liability.
- *Find out if follow-up activities are part of the program,* either formal or informal, as a means to reinforce learning over time or to support an ongoing network among faculty and participants.

Quality Control

- *Look for clear and detailed program learning objectives* that describe specific ways in which attendees will benefit from their participation.

- *Evaluate sample program materials* both for substance and with regard to the overall written quality of the documentation.
- *Contact previous users of the program* for their views about the strengths, weaknesses, and ultimate value of the program, both colleagues at other organizations who have sent participants as well as the participants themselves.
- *Visit program sites and audit individual programs* whenever possible, particularly when you are considering sending several executives or using the program on an ongoing basis.

Reprinted by permission of Peterson's, P.O. Box 2123, Princeton, NJ from *Bricker's International Directory: University-Based Executive Programs 1996*.

Summary – EMP

It can be noted from this analysis that an open-enrollment program like the EMP may be best characterized as a developmental experience, one which challenges the beliefs, skills and values of participating managers and creates greater awareness of the leadership challenge. Through this type of experience, participants are given the opportunity to rethink their values and views across many dimensions. Through their interaction with a diverse group of peers, they are encouraged to broaden their perspectives and develop a greater openness to diversity and change. These outcomes are perhaps best summarized by one EMP graduate:

❝ *EMP will go down as an experience of a lifetime. I am back at work invigorated, ready to take on the world.* ❞

The Conrail Management Program

The same university that sponsors the EMP, Penn State, is also the sponsor of a two-week general management program designed specifically for the Consolidated Rail Corporation (Conrail). The Conrail Management Program (CMP) is a two-week general management program aimed at middle and upper-middle managers from that company. Like the EMP, the CMP is typical of many similar company-specific programs developed and delivered as a joint venture with a university business school.

The CMP is offered twice each year on the Penn State campus to carefully selected groups of about 30 Conrail managers. Participants are, on average, in their late 30s, with seven to eight years of management experience in one functional area. The participants must be nominated by a senior officer and approved by the chairman and CEO. This nomination process has caused the program to be seen not as a remedial experience among Conrail managers, but rather as a developmental experience designed to facilitate continued career progression. In addition, Conrail has developed an allocation system across departments and divisions to ensure organization-wide representation within each session of the program. A company-specific focus and cross-functional representation are crucial components in addressing the program's objectives of extending the awareness and understanding of Conrail's strategy and building a team-oriented culture.

Background

As we have seen, Conrail has emerged from a floundering position to one of financial stability and growth. A major factor in this corporate turnaround was the development of a radically new (for Conrail) strategy with a distinct market-driven focus. This strategy differed greatly from the operations-driven focus that had dominated the US rail industry for many years. Conrail's senior management realized that it was essential to communicate this new set of strategic imperatives clearly throughout the organization, and that it would be necessary to mount efforts to help managers understand this strategy and its implications for organizational change and development.

To this end, Conrail launched a three-pronged effort to immerse management at all levels in the concepts of marketing, innovation and effective management. First, Conrail sent senior-level managers to traditional executive education programs like the EMP. Sending top-level people to longer term programs at prestigious institutions sent a clear message throughout the organization that standard operating procedures were going to change, and that fresh thinking and new ideas would be required. Second, a first-level supervisory program was developed and delivered internally. This program was designed to familiarize new managers with company goals and newly defined management practices. While those programs were being established, Conrail began working with Smeal College on the third prong of the effort, the launching of the CMP.[14]

The design and content of the program were collaboratively constructed through a series of interviews and meetings between Penn State faculty and Conrail management. During these sessions, the university gained a detailed insight into the strategy, structure, process and culture of Conrail, and were then able to translate this understanding into an educational experience designed to facilitate the transformation and development of the firm. These meetings have continued over the life of the program, and are an ongoing force for its continued evaluation and improvement.

In many ways, the program is designed to facilitate a deepened *conceptual* understanding of where Conrail is going and what it and its leaders need to do to be successful. The program also makes extensive use of simulation, and includes an outdoor leadership development experience to help facilitate the transfer of learning and the personal growth of participants. But, while the program is expected to facilitate the personal growth of participants, it is expected even more to facilitate the "collective growth" of the new Conrail culture.

Program Process

The program curriculum emphasizes several core themes. The first is the importance of customer awareness and service in Conrail's highly competitive environment. The second is the need for greater interaction and co-operation across Conrail's traditionally isolated departments in order to become more market-driven. The third is cross-functional awareness of the contributions made to corporate effectiveness and success by each of the various departments and divisions represented in the program.

Rather than encouraging participants to look at many different business approaches and managerial perspectives (as is the case with the EMP), the CMP is designed to help Conrail managers learn to blend operational efficiency and a market orientation into a new Conrail structure. To ensure the success of the effort, faculty structure sessions around the strategic imperatives of the firm, several Conrail-specific cases are used in the program, numerous Conrail executives participate as faculty members, often co-teaching modules with core program faculty, and several Conrail senior officers (usually including the CEO) conduct open discussion sessions during each program. Simulation is used heavily, both for practice in putting new concepts to work and as a team-building process. Similarly, an outdoor leadership development experience is built into the program to help group interaction.

Like most internally sponsored programs of this type, the CMP's focus is less on perspective-building and broadening than it is on awareness of corporate directions, internal team-building, and cross-functional understanding – a focus that is *internal* to the company, directed toward the understanding and implementation of the organization's strategic imperatives, and intended to clarify company expectations for effective leadership. This type of enhanced internal perspective can be a major catalyst for organizational change and development.

Program Outcomes – Participant Reactions

CMP participants surveyed some time after the program give an indication of the impact of the experience. These reactions cluster around the themes of *confidence building, organizational awareness/team building,* and *transformation.*

Confidence Building   Like the EMP participants, CMP alumni often talk about the value of interacting with other Conrail employees as a real confidence builder. The difference, however, is that the confidence is as much or more in the organization as it is personal. Much of this new-found organizational confidence could be related to networking. As one participant said, "When you've got a name and a face and a relationship with somebody that you can call … it's amazing!"

Organizational Awareness/Team Building   In the CMP-type program, it often becomes difficult to separate confidence building from organizational awareness and team building.

> ❝ *The interaction achieved by being at a program such as this with peers from various departments was very beneficial. We were reminded that we are all on the same team with the same common goal... For some it was a first chance to talk openly with managers from other departments, and thus break through walls that hinder communication.* ❞

Transformation   Other reactions of many participants focused on the role of the program in facilitating the implementation of strategy, as well as organizational change and transformation.

> ❝ *The program helped me recognize the corporation's short-and long-term objectives and the important contributions made by each individual department to achieving those goals… Now I can more knowledgeably talk about why corporate structure has changed with time and why certain structures are more effective than others. I can build into my conversations an 'advertisement' for the importance of marketing and what Conrail must do to survive.* ❞

Transfer of Learning

When asked why they use company-specific programs like the CMP, organizations generally mention both specificity to critical organizational issues and the opportunity to launch or add momentum to organizational change processes.[15] These objectives alone suggest that the transference of learning from a well-crafted company-specific program to the work environment is a far easier task to manage. That is because the development context is managed right from the start. The program has clear objectives related to the strategic imperatives of the firm, the content is focused on issues critical to the firm and its leaders, and the interaction helps to put in place the sort of "glue technology" we encountered in Chapter 3. For Conrail, the value of this type of process can best be described in a quote from a story written on the CMP:

> *For two weeks Conrail managers from across its entire system come together in a relaxed atmosphere to think about the railroad in a broader perspective. Men and women who work in transportation, marketing, finance, engineering, and a variety of other functions come together to share opinions, perspectives, and transportation industry knowledge.*
>
> *It is an opportunity for Conrail people to step back from their everyday jobs – phone calls, memos, meetings – and learn new perspectives. Perhaps more importantly, the sessions facilitate a great deal of knowledge transfer, from session faculty to "students", and from employee to employee. It provides a real chance for Conrail managers to talk with one another, and to ask the questions that have been on their minds for a long time.*[16]

The systems model presented in Chapter 4 provides a solid framework for crafting effective company specific programs like the CMP. When an organization starts with the strategic imperatives of the firm, links those imperatives to a set of developmental objectives, matches those objectives to the most appropriate methods and provider partners to design a developmental process, then links that process to the HR systems of the company (selection, appraisal, reward, and development systems), purposeful leadership development is likely to take place.[17] Because the selection of provider partners is so critical to making this process work, Chapter 7 is devoted to that issue.

Summary – CMP

CMP is an experience that promotes team building and corporate spirit across managerial ranks. Such programs appear to be very effective at promoting team-building and networking, providing a focus on strategic directions, setting expectations, and driving change and transformation throughout the organization.[18] An early graduate of the CMP sums it up:

> " *By teaching managers the value of working together, understanding and respecting each other's roles, and adapting our individual styles to fit the company, the program has brought each of us, and Conrail, a step closer to reaching our corporate vision.* "

Executive Conference II at Johnson & Johnson

As we saw in the introduction, when CEO Ralph Larsen of Johnson & Johnson was planning a leadership development effort for the top 700 people at his firm in 1992, he was driven by the importance of thinking about the future along with the dangers of trading on past successes. Larsen appointed a committee of key executives, gave them access to information on the future of Johnson & Johnson gathered through interviews with over 100 of their colleagues, and charged them with developing a plan for his proposed initiative. Their work resulted in the company's first Executive Conference, a very successful initiative built around the theme "Setting The Competitive Standard." This highly interactive series of programs was coordinated by the Center for Executive Development, a consulting firm from Cambridge, Massachusetts.

Based on the success of the first Executive Conference, J&J decided to launch a second initiative in 1993. The program director, Dr. Myron Goff, interviewed representatives from approximately a dozen university-based business schools and independent consulting firms to find a partner for the initiative. Goff decided to create a network of independent providers (both individual university faculty and independent consulting firms) rather than select a single entity because of what he perceived as opportunities for greater flexibility and responsiveness to demands for the high degree of custom work required by the initiative. One of the authors was selected as course manager and selected professors from two US and two European universities, as well as one independent consultant, to work on the program.

Through the interview process and a series of wide-ranging discussions, a number of ideas and issues were brought to the forefront of the agenda for Executive Conference II. The program steering committee eventually identified the four most important objectives for the initiative which was then called "Creating Our Future":

1 To acquire the tools to create a future full of new opportunities for success.
2 To challenge basic assumptions.
3 To reflect on feedback from self and others that can lead to personal change.
4 To develop the competence and courage to lead changes that bring about a successful future.

Goff insisted that some of the principals who designed the program should also be involved in the delivery of the content. The faculty members conducted interviews with J&J executives in six countries and helped to develop the course design and materials. These included computer-assisted discussion exercises; an original future scenario case called "J&J 2002"; a comprehensive, integrative "Merlin Exercise" (described later) that resulted in presentations to the CEO or member of the J&J Executive Committee; and individualized 360-degree feedback sessions conducted by professional psychologists based on leadership profiles completed by peers, subordinates and superiors. Because of the extensive involvement of university-based faculty members, the development cost for this program was at the upper range of costs reported in surveys of the field. Yet, faculty members agreed to participate in the development process at half their usual billing rates to take advantage of the opportunity to participate in an extensive number of programs over a three-year period – a total of 23 sessions in all – in the unique format described below.

> *We insist that our partners in a major learning initiative be prepared to relate to the uniqueness of our executives. We spend more on the developmental process than many groups because we do not want "off-the-shelf" presentations.*

> Myron Goff, Director of Executive Conferences,
> Johnson & Johnson

Program Process

The content and flow of the program was designed to build on what preceded it. Consequently, faculty members were not allowed to switch days to suit their own convenience. All 23 iterations of this program were conducted with exactly the same program design and content. A designated faculty coordinator began each day by leading the group in a discussion around some of the major learning outcomes of the preceding sessions. This provided integration and made the program seamless.

The program design called for an integrative exercise to tie its various aspects together. This was the "Merlin Exercise" and it involved participants each day in applying course concepts to the creation of a future vision of the firm.[19] In addition to integration, the Merlin Exercise also provided an opportunity for participants to interact with the CEO or Vice Chairman at the conference conclusion through a series of presentations. Traditionally, participants had been given the opportunity to challenge the company's most senior officers with questions about the present status or future direction of the firm but their concerns were often presented in a somewhat critical manner which frequently placed the respondent on the defensive. The Merlin Exercise avoided this problem by asking people to describe a future they would recommend to senior management, one that they would feel fully committed to supporting with their own efforts. Senior management could then engage in an open discussion around these future scenarios, thus eliminating defensiveness while still challenging the basic assumptions of the firm.

In addition, the firm had recently begun to use *Lotus Notes* as a communications/networking tool. The J&J Information Systems Group saw the program as an opportunity to demonstrate the power of the network, and offered their expertise in the development of exercises to enhance the team-based interaction called for in the course design, including the provision of coaches to teach the system to participants with relatively little computer proficiency. Ultimately, ten computer-assisted discussion exercises were created and built into the conference design. Coupled with a futuristic "J&J 2002" case, these exercises helped participants develop their perceptions of the future of the company and perspectives on how J&J could capitalize on those future scenarios to carry on its legacy of success.

A unique feature of the conference was that each person had an individual session with a professional psychologist who helped interpret data from a 360-degree feedback assessment. Taking a coaching role, the psychologists also helped participants to develop personal action plans for improvement. In addition, most of them were involved in analyzing the 100-plus feedback reports and were adept at giving sensitive and helpful interpretations of the data. The ability to place the issues in a practical and meaningful context for individual participants was a key objective of the program. They were there not just to talk about the future, but to take action to create it.

Program Outcomes

Participants in the Executive Conference were asked to evaluate the degree to which the program met their own expectations as well as the stated objectives of the program. After the first ten sessions had been conducted, an outside firm was engaged to survey previous participants to determine the real and lasting value of the program. The category clusters were:

- broader horizons for thinking and planning
- personal insight about areas for change, and
- overcoming the complacency often associated with long-term success.

More important than the participants' comments were reports of three new businesses generated as a result of the Merlin presentations and the use of tools acquired in the conference at lower levels within the organization.

Widened Horizons Many participants reflected on the fact that the program provided an unusual opportunity for them to step out of the day-to-day pressures of their operating responsibility and think about the truly critical responsibility for creating a future for the company.

> 66 *The session was successful in allowing me to begin declaring a future and understanding what is needed to achieve this vision ... an opportunity to envision J&J unencumbered by the constraints of our world today.* 99

This unrestricted way to "declare" the future was invigorating and thought provoking. The interaction with other companies outside the franchise group was also very informative. Many participants describe Merlin as "a unique way for dealing with future possibilities." Another participant wrote that the significance of participation in Executive Conference II was:

> 66 *understanding the tools of anticipatory learning and being given very vivid examples of how breakthroughs can direct markets and completely change the way we do business. These breakthroughs then create new standards that become widely accepted. A real challenge for us.* 99

Personal Feedback An important part of any change initiative is recognizing the need to make revisions. Individualized feedback based on data collected from peers, subordinates and bosses provided participants with real data about how they were perceived by others. Some had difficulty in recognizing that, even at the top of the organization, there are variations in performance and behavior. All of the participants could not be above average in their peer group. One participant wrote, "It was the best personal feedback I have had in 21 years with the company. It was relevant given the way it was structured." Another participant commented on the importance of being able to "see the boss's feedback, unadulterated and undiluted." Another appreciated "getting feedback from direct reports. This motivation for positive change by a personal action was invaluable."

Overcoming Complacency   One of the chairman's original reasons for setting up Executive Conference II was the fact that Johnson & Johnson had been consistently successful for such a long period of time.[20] While the company had a wonderful heritage, Ralph Larsen had seen industry leaders like IBM and General Motors begin to founder and lose ground because of what was perceived by outside observers as arrogance or complacency. In fact, former CEOs at these firms served on his board of directors. Participants were given opportunities to discuss what dangers they saw in various parts of the Johnson & Johnson family of companies.

> One participant described the need to "always look at yourself as others see you. You can become complacent when you are doing well. Always challenge your strategy. Make sure that you are looking forward and don't get lost in the present."

Each participant was expected to interview a customer about the perceived future of their industry before coming to the conference. These interview profiles became a database for reference by other participants. One participant said, "he enjoyed the discussion relative to the successes and weaknesses of tomorrow ... and also the discussion of products and the perceived value of our customers was informative." A summary of the value of these concepts was captured by a participant who wrote about the "important concepts of how past successes can easily predispose an organization to future failures. We must avoid this."

Summary

Comments from participants captured some of the ways that a custom program design can address specific challenges which face an already successful organization. The program established an important dialogue between various parts of the almost 200 separate companies within the J&J organization. It provided exposure to cutting-edge ideas and an opportunity to apply those ideas directly to the entire company as well as to the specific portion which each participant represented.

> Forcing us to look out in the future is clearly the right direction. This should be used at the individual company level to help develop a common vision and identify the core competencies required to achieve it. This can then be shared with franchise groups to explore opportunities.

Perhaps the most important conclusion about the success of this initiative came when the faculty coordinator congratulated a former participant on a very significant promotion. The response was, "It took six months to make it happen, but I finally got my Merlin." This individual had seen the final conference presentation as more than an intellectual exercise. He continued to push for the establishment of an integrative healthcare system that was broader than anything within the company portfolio at the time. By leveraging the work done in the conference, an important new business began and a significant promotion was the personal reward for applying program concepts to the competitive environment.

A Comparative Discussion

By analyzing the brief cases presented above, one can begin to grasp the impacts and implications of both open-enrollment and company-specific executive education/leadership development experiences. The traditional open-enrollment program, typified by the EMP, is a broadening experience. It enhances participants' confidence, challenges their assumptions, encourages them to rethink their own and their organization's traditional values and viewpoints, and makes them more aware of the leadership challenge. Appropriately designed and presented, it is a perspective-building experience that can revitalize a leader's career and position him or her for continued development. However, an open-enrollment program is less likely to develop specific skills or reinforce specific corporate values or operating styles. Rather, the experience often serves as a catalyst for change and innovation in individual management styles and perspectives, and as a tool to aid the transition from a managerial mind-set to a leadership mind-set. We can see from the comments of the EMP participants that the experience challenges the individual to look beyond the routine and habitual elements of his or her job towards a more comprehensive view of the leader as strategist.

Company-specific programs, typified by the CMP and Executive Conference II, generate somewhat different outcomes. Perhaps the most significant of those outcomes are the encouragement of teamwork, the development of new lines of communication, and the clarification of organizational style, strategy and culture. Participants learn more about their respective company, more about its competitive strategy, and more about each other, but focus less on issues apart from the specified corporate agenda. Thus, they are less likely to experience a challenge to their organization and/or its operational status quo unless that challenge is planned for or orchestrated through action learning projects or some other technique.

When designed appropriately, a company-specific executive program is also a perspective-building experience, but for different reasons than an open-enrollment program. The company-specific program assists managers at all levels to develop a working understanding of an organization's current and desired strategy and culture. It helps managers to feel better informed and more aware of the internal workings of the firm. As such, they are better prepared to provide leadership and direction and to facilitate desired organizational changes. Comments made by the CMP and Executive Conference II participants show how this type of program can serve as a conduit for organizational communication, and a catalyst for team building and organizational transformation. Furthermore, the applications/action planning focus typified by Executive Conference II can help initiate both dialogue and action that can fuel transformation and change within the sponsoring organization.

Based on this analysis, we believe internal and external programs generate different kinds of outcomes and clearly are not substitutes for one another. Whether they are complementary or conflicting depends on the ability of an organization to understand and acknowledge their respective contributions to leadership and organizational development and choreograph their use appropriately. At the right times in an individual's career or in an organization's developmental cycle, each can have a dramatic effect on individual and/or organizational effectiveness. A better understanding of the impacts and implications of both types of programs can ensure that each type of educational experience is more effectively matched with the executive development objectives of individual managers and the organization as a whole.

As a side note, the consortium-type program discussed elsewhere in this book is an attempt to bridge these two approaches by melding teams of leaders from four or five companies together in a program customized to the collective needs of the participating companies. It does seem to be a model worthy of further examination as it attempts to draw on the best of both worlds.

Summary

The debate about internal and external programs rages on. Our research shows that both have their strengths and their place in the arsenal of tools for leadership development. By understanding the nature of the experiences, companies should be in a better position to maximize the contributions of each approach. External programs can provide a rich developmental sabbatical for participants through which they are exposed to leading-edge thinking, multiple approaches to doing business, and a potential network of diverse colleagues. Although most participants find such experiences stimulating and refreshing, the benefit to both the individual and the company will be greatly increased through the kind of briefing, preparation, and follow-up discussed in this chapter.

Internal programs can be an engine for transformation, a vehicle for changing the way an organization operates. By helping people develop a deeper understanding of the organization as a whole, and by helping to form and maintain internal networks, these programs can play a critical role in the organizational development process. But for that to happen, senior managers of the company, like those at Conrail and Johnson & Johnson, must play an active role in the process. And to truly leverage the experience, the company and its providers must work in partnership to create the most effective, relevant experience possible. The following chapter is focused on the assessment and selection of provider partners.

Endnotes

1 The EMP and CMP analyses are adapted and updated from Vicere, A.A., "Universities As Providers of Executive Education," *Journal of Management Development*, **9**(4), 1990, pp. 23–31.

2 *Bricker's International Directory of University-Based Executive Education Programs*, Princeton: Petersons, 1995.

3 See Conger, J. *Learning to Lead*, San Francisco: Jossey-Bass, 1992.

4 Ibid.

5 The *piper* is an element of the EMP program orientation given to participants on the opening day of a session.

6 Conger, 1992, op. cit., p. 170.

7 Vicere, A.A., M. Taylor, and V. Freeman, *Executive Education in Major Corporations*, University Park, PA: Institute For the Study of Organizational Effectiveness, 1993.

8 Conger, 1992, op. cit., p. 180.

9 Vicere, Taylor and Freeman, 1993, op. cit.

10 See sections three and five of Vicere, A.A. (ed.), *Executive Education: Process, Practice and Evaluation*, Princeton: Petersons, 1989.

11 Vicere, Taylor and Freeman, 1993, op. cit.

12 Vicere, A.A., "Foreword," *Bricker's International Director of University-Based Executive Education Programs*, op. cit.

13 Vicere, Taylor and Freeman, 1993, op. cit.

14 MacQueen, C. and A.A. Vicere, "Conrail's Development Program: On Track Toward the Company Vision," in Vicere, A.A. (ed.) 1989, op. cit., pp. 91–97.

15 Vicere, Taylor and Freeman, 1993, op. cit.

16 Zimbler, H. "Leadership in Action," *Alumni Exec*, Winter 1993, p. 3.

17 Ulrich, D. and D. Lake, *Organizational Capability*, New York: John Wiley, 1990.

18 See Vicere, Taylor and Freeman, 1993, op. cit.; Vicere, 1989, op. cit.

19 See Fulmer, R.M. "A Model for Changing the Way Organizations Learn," *Planning Review*, **22**(3), May–June 1994.

20 See Brian O'Reilly, "Johnson & Johnson is on a Role," *Fortune*, **130**(13), Dec. 26, 1994; Michael Treacy and Fred Wiersrna, "How Market Leaders Keep Their Edge," *Fortune*, **131**(2), Feb. 6, 1995, pp. 88–89; and "Dusting the Opposition," *Economist*, **335**(7912), April 29, 1995, pp. 71–72.

7

SELECTING PROVIDERS

Corporate expenditure on various forms of leadership development has grown to over $45 billion during the past decade. Arthur Andersen spends well in excess of $300 million a year on its learning initiatives. Motorola invests more than $100 million each year on its various educational activities. Many corporations have multi-million dollar budgets for educating their key managers and many programs are targeted at more than 1000 executives in a single firm.[1]

With the stakes in the corporate leadership development marathon so high, it is surprising that so little systematic work has been done on the process of evaluating potential providers and the programs they offer. This chapter deals with that challenge.

The Selection Process

Word of mouth still appears to be the major means by which specific providers gain their reputation. Universities still have a leading role in the process since alumni from their regular degree programs and public executive education courses are apt to nominate their alma mater for consideration. Was it coincidence that in 1995 when Jack Snow, CEO of CSX and a University of Virginia (UVA) alumnus, announced plans for a "world class" commitment to organizational learning, UVA's Darden School was designated as the principal provider of a two-week leadership development program for its top 500 executives?

It also appears that being mentioned in print as one of the leaders in executive education has an undetermined, but very real, positive impact on credibility and opportunities. Marshall Goldsmith reports that after having been identified as one of the top ten independent executive education consultants in *The Wall Street Journal*, the number of inquiries received by his office tripled almost immediately. Universities report similar results when they are listed at the top of various rankings of executive programs.

The systems approach discussed in Chapter 4 offers insight into how the process of selecting providers typically works. A "virtuous cycle" is created when a provider has been involved in a successful leadership development program. This is particularly crucial for new providers trying to break into the competitive arena of high-level executive programs. Until a provider has delivered a successful program, no one knows for certain if they have the capability to do so. An individual who has been successful in delivering portions of a program as a platform presenter or facilitator may have some credibility. Yet the ability respond to client requests, develop or select appropriate materials for a larger scale initiative, then manage the logistics of the people and materials required to successfully and repeatedly deliver that initiative requires a totally different and much broader set of capabilities.

Thus, there evolves a virtuous cycle that can be described as follows: "experience builds success ... success builds a reputation." Few users are going to trust a new provider with a major initiative or with groups of experienced leaders. Consequently, the selection of providers can become a process in which an organization continually repeats what has always worked in the past, either for them or for other clients of an experienced provider. Without care, an organization can find itself in the business of merely buying programs from proven vendors as opposed to selecting provider "partners" who work to understand the organization, its strategic imperatives, and its developmental objectives. Therefore, to ensure the creation of purposeful leadership development initiatives that are driven by the strategic imperatives of a firm, it is important to craft a process for selecting provider partners.

At AT&T, we really believe that people hold the key to our future success. So, investment in people is a priority here, as is the development of

> *systems and processes that will enable us to get the greatest return on that investment.*
>
> Don Kuhn, former Director Employee Development,
> AT&T

Three Key Questions

The process of narrowing the field of potential providers for a major initiative can be marshalled through the following questions.

1 What Have You Done?

Almost every "request for proposal" (RFP) asks about previous projects, solicits specific examples of program design, and requires a list of previous clients served. Respondents who give evidence of having done interesting work of a comparable scope are considered worthy of further consideration and moved on to the next step.

2 What Else Can You Do?

This question is used to examine the depth and potential of providers. Some corporations may want a provider to conduct a needs assessment. Others may want detailed development of original program materials, including cases, simulations or other exercises. Clients often are (and should be) concerned about "back office support." Is the potential provider or an associate likely to be available or accessible to respond to questions and handle problems given the travel and time demands of their work?

It is also important to examine what the provider is really good at. Some firms have a specialty they pursue with great dedication and excellence. They have, by choice, decided not to compete on a wide range of topics or projects. A group that specializes in outdoor adventure learning or in providing 360-degree feedback may not be a viable candidate for a broad-scale program on global competitiveness. On the other hand, some relatively small firms are able to offer a wide range of program designs due to their extensive network of contacts and knowledge of the industry.

For example, even after downsizing his organization to two full-time people, Jim Bolt's Executive Development Associates is still considered a potential provider for a wide variety of programs because of its network of intellectual resources. As mentioned previously, Global Access Learning, with less than a dozen full-time employees, talks of having utilized 60 academics from 25 institutions for programs on six continents. Universities tend to have broad networks as well. The network a prospective provider can tap into can be a very valuable resource to a client.

3 What Will You Do For Us?

The issue addressed by this final question is flexibility. Academic institutions and established consulting firms often have distinguished track records and the resources to do almost anything a company needs. Yet, because of conflicting pressures on principals and/or faculty resources, they may be wary about program initiatives that require a significant degree of customization.

Universities are often seen as being best at making minor adaptations to relatively successful public programs which can be offered to a large number of executives in a single firm. For example, the Darden School of the University of Virginia will offer "Creating the High Performance Work Place" four times each year as an open-enrollment program. A similar version of the program will be offered a comparable number of times to specific company groups.

Perhaps due to their success in public programs or in adaptating existing course offerings, some universities do seem to lack the flexibility required to respond to requests from clients who may ask for the creation of original cases, computerized exercises, video vignettes, or integrative exercises to tie a program together. Not all universities are so constrained, however, and many have developed impressive portfolios of custom and customized program clients.

> The real issue here is whether the provider is willing to work with the organization to develop an initiative that is tailored to the needs and demands of the organization, whether the provider is truly willing to be a *partner* with the sponsoring firm.

Formal Proposals

To ensure some degree of objectivity, as well as to focus their own thinking, many firms have developed a formal "request for proposal" (RFP) process. Creating an RFP can be an arduous assignment in itself. It is difficult to think through, in advance, all of the factors likely to be important in making the decision about a program designer or deliverer.

At least in the early stages of a selection process, most corporate clients have a sense of the providers they would be most comfortable with. They may have had successful experience working with some of them in the past, or received good reports on them from colleagues in other firms. Most HRD professionals have well-developed networks of contacts they utilize on a regular basis in order to gather information about the perceived strengths and/or weaknesses of various potential providers. Many corporate executives maintain one or two memberships in networks created as forums for sharing "best practices" and concerns with colleagues. For example, Jim Bolt of Executive Development Associates created and still maintains a client network in addition to his own consulting practice. One of his purposes is to bring together prospective buyers and sellers to discuss the evolving marketplace for his firm's services.

While one of the authors was Director of Corporate Management Development at Allied Signal, he regularly talked with colleagues at AT&T, IBM, GTE, Combustion Engineering, Beatrice Foods, Borg Warner and Coca-Cola. Representatives of these firms agreed to meet for one or two days every six months with an almost unstructured agenda and no outsiders present. The first meeting of what came to be called the "Executive Education Exchange" was conducted at the Allied-Signal Pleasantdale Farm facility. Six months later, the group reconvened for a day and a half at the GTE Conference Center in Norwalk, Connecticut. Typically, the host institution began the session by outlining the scope of their program offerings, problems, and plans. In open, candid discussions, members outlined the challenges they faced, reviewed successes with particular vendors, or highlighted problems other members might need to address. The meetings usually involved only one night away from home/office and provided an uncensored opportunity to share ideas and concerns, along with best practices, with a selected group of peers.

Universities often create and maintain networks, frequently through business-school sponsored research institutes, that can be veritable fountains of information for HRD professionals, providing access to leading-edge information as well as knowledge of potential resources. In addition, more formal networks, like the International Consortium for Executive Development Research (ICEDR) based in Lexington, Massachusetts, are engaged in facilitating think-tank type interaction among leading researchers in the field and corporations.

A Model Request for Proposal

Regardless of the amount of networking done by an HRD professional, the creation of a formal RFP process will add clarity to both the design and selection process. Figures 7.1 and 7.2 provide some details from an unusually comprehensive RFP developed by Ron Meeks at Hoechst Celanese Corp. An interesting factor in this RFP is the company's quantification or weighting of several key selection criteria. Meeks would admit, however, that a great deal of subjectivity is involved in the assignment of the various weights.

A system similar to Hoechst Celanese's could be used to compare provider proposals using the format shown in Figure 7.3. In today's competitive world it is not uncommon for two consulting firms to considered as potential providers along with two or more business schools. A visible comparative process can help clarify which provider would make the best partner, thereby adding a bit more objectivity to the process.

Most of the selection criteria listed in Figure 7.3 are self-explanatory. The first two items deal with the experience and reputation of a provider. Teacher/faculty access refers to the degree to which an individual supplier is willing to use the best available person for a program module, regardless of institutional affiliation. For example, in their Middle Management Leadership Program, Hoechst Celanese attached a great deal of importance to one provider's willingness to use independent consultants as well as professors from a variety of academic institutions rather than restricting its choice to the faculty of a single business school. Depending on whether or not this is a critical issue in the company's selection process, the weighting of this factor can be adjusted accordingly.

Overall expectations: The consultant(s) will assist Hoechst Celanese Corp. (HCC) to define its specific purpose and scope for the Continuing Leadership Education Forums, and will provide expertise in:

A A structured "needs analysis" methodology for (1) identifying the key business issues and challenges, (2) the related leadership behaviors, skills and knowledge required to meet those business challenges, (3) identification of the segments of the leadership levels requiring those competencies, and (4) the "gap(s)" which, in general, need most emphasis.

B Methodologies for designing specific "interventions" targeted at each priority issue (priority to be defined by HCC). Such methodologies will be subject to context, cost and time considerations to be managed at HCC.

C Access to "leading edge faculty". Will help identify the appropriate choices; will guide in selection; and will serve to orient the faculty initially to HCC's needs, expectations, and opportunities. Will manage the contractual arrangements between the external faculty and HCC.

D Program evaluation methodologies to determine effectiveness of the interventions in both "participant reaction" level as well as "application and behavior change" level.

Hoechst Celanese and its representatives (specifically HRD personnel, Leadership Development Steering Committee) will be responsible for:

A Guiding consultant(s) in the expectations of Continuing Leadership Education, and in specifying "operating and design parameters" such as time, cost, frequency, etc. for both design activities and delivery.

B Leading processes for setting priorities on Continuing Leadership Education forums, in defining "target audiences" and in establishing communications to target participants.

C Approving the methodologies and content of the forums once a scope and context have been agreed to.

D Soliciting and orienting "internal expertise" to be used, as well as arranging specific HCC information and materials incorporated in the design.

E Arranging logistics and administration of meetings related to design and delivery of the forums.

F Assessing overall program interest and effectiveness

Figure 7.1 Criteria for Selection of External Providers

Reputation: (A)
Experience in executive/management education: (A)
Teacher/faculty access process: (A)
Time availability: (A)
Cost/cost effectiveness: (B)
Support resources: (B)
Geographic proximity/ready access: (B)
Support resources: (B)
Serves as faculty sometimes: (C)
Flexible but systematic: (A)
Ability to adapt to HCC cultural expectations: (A)
Industry/business experience: (B)
Creative/innovative methodologies: (B)
Commitment to HCC – existing "supplier": (B)

(A) = Major importance: weighted value of 3 points
(B) = Would significantly improve our confidence: weighted value of 2 points
(C) = Would be nice to have this attribute, not critical: weighted value of 1 point

Figure 7.2   Specific Selection Considerations

In addition, some program providers like to view program modules as interchangeable parts. Others take the view that each component should build on the other. Consequently, modules scheduled for Wednesday cannot be shifted to Monday in order to accommodate the presenter's schedule since it might undermine the integrity of the original program design. This challenge can be addressed in one of two ways, both of which have been used in Johnson & Johnson's Executive Conference series. During the first three-year initiative (built around the theme "Setting the Competitive Standard"), program design and sequence were sacrosanct. The Center for Executive Development developed a core faculty for this program but coached alternative faculty members who were available in the event that a particular instructor was not available for a particular session. In the second Executive Conference, ("Creating Our Future"), the 23 sessions were conducted over a three-year period with the same instructors being used in the same

	Providers					
Decision parameter (weighing)	1	2	3	4	5	Total score
Reputation/track record: (3)						
Experience in executive/management education: (3)						
Teacher/faculty access process: (3)						
Time availability: (3)						
Cost/cost effectiveness: (2)						
Geographic proximity/ready access: (2)						
Support resources: (2)						
Serves as faculty sometimes: (1)						
Flexible but systematic: (3)						
Ability to adapt to HCC cultural expectations: (3)						
Industry/business experience: (2)						
Creative/innovative methodologies: (2)						
Commitment to HCC – existing "supplier": (2)						
Willingness to confront customer when needed: (2)						
Total points:						

On a scale of 1–5 (1 = weak, 5 = strong), rate each resource against the parameter. Multiply the rating by the weighing factor for the total rating of each parameter.

Figure 7.3 Proposed Selection Model

sequence in every session. Instructors and facilities were scheduled two years in advance and the program operated like clockwork.

"Time availability" simply refers to how important the client will be to a provider. All clients like to believe that their project is the most important program the provider has to deal with. However, the most successful providers are likely to be involved with several projects simultaneously. The best potential provider organization may not get a project if the client lacks assurance with regard to the access to key resources throughout the program. A respondent in our field interviews reported a cautionary experience with a business school. When one particular program was first offered, world-class faculty members were used but, during the second or third iteration of the program, different (although still experienced) presenters were used because the "super-stars" had become unavailable. This observer concluded, rather cynically, that by the time the program was a couple of years old, the business school was struggling to get even junior faculty involved. We encountered similar stories about consulting firm principals in various projects.

An issue similar to this is addressed in the model RFP under "commitment to HCC – existing supplier" Consultants or business schools that have worked with a client previously have already moved up the learning curve. They know something about the culture of the organization and the expectations of that client, and they are more of a known quantity. As a result, if there is ongoing access to key provider faculty and other intellectual resources, it can be a great advantage to clients. On the other hand, a provider that has become too familiar with an organization can become too much like one of the gang, and not challenge participants to the necessary extent. One of the major themes discussed at the 1996 conference of the International University Consortium for Executive Education (UNICON) was the need for providers of leadership development to focus on developing deeper relationships with a few corporate partners rather than attempting to be generalists who provide limited engagements for large numbers of clients.

For consulting firms, the issue of support resources or "back office" staff is important. A client wants to know that the less glamorous but essential jobs (like preparing notebooks and getting materials to the appropriate place on time) will be competently handled. While this is typically one strength of university providers, it is often a major challenge to a smaller firm. In addition, some companies prefer a particular provider to be totally involved in the design of a program but contract out delivery obligations to other individuals. Conversely, some clients want to be sure that the person or people who coordinate the project have the ability to design *and* to deliver. These expectations must be clarified if a working partnership is to develop.

Finally, many customers of leadership development programs will speak openly about the "chemistry test." Despite the credentials offered by some providers, the decision-maker knows, almost intuitively, that certain providers will mesh with the corporate culture – that there is good chemistry between the two organizations. This is seldom just a matter of liking a principal's personality. It is usually intuition based on years of experience in attempting to articulate what it is that makes programs successful or unsuccessful within a given organization.

Can Universities Deliver?

Universities have always been a major provider of executive education/leadership development programs. Even with today's proliferation of providers, a relatively small group of universities still control over 25 percent of the highly fragmented market for leadership development services.[2] Yet, throughout our research, it has become clear that there is a significant movement away from external, open-enrollment programs toward customized programs. It is also clear that an increasing amount of corporate executive education and leadership development dollars (approximately 75 percent) are being spent internally or going to non-university providers. In the Appendix, we quote Jim Baughman of Morgan Guaranty who said, "University programs are too long. They are not flexible enough. They are too expensive, and they lack action learning."[3]

Fortune's Brian O'Reilly, encouraged his readers to: "Ask a lot from the business schools, colleges and professors that do work for your company. Plenty are greedy, lazy, or incompetent. Because executive education is so profitable for universities, many have rushed into the business. The teachers they provide may be academic drones without the temperament of solid consulting experience needed to satisfy veteran executives."[4]

Although highly regarded as providers of executive education/leadership development, universities have yet to achieve their full potential as critical components of the corporate leadership development process. It appears that a market economy is developing in the field and this should yield substantial improvements in both university-based and corporate-directed executive education/leadership development over the next few years.[5] These improvements will be directly related to a steadily increasing corporate sophistication in their use of executive development as a means of organizational development. Based on recent research, we can identify the following two critical observations about the role of universities in the field.

|| *1 University-based executive education/leadership development has yet to achieve its full potential, a state resulting from unintentional collusion between the supplier and customer communities.*[6]

A growing percentage of the corporate community sees the development and dissemination of state-of-the-art research that frames critical issues for leaders as a primary role for universities (see Figure 7.4).[7] There is also a growing interest among corporations in engaging universities as partners to provide quality instruction in these leading-edge areas. These research findings reflect a dramatic shift over a ten-year interval away from the traditional view of universities as centers of undergraduate education and academic research toward a more collabo-

Role	*1982*	*1987*	*1992*
Develop and present state-of-the-art research and issues	32%	45%	58%
Provide quality instruction and faculty	27%	10%	25%
Revitalize, challenge, and stimulate in environment of reflection	7%	10%	21%
Broaden and develop managers for the future	7%	43%	21%
Respond to needs of business as partner, consultant, and resource	14%	15%	21%
Provide external contacts and dialogue exchange	8%	14%	15%
Be pragmatic and relevant through experiential learning		10%	10%
Teach specific or functional skill	5%	12%	8%
Provide background prior to emploment	18%	2%	4%

Figure 7.4 Perceived Roles of Universities in Developing Management Talent
Source: Vicere, A., Taylor, M., and Freeman, V.,
Executive Education in Major Corporations, University Park, PA:
Institute for the Study of Organizational Effectiveness, 1993.

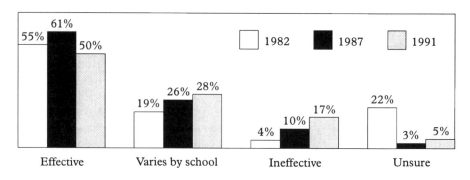

Figure 7.5 Perceived Effectiveness of Universities in
Management Development
Source: Vicere, A., Taylor, M., and Freeman, V.,
Executive Education in Major Corporations, University Park, PA:
Institute for the Study of Organizational Effectiveness, 1993.

rative role in business and organization development. There is also a
small but growing percentage of potential customers who feel that
universities are ineffective in their provision of state-of-the-art leadership
development programs (Figure 7.5). It should be noted that while a
majority of respondents view university contributions to executive
development as effective, the percentage rating them as ineffective has
increased consistently over the same ten-year period.

In a recent study, Doug Ready, Executive Director of the International
Consortium for Executive Development Research, found that corporations desire stronger links between executive education/leadership
development programs and the *realities of work.* In addition, these same
companies are interested in new and innovative approaches to teaching
and learning, and are demanding that university programs and services
be more responsive and customer focused.[8] Interviews conducted by
Alan White of MIT support these findings and note further that, in
general, universities have been far too slow to change. It seems that many
universities are perceived to have continued to use outdated materials
and/or be simply out of touch with the realities of competing and
managing in today's environment.[9]

Two related corporate behaviors and conditions appear to have
contributed to this:

1   Until recently, corporations have tended to lack the internal capability to provide a viable alternative to university-based programs

2   At the same time there has been a steady to growing expenditure on university programs by corporations, which may have sent the wrong message to universities.

These factors have created an unintentional collusion within the marketplace, creating no incentives for universities to change given that their traditional programs were operating at full capacity.

As executive education and leadership development have emerged as important levers for crafting competitive advantage, companies have increasingly begun to pay more attention to these processes. They have hired professionals to run the education/development function and asked them to calculate the returns on their investments. This has resulted in a significant professionalization of the field over the past decade, along with a corresponding increase in the internal executive education and development capabilities of many companies.[10] As a result, a growing sense of corporate dissatisfaction, coupled with a marked improvement in internal program development and delivery capabilities, has led to a visible decrease in the use of open-enrollment, university-based executive education programs over the past decade or more.[11]

This is not meant to suggest that all institutions have been blind to the need for change or to the importance of being focused on the customer. For instance, it can been shown that although the overall perception of university effectiveness in developing management talent is declining, there is a steadily growing perception that effectiveness varies between institutions (see Figure 7.5).[12] This assertion is clearly supported by other researchers.[13] These conditions suggest that there is great potential for a shakeout among universities in the executive education/leadership development business over the next few years. Institutions with carefully crafted strategies that focus on leveraging their core competencies, coupled with a fierce dedication to quality, teaching excellence, innovation, and *measured* market responsiveness will not only survive, they will also be very likely to flourish in partnership with the corporate community. This perceived opportunity for the university community is the cornerstone of our second observation.

> 2 *As a consequence of inefficiency in the marketplace, a market economy is emerging within the field. This market economy should yield substantial improvements in all forms of executive education/leadership development in the future.*[14]

At its core, a market economy is characterized and driven by supply, demand, price, and competition. Changes among any of these variables usually stimulate changes in the dynamics of the market, in this case the executive education market. When markets are efficient there is relative stability among these variables; when they are inefficient, there is significant instability.

An Inefficient Market

We believe that an inefficient market currently exists in the field of executive education/leadership development. Many indicators point to a significant increase of institutional suppliers or competitors.[15] *Bricker's International Directory of Executive Education Programs* reported that 52 new executive programs were on offer in 1996, up from 41 in 1993.[16] This proliferation of offerings comes at a time when demand for such programs seemed to be waning. On a practical level, companies have indicated to us that it is becoming increasingly difficult to distinguish the serious players from opportunists because so many new providers have recently entered the market. And this does not even take into account the additional private sector competitors that have emerged.

If demand were reasonably stable for university-based programs, this increased competition could be explained as a response to unmet customer needs. However, several researchers have identified a clear shift away from external programs toward internal, company-specific programs.[17] Furthermore, one study indicated that only a fraction of that shift would be likely to become business for universities as custom or customized programs.[18] Despite this, many universities seem to be shedding their portfolio of open-enrollment programs in favor of custom programs in the hope of capturing what appears to be the only growth segment of the market.

This shift toward customers (companies) controlling channels of distribution (running their own internal programs) reflects a classic case for scenario planners in that the customer has become one of the supplier's most formidable competitors in the business.

Corporations today seem to be looking less for programs and more for educational process partners to help create development systems that promote continuous improvement, continuous innovation, and continuous learning for both individual leaders and the organization as a whole. This emerging demand provides a new window of opportunity for universities and for all providers.

Coordinating the Process: The AT&T Approach

AT&T has made as strong a commitment to ongoing leadership development as any organization in the world. The company's strategy for coordinating its impressive investment in external executive education, and the way it attempts to maximize the return on its investment, provides a useful benchmark.[19]

Background

AT&T has had long-standing commitments to providing in-house education and training for all levels of employees. This includes: offering tuition support to employees for out-of-hours study; supporting release time programs for specially selected individuals (typically executive MBA programs or advanced technical degree programs); conducting executive education programs internally using university faculty, consultants, and corporate executives; and sending high-potential managers to university-sponsored executive education programs. Annually, approximately 300 middle and upper-middle managers attend AT&T designed and administered executive education/leadership development programs. In addition, approximately 500 managers at the same levels and higher (directors and officers) attend university-based programs.

There are three components of AT&T's human resource management system that have a direct bearing on involvement in executive education/leadership development and what form it will take:

1 *Performance Management* This is a process for ensuring that corporate and organizational goals are defined and communicated, and for determining the basis for setting individual objectives; how performance should be measured against those objectives; and the developmental needs of the individual that must be addressed in order to enhance achievement of current objectives and ensure longer range professional growth.

2 *Career Planning* While defined as the primary responsibility of the employee, career planning at AT&T is viewed as a three-legged stool: the employee defines his or her values, goals, and interests; the supervisor provides instruction, support, and feedback; and the organization defines longer term needs and provides education and training resources.

3 *Leadership Identification* Based on defined leadership competencies or dimensions, individuals are identified by their organizations as having potential for accelerated movement to higher level positions. Typically, organizational "round-tables" are used for reviewing candidates. Once identified, high-potential managers are viewed as the primary (but not exclusive) group from which to select executive education participants.

Corporate policies and programs in support of these three aspects of career development are defined and made available to individual business units. The units have full cost responsibility, and can buy or not as they see fit. Typically, all business units participate, modifying approaches to suit their own business needs. One area in which they have somewhat less freedom is in the use of university-sponsored executive education programs, as will be explained below.

Development Philosophy

The preferred executive education route in the high-potential individuals' development plan is to have managers participate first in an internal AT&T program early in their careers. Working with a class of 30 to 40 colleagues from all parts of the corporation, these individuals learn more about AT&T, gain an insight into synergies that exist across organizational lines, and have the opportunity to develop internal networks. After the individual has completed this internal experience, further developmental initiatives rely heavily on university-based programs and the AT&T School of Business (discussed later). In this respect, AT&T is unlike many corporations that have pulled away from open-enrollment university programs. AT&T sees great value in having its high-potential managers work alongside peers from other industries and countries in open-enrollment programs as a way to expose them to alternative organizational structures, leadership styles, and business development approaches.

While executive education is managed at the corporate level, business units are also involved in leadership development. Change seems to be a dominant issue in the management literature today, and AT&T is clearly no stranger to the process. Since change dominates the agendas of business units, programs related to change are the responsibility of those business units. Typically, they involve one-week courses attended by all managers at a particular level or within a particular group. These programs are conducted in addition to corporately managed executive education, not in place of it.

Organization of the Executive Education Function

Responsibility for executive education policy, liaison with schools, enrollment, administration, and program evaluation rests with a corporate manager at the head office. Within each of the business units (approximately 40) there is a person designated as the executive education coordinator for his or her unit. Responsibility for conducting in-house executive education programs resides with the AT&T School of Business, but admission to such programs is overseen by the corporate manager. The AT&T School of Business provides all internal general management and skills training for AT&T employees worldwide. Programs are offered for clerical through director level employees. The School of Business coordinates its educational offerings with those of other functionally oriented AT&T training organizations. Programs are designed in partnership with providers, usually external, who develop specific programs that are marketed throughout the organization. These providers may be individuals, consulting firms, or universities.

Process

The corporate manager runs an annual conference for the business unit coordinators at which the internally generated AT&T executive education course catalogue is reviewed. The catalogue is sent to all officers, human resource heads, and coordinators. Its prefatory material explains the basic philosophy and linkages to performance management, career planning, and leadership. It lists both internal and university programs available for the next year, their broad content, and the intended audience, along with costs and session dates. Over 75 general management and 60 functional programs were listed in the 1996 catalog. Business units are allocated a rough number of seats based on the size of the unit and historical participation in various programs. With respect to university programs, AT&T (like university executive education program directors themselves) does not want to dominate sessions numerically, and so limits the number of participants who can attend any one session at a given school. Such factors are taken into account when seat allocations are made.

Coordinators return to their organizations and, working with line executives, line managers, leadership and development staff members, and high-potential employees, develop the list of people the unit will support for education during the following year, as evidenced by an officer's approval. The coordinators submit applications to the corporate manager, usually suggesting up to three programs that appear to match the developmental needs of each nominated individual. The corporate manager and staff review the applications to ensure candidates appear to be appropriately matched with programs, and then attempt to allocate seats based on coordinators' recommendations. Formal notification is given to the organizations, listing which programs candidates have been approved to attend and providing instruction to line supervisors as to how they should brief the individual prior to and following the program.

The corporate manager also notifies the universities as to how many AT&T candidates they can expect for the following year's approved programs. Arrangements have been worked out with most universities to accept the AT&T executive education application form in lieu of having the student make separate application to the university. This is because AT&T has agreed with the universities it uses that all contacts with the individual school will be through the corporate manager or his or her staff. This relieves universities from having to deal with multiple business units. It also facilitates discussion of program evaluation, as is discussed below. A database is used to manage all administrative and valuative aspects of the process.

Program Selection and Evaluation

Major universities around the world have programs included in the AT&T internal catalogue. The corporate manager determines which programs will be listed. He or she bases selection on the school's reputation as well as the experience of AT&T managers who have participated in prior sessions. New programs are usually added in one of two ways. As new offerings are made by universities, the corporate manager asks a coordinator to identify someone who might benefit from the experience, and who would be willing to provide the company with a detailed evaluation of the program. The second approach is involvement in consortium programs where AT&T participates with other companies in the development and guidance of a program for managers from member companies.

The corporate manager attempts to visit as many schools as possible each year. In addition, regular contact is maintained with university representatives to ensure that the company stays abreast of new programs or revisions to existing programs. More importantly, the feedback from individuals who have attended programs is taken very seriously. Each student is asked to complete a multi-page evaluation which covers program content, level of fellow participants, faculty, facilities, and so on. The ratings by students are entered into a database and are used to provide feedback to university representatives. If a program receives consistently low rating it is dropped from the catalogue. Additionally, if programs included in the catalogue draw little interest, they too are dropped.

The AT&T example demonstrates the value of developing both a strategy for executive education and leadership development, and a well-defined process for implementing that strategy. Because of their orchestrated approach, AT&T is able to catalogue information about potential providers as well as potential participants. This leadership development database enables AT&T to maintain both focus and quality in its leadership development initiatives. Individuals are more likely to be placed in appropriate programs. There is a greater likelihood that learning from the program will be transferred back to the workplace. Sound data can be collected on potential providers and/or resources for internal programs. Better relationships can be built with university providers. Better internal programs can be developed. All of this information enhances the value of leadership development to the organization.

> *At GE and BMG, I have found that providers of educational programs perform better if they have a sense of "partnership" or long-term association with us. It becomes a "win-win" relationship where each party benefits because of the mutual trust and knowledge that has developed over time.*
>
> Joe Isenstein, Sr. VP Human Resources,
> BMG Entertainment

Making the Final Selection

There is little question that the common ingredients for provider success in the new, emerging paradigm for executive education and leadership development include quality, teaching excellence, innovation, and market responsiveness. However, we believe that the most effective providers are likely to be those that have mastered the process of defining and optimizing their core capabilities. Providers must build from their strengths in order to effectively meet customer requirements. If a provider enjoys a world-renowned reputation for research in technology development and manufacturing, then the most plausible scenario for their success would be to leverage those strengths by finding a set of customers with needs for such capabilities instead of trying to launch a finance for non-financial managers program because a company asked them to do so.

Providers, like the corporations they serve, have limited resources and therefore decreasing opportunities for investment in the future. It is vital that those investments be made strategically. Being market responsive and customer focused should mean more than a willingness to try to deliver a service. It should also mean the provider is actively engaged in becoming a world-leading supplier in its areas of expertise. By applying these and other standards, providers can make great strides in developing executive education/leadership development programs and other services that serve both their themselves and their customers quite well. By holding providers to those standards, corporations enhance the capability and capacity of the entire field.

Moving Forward

In assessing the opportunities and challenges of creating initiatives in strategic leadership development, users *and* providers of executive education/leadership development may wish to keep the following observations in mind.

- Users are turning "internal" to meet executive education/leadership development needs. However, they seem unsure as to what actions are needed and often question their ability to develop and deliver those actions in an effective, timely manner. This suggests that the need for process consulting services from the top providers may be growing, providing new opportunities for those providers willing to share both their educational *process* and their *content* expertise with the user community.
- Users are sure that courses on issues such as change management, leadership, and process and performance management are needed quickly to help adjust to the demands of a changing world. They are less sure of what their leadership development needs will be in the future. Based on their research, universities are being asked to look into their crystal ball to help organizations define and address emerging opportunities. The demand, however, is less for basic research and more for outcome oriented applications – processes that contribute to change and transformation. This is a challenge to universities who have tended to view themselves as the *creators* of new knowledge and ideas, and not consultants on the *implementation* of those ideas in the corporate world. The dramatic growth of corporate/university research consortia in recent years suggests that universities may be slowly but steadily learning to better blend societal needs for essential basic research with

corporate needs for rapid application of that research to solving real-world problems. In the meantime, consulting firms are demonstrating that they, too, have the ability to do research and publish, as witnessed by the recent, if not controversial, wave of best-selling books emanating from consulting firm authors.[20]

- Users are increasingly interested in educational experiences that are tied to the work environment and are growing more convinced that the action learning model is a powerful framework for leveraging investment in executive education. At the same time, users must not forget the need to continue to build strong individual skills among high potential/key managers even while faced with the need for overwhelming organizational reforms. There is danger that leadership development processes could become too insular if focused only within a particular organization and only on its current competitive environment. Researchers, in particular, should give careful consideration as to whether the pendulum may have swung too far in the direction of targeted educational interventions, and whether there is a need to promote more debate on the appropriate balance between open-enrollment and company-specific executive education experiences.

- Providers must recognize that key supply/demand partnerships will be established over the next decade. It appears that comparative advantage will (and should) go to those providers willing and able to develop innovative mechanisms for establishing such partnerships with both the corporate community and with fellow providers who can add complementary capabilities or additional capacity to address corporate needs.

- Finally, users must demand that providers practice what they preach. They must be required to identify their core competencies, focus on those areas where they can leverage their value and uniqueness in the marketplace through partnerships, establish those partnerships, and help their clients rethink the meaning of executive education and leadership development for the 21st-century economic environment. They must help their clients plan for success in a world where continuous learning is the ultimate competitive advantage.

By understanding the strategic context for effective leadership development, and by orchestrating a process for selecting providers who have the focus and flexibility to address the critical leadership development issues faced by their organization, clients are in a much better position to add real value through an investment in purposeful leadership development.

Endnotes

1 Fulmer, R.M. and A.A. Vicere, *Executive Education and Leadership Development: The State of the Practice*, University Park, PA: Institute For the Study of Organizational Effectiveness, 1995.

2 Ibid.

3 Reference quoted from Lori Bongiorno, "Corporate America's New Lesson Plan," *Business Week*, October 25, 1993, p. 102.

4 O'Reilly, B., "How Execs Learn Now," *Fortune*, April 5, 1993.

5 Ready, D., A.A. Vicere, and A. White, "Executive Education: Can Universities Deliver?" *Human Resource Planning*, 16(4), 1993, pp. 1–11.

6 Ibid.

7 Vicere, A.A., M. Taylor, and V. Freeman, *Executive Education in Major Corporations*, University Park, PA: Institute for the Study of Organizational Effectiveness, 1993.

8 See Ready, D., A.A. Vicere, and A. White, *The Role of Executive Education in Executive Resource Planning*, Lexington, MA: International Consortium For Executive Development Research Working Paper, 92/3, 1992.

9 Ibid.

10 *Wall Street Journal,* special supplement on executive education, September 10, 1993.

11 Ready, D., "Executive Education: Is It Making the Grade?" *Fortune*, December 14, 1992, pp. 39–48; Vicere, Taylor, and Freeman, 1993, op. cit.

12 Vicere, Taylor, and Freeman, 1993, op. cit.

13 Ready, 1992, op. cit.; Ready, Vicere, and White, 1992, op.cit.

14 Ready, Vicere, and White, 1993, op. cit.

15 *Wall Street Journal,* 1993, op. cit.

16 *Bricker's International Directory of University-Based Executive Education Programs*, Princeton, NJ: Petersons, 1993, 1996.

17 Ready, 1992, op. cit.; Vicere, Taylor, and Freeman, 1993, op. cit.

18 Ready, ibid.

19 This section was developed from personal correspondence with Don Kuhn,

former Employee Development Director with AT&T, and now Executive Secretary with UNICON, the International University Consortium for Executive Education.

20 McGinn, D., "Business by Best Seller," *Newsweek*, April 3, 1995, p. 47.

8

EVALUATING IMPACTS

The evaluation of leadership development programs is one of the most perplexing challenges facing human resource development practitioners. Most of the work done on evaluation has focused on lower level training initiatives where it is easier to quantify learning. While the challenge is greater for assessing programs aimed at corporate leadership, many of the same principles apply.

Rothwell and Kazanas defined evaluation as the process of assigning value and making critical judgements on the impact of leadership development on organizational, group, or individual performance. They suggested evaluation should answer the following questions:[1]

- What changes resulted from the program or its various methods?
- How much change resulted from the program or its methods?
- What value can be assigned to those changes?
- How much value can be assigned to those changes?

In a presentation to the National Society for Sales Training Executives, J.P. Huller of Hobart Corporation noted that the ability to document impact was directly linked to the credibility, and therefore the influence, of the HRD function. Huller outlined the value of such credibility:[2]

❝ *When you are accepted, trusted, respected and needed, lots of wonderful things happen:*
- *Your budget requests are granted.*
- *You keep your job (you might even be promoted).*
- *Your staff keep their jobs.*
- *The quality of your work improves.*

- *Senior management listens to your advice.*
- *You are given more control.* **"**

If all these wondrous things can happen when there is an effective design for evaluating leadership development efforts, there should be great interest in enhancing the caliber of evaluation techniques. Without doubt, program assessment is a source of considerable stress in HRD departments. One of our interviewees commented, "A provider of programs that are well received is 'managerial Sominex' – if the evaluations go well, I can sleep at night." In a more serious vein, initiatives are evaluated in order to determine whether or not they should be supported, or whether a particular session or facilitator should be changed, eliminated, or given an expanded role. Credible evaluation processes also help to identify ways of making future programs even more effective, and help to justify the continuance or expansion of development efforts. Perhaps most importantly, in an age of continual cost-cutting and relentless expenditure justification, continued corporate investment in leadership development is predicated on the availability of credible assessment data that verify the efficacy of those investments on enhancing individual and organizational performance.

Two approaches to evaluation are essential to effective assessment of leadership development.

1 *Formative* evaluation is conducted before and during an initiative to ensure it stays on target. This includes ongoing reviews of objectives; assessments of methods, approaches, and materials; previews and pilot testings of programs, providers, and techniques; and benchmarking best practices for comparative purposes.

2 *Summative* evaluation occurs after the fact, either following each aspect of an initiative in progress, and/or at the conclusion of the overall experience.

Although most evaluation efforts are devoted to summative evaluation, it is formative evaluation that ensures the integrity of an initiative's initial design. We discuss both approaches below.

Getting Started

Leadership development initiatives are mounted not to "run programs", but to address potential gaps in leadership skill-sets that could impair an organization's ability to achieve its strategic imperatives. Therefore, it is essential that evaluation and assessment focus on performance, both individual and organizational. The first step in the evaluation process, then, should be an assessment of the leadership development task at hand. A plan of action should draw heavily on our discussion of systems frameworks for leadership development in Chapter 4. Those frameworks root leadership development in the strategic imperatives of the firm. Objectives are then created for development efforts that facilitate progress toward the strategic imperatives. Based on those identified objectives for development, methods and providers are selected, initiatives developed, and linkages made with corporate human resource management systems in order to reinforce the process. Finally, techniques for assessing and evaluating effectiveness are built in throughout the system to ensure its integrity.

Thus far in this book, we have devoted a considerable amount of discussion to linking leadership development to strategic imperatives. For our present purposes, then, we will assume that the firm's strategic imperatives have been identified and broad-based objectives for development have been formulated based on these imperatives.

A Framework for Assessment

Figure 8.1 presents a simple framework for the up-front assessment of leadership development initiatives.[3] It starts with a set of identified objectives for development. Various ways to address those objectives can be considered by working through the model.

The first level of assessment involves determining whether the best way to address a defined objective is through some form of instruction, or through alternative techniques like coordinated work experiences, task force/project team assignments, or coaching/mentoring. If instruction seems like the most viable solution, then the next level of assessment involves considering whether or not the classroom is a viable delivery mode. If the classroom is found to be viable and appropriate, then ways to enhance the classroom experience can be assessed. If the classroom

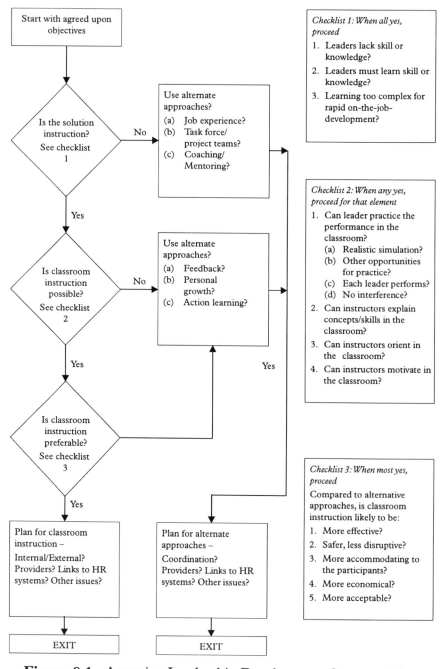

Figure 8.1 Assessing Leadership Development Opportunities

Adapted from: S. Yellon, "Classroom Instruction," in Stolovitch, H. and Keeps, E. (eds.) *Handbook for Human Performance Technology*, Washington: The National Society for Performance and Instruction, 1992, p. 385.

does not seem viable, then the feedback, personal growth, or action learning approaches discussed earlier can be contemplated. Once all of these issues have been considered, then plans for leadership development initiatives as well as methods of evaluating the effectiveness of those initiatives can be developed.

Benchmarking

Either in advance of designing a leadership development initiative, or in an effort to keep an ongoing initiative vital and on the leading edge, benchmarking best practices can be an effective tool for enhancing the effectiveness of the effort. Jac Fitz-Enz, president of the Saratoga Institute, defined benchmarking as:

> ❝ *an investigative process that seeks out high-performing business units, inside or outside the company, for the purpose of learning how they have achieved their exceptional results.*[4] ❞

When Westinghouse decided to redesign its leadership development process, benchmarking was used extensively to help frame the company's efforts. The company already had a well-defined leadership development process in place, but Jack Murphy, former Director of Education and Development, described that process as "traditional and low risk." Although the company had a highly mechanized succession planning process, and although candidates for executive education and leadership development programs were selected via that process, there was little accountability for actual performance against development plans. In addition, the company had no effective method for adequately measuring effective behavior and performance in leadership positions. As a result, Murphy noted, "the corporation didn't really enjoy much behavior or performance change. It was a case of information transfer coupled with 'ticket punching'."[5]

To help rectify this situation, Murphy launched an effort to identify and benchmark best practice companies in the areas of succession planning and leadership development. He drew upon his extensive network of contacts both within and outside Westinghouse to identify a group of target companies for visits. He then identified a group of high-potential leaders, organized them into a task force, and set out on the project. In a sense, Murphy initiated Westinghouse's first foray into action learning through this benchmarking process design.

Ultimately, the task force visited 13 companies in the US and Europe, and developed a set of "lessons learned" that heavily influenced the development of the integrated model we discussed in Chapter 5. According to Murphy, the four most critical lessons were:

1 The quality of leadership development is directly proportional to the level of interest and involvement of senior management. And CEO commitment is essential.

2 Most learning comes from actual experience on the job. As a surrogate for experience, many companies are experimenting with "action learning" in a variety of forms.

3 We must identify and develop employees with high potential early in their careers in order to create a "talent pool" within the organization.

4 Performance reviews should be frequent and focused, potentially involving the use of 360-degree assessment.[6]

Armed with these lessons, Westinghouse set out on a course to revamp its executive education/leadership development process. The information gleaned from the benchmarking study was used to determine what the company was doing right as well as what it could improve. Interestingly, when disaster struck in 1992 and the massive reorganization described in Chapter 5 began, the information from the benchmarking study was very useful in assessing how the company could use executive education and leadership development as an instrument of the transformation process.

Moving Forward

Once assessment has been conducted, benchmarking accomplished, and an initiative designed, methods for ongoing evaluation must be developed. The standard system for classifying approaches to evaluation was developed by Donald A. Kirkpatrick. In 1959, he wrote a series of four articles entitled "Techniques for Evaluating Training Programs," published in *Training and Development Journal*.[7] These articles described the four levels of evaluation he developed while working on his Ph.D. dissertation. Although Kirkpatrick's focus was on *training*, he argued that the system he outlined applied to all "courses and programs designed to increase knowledge, improve skills and change attitudes, whether for present job improvement or for development in the future."[8] Kirkpatrick's early work is still cited regularly, and his four levels have become a standard model for the evaluation process.

The remainder of this chapter will focus on the four levels of evaluation with examples of how each can be utilized in a more effective manner. The levels should be viewed as a sequence of increasingly sophisticated approaches to evaluation. Each level has its role and importance. Moving from level I to higher levels becomes increasingly challenging and time-consuming. Yet, higher levels of evaluation provide more credible data on the real returns on leadership development investments. The four levels of evaluation to be discussed are:

Level I – Reaction Evaluation
Level II – Learning Evaluation
Level III – Behavior Evaluation
Level IV – Results Evaluation

Level I – Reaction Evaluation

The most common and basic technique for evaluating programs is by assessing the reactions of participants. In essence, this approach is a "customer satisfaction index." It lets the program designer know whether participants are satisfied with the program content and methods of delivery. Many individuals refer to reaction evaluations as "smile sheets." This label could be related to the phenomenon of program designers enlisting speakers who are good "closers" in order to ensure that participants leave the program happy. As a result, participant evaluations are often influenced by a "recency effect" – since the most recent speaker was good, the program was just fine! Because of this, and because of the simplicity of the method, reaction evaluation sometimes is not viewed seriously, despite its almost universal use. Yet, monitoring participant reactions to an initiative and its various components does provide valuable feedback which helps assess the "perceived value" of that initiative. If people are not satisfied with the learning experience, they probably will not use what they have learnt and are likely to advise others that the program has little value.

To maximize the impact of this kind of evaluation, it is important to articulate what participants are really expected to learn or accomplish. If there are stated program objectives, it will be more helpful to ask participants about the degree to which this session or program met those objectives than to ask about enjoyment or even perceived relevance. Figure 8.2 is an example of a daily evaluation sheet that related presenter performance to both session objectives and traditional performance indices. Figure 8.3 gives examples of reaction feedback that has been quantified according to whether the objectives of a program or various segments of a program were met.

> *The "smile sheets" collected at the end of a program help measure entertainment value, but they don't help measure real impact.*
>
> Participant, HRD Planning Conference

A good reaction evaluation form should quantify as many measures as possible, but still provide an opportunity for open-ended input from participants. Simple questions such as "how could this session have been improved?" or "what were the most valuable aspects of the session?" are examples of typical queries that provide focused, but open-ended responses. Analysis of these open-ended responses can add useful context to numerical evaluations, helping to explain discrepancies or clarify concerns.

To avoid the problem of non-response bias, every participant should submit an evaluation. Most practitioners agree that the best way of achieving this is to insist that participants complete their evaluation *before* they leave the session because it seems that, despite their best intentions, individuals who say they want time to think it over and then return it by mail are not likely to do so once they have returned to the hectic demands of their regular schedules. A similar way of handling this challenge is to encourage people to complete a portion of the evaluation at the end of each day. In this way, impressions are still fresh and when the program comes to a close, only a small portion of the assessment remains to be completed. Information collected on an ongoing basis can be more current and can be useful for formative evaluation of an experience. However, frequent collection of data can make the experience routine

"Leadership in Transforming Organizations"

1   Listed below are the key objectives for this segment of the Program. You are asked to evaluate how well the presenter fulfilled these objectives.

Objective A   Be able to discuss the nature of effective leadership in the company.
Excellent _____ Good _____ Fair _____ Poor _____

Objective B   Be able to articulate the challenge of building competitive capabilites within your business.
Excellent _____ Good _____ Fair _____ Poor _____

Objective C   Be able to describe the leadership implications of the life-cycle stage of your business.
Excellent _____ Good _____ Fair _____ Poor _____

Objective D   Be able to profile the organizational development challenge faced by your business using the High Flex Organizational model.
Excellent _____ Good _____ Fair _____ Poor _____

Objective E   Be able to articulate the key strategic leadership issues you face in today's environment of change.
Excellent _____ Good _____ Fair _____ Poor _____

2   What points were made in the presentation that were the most valuable or meaningful to you?

3   Presenter's effectiveness

	E	G	F	P
Presented subject matter clearly; explained and illustrated key points				
Kept session moving and on track				
Knowledge of subject matter				
Visuals (slides/videographs) readable and clear				
Instruction materials (handouts/exercises/case studies) useful				
Encouraged participation and answered questions satisfactorily				
Overall opinion				

E = Excellent   G = Good   F = Fair   P = Poor

Additional Comments

Figure 8.2   Evaluation

Monday: Monday's activities were to focus you on thinking about our long-term future in nontraditional ways.

1.	Relevance of the content to the challenges facing GHP	*Mean score* = 4.07
2.	Value of the content to you	*Mean score* = 4.07
3.	Quality of presentation and group discussion	*Mean score* = 3.94
4.	Effectiveness of the case, GHP 2002	*Mean score* = 3.85

360-degree feedback report: The report and your one-to-one meeting with the coach/psychologist were to provide you with insights into your leadership strengths and opportunities for personal improvement.

1.	Relevance of the 360-degree feedback survey to the challenges facing GHP	*Mean score* = 4.23
2.	Value of the 360-degree feedback survey to you	*Mean score* = 4.32
3.	Quality of Tuesday's presentation of the survey report	*Mean score* = 3.91
4.	Effectiveness of the one-to-one meeting with the coach-psychologist	*Mean score* = 3.77

Objectives: There are four major objectives of the conference. Rate the extent to which each objective has been achieved.

28.	To acquire tools to create a future with new opportunities for success	*Mean score* = 3.96
29.	To be able to challenge basic assumptions	*Mean score* = 4.13
30.	To reflect on feedback from self and others that can lead to personal change	*Mean score* = 4.17
31.	To develop the competencies and courage to lead changes that bring about a successful future	*Mean score* = 4.03

CONFERENCE OVERALL

32.	The overall quality of instruction	*Mean score* = 4.26
33.	The quality of the instructors' interaction with participants	*Mean score* = 4.07
34.	The quality of the support staff's responsiveness to participants' needs	*Mean score* = 4.55
35.	The quality of the educational facility	*Mean score* = 4.42
36.	The effectiveness of the executive conference overall	*Mean score* = 4.26

Merlin: The Merlin exercise is intended for you to experience a process of creating breakthrough business opportunities and to communicate them to top management.

1.	Effectiveness of the Merlin process as a tool for stimulating discussion of breakthrough thinking	*Mean score* = 4.23
2.	Effectiveness of your Merlin group focused on our long-term future	*Mean score* = 3.91
3.	Quality of the presentation by the Merlin group	*Mean score* = 4.29

Figure 8.3 Sample Feedback: Level 1 (Quantified)

and mechanical for participants, further encouraging the "smile sheets" mentality.

Some organizations have experimented with daily and end-of-program critiques, or open discussion sessions with participants. Most have found these sessions to have more negative than positive consequences. Some of the negative consequences are that quieter people tend not to get involved in the discussions, participant's true feelings seldom emerge, and the critique can turn into a bashing session. As a result of these and other concerns, the value of this technique is uncertain.[9]

Following on from this, there is always a question about how to use the information generated by reaction evaluation. Certainly, managers who are responsible for a program need access to the data. The faculty/facilitators should be given a summary of the information that relates to their part of a program. Most companies provide facilitators with a quantitative evaluation of questions pertaining to their sessions, as well as a complete transcript of related written comments, both positive and negative. Many program directors use this information as a way to help facilitators improve their delivery. Obviously, this is particularly important when the program is to be repeated a number of times. Some program directors set a minimum level of acceptability. If a program session does not achieve an overall average of 4.0, for example, the instructor may be given a couple more opportunities to meet that standard before he or she is replaced. Some organizations use participant reaction as a measure of quality control or customer satisfaction. For example, because of GTE's organizational commitment to quality, participants (and their departments) are offered a complete refund of the tuition costs if any program does not meet their expectations. Participants are allowed to make that judgement independently and do not have to justify a negative response, even if other people in the program view it as being successful.

Level II – Learning Evaluation

Level II evaluation adds a level of sophistication to the process by attempting to determine whether or not participants have actually learned what a program was designed to teach, whether participants have internalized the prescribed content, and whether they have mastered the material at the level of some prescribed standard. It is typically administered through some form of testing, demonstration, or role playing technique. Level II evaluation can be viewed as quality assurance for the program.

Kirkpatrick found that there are three things that instructors can teach – knowledge, skills, and attitudes.[10] He added that it is important to measure *learning* since behavioral change is not likely to take place unless new knowledge has been acquired, new skills developed, or attitudes altered in some way. Moreover, it is difficult to assess the meaning of a lack of behavioral change (level III evaluation) unless there is knowledge about the degree to which learning *has* occurred . In other words, if a program results in little or no behavioral change it is important to know whether that is a consequence of a lack of learning or whether something in the environment prevented participants from applying new concepts to their work.

It is inherently more difficult to measure the knowledge gained during a leadership development experience than to determine if, for instance, a person has improved his or her ability to apply methods of statistical process control to their job. However, certain programs such as "Finance for the Nonfinancial Manager" or "Quantitative Tools for Decision-Making" do lend themselves to level II evaluation. Most university credit courses use this type of assessment in the grading process. Because of the subjectivity associated with level II evaluation, this may the most difficult part of being a university professor. Douglas D. Anderson, Managing Partner of The Center for Executive Development, contrasted his experience as a member of the Harvard Business School faculty with that as a principal with a major consulting firm by referring to Shakespeare's line, "The test of a vocation is the love of its drudgery." Anderson added:

> "I can't say that I always passed that test at HBS; for although I loved the teaching, learning and colleagueship of the university, I did not love the grading of exams, the attending of committee meetings, and some of the other duties associated with the academy. Now, I don't have to do any of those things. I feel like I have found the Shangri-La of teaching."[11]

Assessment centers focus on the bridge between Level II and Level III. They are "competency demonstrations" that provide learners with an opportunity to demonstrate what they have learnt while being observed by an evaluator. Robinson and Robinson described this as being similar to "auditioning actors for the cast of a stage production."[12] In auditions, actors are usually given pages of script to read and deliver in a believable manner, thus demonstrating their acting skill. Similarly, simulations or activities that require participants to demonstrate how they would respond to specific situations requiring knowledge of concepts discussed in an earlier part of a program can provide evidence of learning that can be observed and assessed. Additionally, the simulation may also serve as a reinforcement for the concepts that were taught.

Scales with behavioral anchors provide an added level of sophistication for assessing performance. In this system, each anchor describes a particular level of competence. A *behaviorally anchored rating scale* (BARS) provides a means of assessing the differences in skill levels possessed by learners. This technique can help to eliminate some of the subjectivity in observer evaluation and can be used as a feedback tool for participants. An example of a simple BARS scale is shown in Figure 8.4.

The Search For Objectivity

The achievement of objectivity in assessment center evaluation is an elusive goal that has challenged university professors as well as HRD professionals. Most organizations that use assessment centers employ a multi-rater format in which several experts evaluate the performance of participants. Some organizations video-tape simulation exercises so that program managers can go back to review and verify their assessments of individual participants.

An organization that wishes to use level II type assessment would do well to think through the design of the evaluation process while developing the program. Some corporations have found that specialized firms are able to offer assistance and objectivity in building level II evaluation into a program design by providing experienced observers to critique the program itself and to construct evaluation protocols to use with a sample of program participants and their sponsors. A detailed assessment by an experienced outside specialist offers a degree of

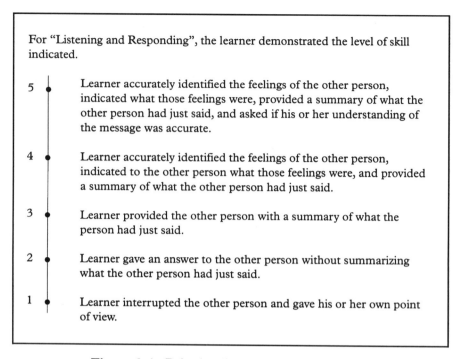

For "Listening and Responding", the learner demonstrated the level of skill indicated.

5 — Learner accurately identified the feelings of the other person, indicated what those feelings were, provided a summary of what the other person had just said, and asked if his or her understanding of the message was accurate.

4 — Learner accurately identified the feelings of the other person, indicated to the other person what those feelings were, and provided a summary of what the other person had just said.

3 — Learner provided the other person with a summary of what the person had just said.

2 — Learner gave an answer to the other person without summarizing what the other person had just said.

1 — Learner interrupted the other person and gave his or her own point of view.

Figure 8.4   Behaviorally Anchored Rating Scale
Source: D.G. Robinson and J.C. Robinson, *Training for Impact*, San Francisco: Jossey-Bass, 1989, p.199.

credibility and objectivity that the sponsoring organization will find difficult to achieve alone.

Level III – Behavioral Evaluation

A critical question for any leadership development program is, "Did the behavior of participants change?" There is no guarantee that newly acquired knowledge or skill will actually be used. Level III assessment attempts to address this issue by determining whether or not an individual has actually changed his or her behavior as a result of attending a program. Ideally, level III evaluation compares behavioral change within a control group with similar change experienced within the group that participated in the learning experience. This can be difficult to do since it is almost impossible to find two groups that are equal in all the factors that could affect behavioral change.

Level III evaluation relies heavily on before and after measures for evaluation since reported impressions of changed behaviors are less reliable than those that have some type of quantitative standard associated with them. However, pre-program assessment is sometimes impossible. When that is the case, it is possible for organizations to interview or survey participants after a program to determine whether they felt the experience had any perceived impact on their behavior. This can be useful, but it is far less reliable than before and after measures. Reliability can be increased if the participants' bosses, colleagues, and/or subordinates are surveyed in an attempt to ascertain whether they have perceived any changes in the participant's behavior that might be attributable to the developmental experience. Remember, though, that in assessing behavioral change there must be enough time for the change to take place. A six-month follow-up is a generally reliable standard and fairly easy to manage.

One of the most impressive approaches to assessing behavioral change, and one discussed briefly in Chapter 5, is 360-feedback. A *Fortune* headline recently asserted "360-Degree Feedback Can Change Your Life."[15] Author Brian O'Reilly described 360-degree feedback as being essentially "feedback from co-workers or multi-reader assessment." Some observers believe that for feedback to truly represent a 360-degree radius, it must include a personal assessment, the rating of a boss, and assessment from peers, subordinates, and key customers. Most formal programs involving 360-degree feedback use all of these perspectives, although many omit responses from customers.

When the Scottish poet Robert Burns penned the words "would the power some gifts give us, to see ourselves as others see us, it would from many a blunder free us," he could have been talking about 360-degree feedback. People seldom have an opportunity to see themselves in such detail as when they are assessed by peers and colleagues on values, competencies, and behaviors that are seen as extremely important to their effectiveness and success. The assessment instrument is likely to gather opinions on indices such as the person's listening skills, whether the person demonstrates a long-term perspective, whether the person is trustworthy, or whether they tend to be abrasive, and so on. The forms are usually computer scored and summarized at an outside agency, and a computer-generated report identifying perceived strengths and weaknesses is provided to participants. Some companies collect copies of the analysis for the individual's career development dossier, while others choose to let the participant own the data and share it with the company only if they wish to do so. Often participants are debriefed on a one-on-one basis by an expert in the instrument. These debriefing sessions sometimes include the individual's boss and/or a corporate HRD staff member.

The Center for Creative Leadership in Greensboro, NC is probably the largest provider of 360-degree feedback instruments and programs. Their *Benchmarks* assessment tool is one of the most highly regarded in the field. With separate specialized forms that are prepared for executive, mid-level and supervisory participants, CCL provides an extensive database against which to compare responses and profile participants' strengths and weaknesses. In addition, CCL has extensive experience in delivering programs around 360-degree feedback, and a reputation for unparalleled objectivity.

An Example of Level III Evaluation

Keilty Goldsmith & Company is a firm that specializes in programs that provide level III type pre- and post-course assessment. It has also conducted some of the most significant research on the impact of feedback and follow-up on leadership effectiveness. The firm's research began with a *Fortune* 500 company that had conducted a "Leadership and Values Course" for its top 100 executives. As part of the program, each executive received feedback from his or her direct reports using a custom-designed behavioral assessment. Based on this feedback, participants were encouraged to:

1 Pick one to three areas for improvement
2 Develop an action plan for desired change
3 Respond to his or her direct reports concerning areas for improvement and ask them for help in changing, and
4 Follow-up with direct reports to check on progress and to receive further assistance.

1. Do you feel this individual has become more effective (or less effective) as a leader in the past 18 months? (Please rate this person on her/his effectiveness concerning aspects of leadership she/he can control. Please do not consider environmental or organizational factors that are beyond this person's control.)

Less Effective	No Perceptible Change	More Effective

–5 –4 –3 –2 –1 0 +1 +2 +3 +4 +5

2. Did this person discuss what he/she learned from his/her previous leadership inventory feedback with you?

_____ Yes
_____ No
_____ Not Sure
_____ This person did not receive prior feedback from me

3. How has this person followed up with you on areas that he/she has been trying to improve?

_____ Consistent (Periodic) Follow-up
_____ Some Follow-up
_____ No Perceptible Follow-up

Figure 8.5 Leadership Inventory Supplement for Direct Reports

Eighteen months later, the direct reports were asked to rate these same executives on their effectiveness as leaders, and on how well they had responded to concerns raised in the assessment and followed-up on them. The follow-up questionnaire is shown in Figure 8.5. This same methodology was subsequently repeated with several other firms to generate a database of over 5000 managers.[14]

> *Our experience with behavioral change is that action plans based on 360-degree feedback and follow-up reporting about progress is most likely to generate perceived change.*
>
> Garland Bolejack, Southeastern HRD Manager
> Hoechst Celanese

Eighteen months after the initial feedback evaluations were completed, 60 percent of the direct reports still had the same reporting relationship with their managers. These individuals were asked once again to complete the form shown in Figure 8.5. The responses from direct reports who did not have the same managers after 18 months were not included in the study.

Research Findings

Figure 8.6 indicates that 18 months later, over 74 percent of the managers who attended the session were perceived by their direct reports as having responded to their feedback. It is possible that some managers in the "did not respond" group actually did respond, but their response had so little impact that their direct reports did not remember it. For those managers that did respond to the feedback, only 11.4 percent of their direct reports noted there had been no follow-up on progress. The most common response was "some follow-up" (41.5 percent) with a substantial group being seen as conducting "consistent/periodic follow-up" (21.1 percent). The analysis indicates that participants who responded to their direct reports after receiving feedback were very likely to follow up about areas they were trying to improve. Moreover, leaders that both responded and followed up were more likely to be perceived as having significantly improved their effectiveness.

This example reflects the power of level III evaluation. This type of detailed assessment makes it possible to both evaluate the impact of an ongoing initiative *and* shape future initiatives for improvement. The implications may, however, have an even more profound significance: if a leader receives feedback, develops an action plan and follows-up periodically, he or she will almost invariably be perceived as more effective by his or her direct reports. *This reinforces the point that a program itself is not the answer.* Each leader in the Keilty Goldsmith study attended the same program taught by the same instructors and received feedback

Direct Reports (18 months' experience)

My manager responded after program	74.1%
My manager did not respond after program	25.9%

Direct Reports (of those managers who responded after the program)

My manager did no follow-up	11.4%
My manager did some follow-up	41.5%
My manager did consistent/periodic follow-up	21.1%

Figure 8.6

from the same inventory. While most leaders were seen as benefiting from the experience to some degree, a few were seen as wasting their time. However, the major variable for change was found not to be the program, but the follow-up process after the program.

Organizations tend to spend a great deal of time planning programs, but almost no time on planning follow-up. Yet, follow-up seems to be an approach that not only enhances the outcomes of a leadership development initiative, but also provides an ongoing mechanism for measuring progress or improvement associated with that initiative.[15]

Item Analysis

The data generated by 360-degree feedback can be used to create categories for benchmarking or development by applying item or cluster analysis. These types of analysis provide objective, statistically based methods for uncovering clusters of similar individuals or patterns of similar behaviors within a larger population. One *Fortune* 500 firm used this technique to analyze data from over 500 participants in a senior leadership development initiative. While individual anonymity was maintained, the analysis of the data revealed six categories or profiles of leaders who had similar patterns of strengths and weaknesses. These included:

- Highly skilled leaders who use moderate pressure to get results
- Highly skilled, supportive, team-oriented leaders
- High-pressure, business focused leaders
- Underskilled leaders with moderately effective problem-solving skills
- Generally underskilled leaders
- Underskilled leaders who apply high pressure[16]

Figure 8.7 provides an example of the information generated by this type of analysis. The data suggest approximately 10 percent of the participants in the sample could be described as supportive and team-oriented. Their weaknesses were in market knowledge and willingness to take risks. Their strengths were in basic people skills. The bottom of the figure suggests potential areas for personal development. Individuals in this category were viewed as being better candidates for mentoring and helping develop younger colleagues than for start-up or turnaround assignments. By similarly analyzing and reviewing all six clusters, the sponsoring company crafted a well-targeted leadership development initiative complete with appropriate measures for effectiveness. In addition, this information was shared with the entire human resource department and was especially helpful in refining the performance evaluation and succession planning systems.

Level IV – Results Evaluation

After assessing the degree of behavioral change, the next logical question is "how have these changed behaviors affected the business?" Line executives want to know if productivity or quality have improved, or if the change in behavior is consistent with the organization's strategy and objectives. Just as in evaluating the benefits of an investment in new equipment, this level of assessment often requires numerous before and after organizational performance measures along with some difficult calculations.

Common techniques for evaluating results are before and after measurements of indices like productivity, customer complaints, cycle times, employee turnover ratios, and employee attitudes. If there is improvement in these indices following a leadership development

Brief description
Supportive, team building executives

Composition

	n	Breakdown within Group 4-R	Composition of Group 4-R	Percentage of whole population
Senior Level	14	30%	6%	10%
Mgt Board Level	33	70%	13%	($n = 47$)

Skill profile

	Low	Average	High
Leadership vision		✓	
Risk-taking/Venturesomeness	–		
Marketplace awareness	–		
Organizational awareness		✓	
Managing complexities		✓	
Employee development		✓	
Team development			+
Information/data support		✓	
Standards of performance		✓	
Push/pressure			✓
Coping with stress			✓
Sharing credit			✓
Cultural appreciation			✓

Characteristics
- Show a combination of high, average, and below-average skills.
- Are especially strong in the people-orientated areas of management.
- Probably manage internal, day-to-day motivational processes well.
- Show weaknesses in knowledge of the market and willingness to take risks.

Implications
- Need to develop externally oriented skills.
- Need to develop greater long-term and visionary planning skills.
- Need to become more effective with the implementation and organizational processes which are more cognitive, analytical and planning-oriented.

Figure 8.7 Group R-4: Perceptions by Reports

initiative, then it can be assumed that the initiative contributed in some way to the progress made. Unfortunately, there are many intervening variables in the environment that can also affect these same indices during the measurement interval, and it is nearly impossible to allow for all of them. To deal with this challenge, Rothwell and Kazanas noted a results-based evaluation process must:[17]

- Identify important measures, on the basis of organizational needs/plans, to be changed as a result of leadership development initiatives.
- Clarify the degree of change sought.
- Control for intervening variables to the extent possible.
- Compare organizational performance after the leadership development initiative to those existing before the initiative took place.

The ultimate evaluation objective of most human resource development programs is to test whether the activity has generated a significant return on investment for the sponsoring organization. Jack J. Phillips suggested that a fifth level of evaluation should be added to the Kirkpatrick model, one focused specifically on return on investment.[18] Programs that affect the bottom line are certainly more significant and more credible than those that simply produce people who enjoyed the experience. However, as with Level IV evaluation, success in business performance is usually related to a combination of variables. Consequently, it is difficult to determine what portion of any type of performance improvement might be directly related to particular developmental initiatives.

Rothwell and Kazanas' four suggestions for creating results-based evaluation systems are equally applicable to a calculation of ROI.[19] The difference is that not only do critical measurements need to be identified, targets for improvement set, and before and after measurements made, but these numbers must be converted to financial indices. For example, no company has made a greater effort to track their return on investments in learning than Motorola. The Board of Motorola University regularly has a third-party audit team assess whether or not specific programs produce a return for the business. Motorola University President, Bill Wiggenhorn, justifies an expenditure of over a $100 million by citing a conclusion recently reached by the company's Vice

President of Finance who reported that the reduction of floor space in Motorola factories and labs that can be attributed to skill enhancement reduced corporate cost by $2.2 billion between 1987 and 1992:

> ❝ *Those audit reports show that when we train the right people, transfer the knowledge and skills back to the (work) environment, the managers change their own behavior by reinforcing the use of these skills, we got a $30–35 return for every training dollar spent. This is the best return on capital that we get in any of our investment schemes.*[20] ❞

Determining such financial returns of a leadership development program requires careful planning and computation. The first step is to identify the impacts of the program in some measurable way. Methods that can be used in leadership development ROI analysis include customer assessments, control group comparisons, and time series analyses of indices. Program participants and their supervisors, subordinates or outside observers can also provide an assessment of the impact of developmental initiatives. When these data have been quantified, it is necessary to convert them to financial values. Hard data, such as quantity, quality, cost or time, can be converted directly. Softer data, such as measures of the impact of programs on issues like productivity, morale, etc., are more difficult to quantify. Some firms have outside auditors prepare analyses of cost savings or increased profit or revenue due to leadership development. Some have their own finance group do the analysis. Others are content with the analysis provided by the leadership development staff.

To calculate leadership development ROI, it is first necessary to calculate the total cost of the initiative. The cost calculation should incorporate all out-of-pocket expenditures for the program, along with participant time, travel, and other related expenses. This includes:

- *Direct costs* such as materials, provider fees, travel, lodging and meal expenses
- *Indirect costs* associated with development efforts but not tied directly to a specific initiative, including administrative support and marketing
- *Development costs* for program and content design, faculty preparation, and pilot testing

- *Overhead costs* associated with corporate charges and facilities/equipment use, and finally
- *Compensation costs* for participants' time while involved in the initiative.

Some firms do not include this last cost in their calculations, while for many others participant travel and lodging expenses are the responsibility of the sponsoring unit and therefore not included in ROI calculations.

The ROI formula, then, is the net program benefits as assessed in the analysis of changes in critical financial indices, divided by the program cost. A simple way of expressing this formula is:

$$\text{ROI (percentage)} = \frac{\text{Benefits} - \text{Costs}}{\text{Costs}} \times 100$$

Figure 8.8 summarizes attempts made by several organizations to calculate the return on investment of various training and development initiatives. Some of these examples focus on lower level training. Many, however, are parts of initiatives that have "cascaded" throughout an entire organization.

A Systems Perspective on Evaluation

As we have seen, the levels of evaluation described above should be viewed not as an individual approach, but as a cascading process of increased sophistication. Each level provides useful and important information. An overall evaluation process that makes use of techniques from each level is more likely to generate useful data that verifies the impact of leadership development on the organization and its members. Figure 8.9 describes how Cigna provides an overall assessment and evaluation of its programs utilizing the four levels of evaluation.

Summary

The approaches to assessment and evaluation discussed in this chapter should not be seen as independent of each other. Instead, they should be viewed as a "chain of impact" for leadership development invest-

Figure 8.8

Setting	Target group	Program description	Evaluation process	Results
Electric and gas utility	Managers and supervisors	• Applied behavior • Management focusing on achieving employee involvement to increase quality, productivity and profits	• Action planning (variety of projects) • Performance monitoring	• 400% ROI • Benefit/cost ratio 5:1
Bottling company (Coca-Cola)	Supervisors	• Eight half-day workshops covering supervisory roles, settling goals, developing the team, etc.	• Action planning • Follow-up session • Performance monitoring	• 1.447% ROI • Benefit/cost ratio 15:1 Variety of measures
Paper products company	Managers, supervisors and hourly employees	• Organizational development program (workshops, action study teams, skill building programs)	• Follow-up interviews • Survey • Performance monitoring	• Variance form Standard: +$106,000 • Waste: 36% improvement • Absenteeism: 35% improvement • Safety: 25% improvement
Health maintenance organization (HMO)	All managers and all employees	• Organizational development program (team building, group meetings, customer service training)	• Performance monitoring • Management estimation	• 20,700 new HMO members 1270% ROI • Benefit/cost ratio 13.7:1
Large commercial bank	Consumer loan officers	• Two-day sales training program (focus on increase in service training)	• Follow-up • Performance monitoring	• 30% increase in consumer loans • 2000% ROI • Benefit/cost ratio 21:1
Information services company	Supervisors	• Twelve 2.5-hour sessions on behavioral modeling	• Follow-up with surveys	• 336% ROI
Bakery (Multi-Marques, Inc.)	Supervisors/administration services	• 15-hour supervisory skills training (including the role of training)	• Action planning (work process analyses) • Performance monitoring	• 215% ROI Benefit/cost ratio 3.2:1
Avionics (Litton Industries)	All employees	• Self-directed work teams	• Action planning • Performance monitoring	• Productivity increased 30% • Scrap rate reduction 50% • 700% ROI

Figure 8.8 (*cont.*)

Setting	Target group	Program description	Evaluation process	Results
Truck leasing (Peaske Truck Leasing)	All supervisors	• 20-hour program on supervisory skills utilizing behavior modeling	• Performance monitoring	• Turnover reduction of 6% • Absentee reduction of 16.7%
Trucking (Yellow Freight System)	Managers	• Redesigned performance appraisal with training on interpersonal skills, communication and coaching	• Follow-up interviews • Performance monitoring	• 1115% ROI • Benefit/cost ratio 12:1
Federal government	New supervisors	• Five-day introduction to supervision course covering eight key competencies	• Follow-up questionnaire	• 150% ROI • Benefit/cost ratio 2.5:1

These cases appear in Jack J. Phillips (ed.) *Measuring Return on Investment*, published by the American Society for Training and Development, Alexandria, Virginia, 1994.

Figure 8.9 CIGNA CMD&T Impact Model

Chain of impact		Research tool		Time period
Opinions	↓	Trainee self-report	↓	Throughout training and at three-month follow-up
	D i f		P o w	
Learning	f	Trainee self-report	e	At end of training
Behavior	i c	Survey of trainee's subordinates	r	Before training and at three-month follow-up
	u l		↓	
Results	t y	Trainee's work unit records, action plan, and BMS workbook		Tracked from three months preceding training to three months following training
	↓			

Adapted from D. Kirkpatrick, *Evaluating Training Programs*, Alexandria, VA: American Society for Training and Development, p. 194.

ments. First, learning must be rooted in the strategic imperatives of the firm . Then it must be designed to take full advantage of the various techniques, methodologies and providers available. The design must be benchmarked against "best practice" companies. It must be accepted and embraced by participants. It must change participants' knowledge and attitudes. It must help them to change their behavior back on the job. It must show that these changed behaviors have led to improved results for the organization.

Nicholas S. Merlo of Hughes Aircraft Corporation reported that his firm had generated returns of over 3000 percent from performance improvement related to training. While his numbers are challenging, Merlo felt the approach used to obtain them was conservative and pragmatic.[21] He suggested that the findings call for HRD professionals to reorient their thinking.

> Perhaps our primary concern should move beyond what is being taught and how many managers are being developed. Instead, a shift to "is what we are teaching improving performance?" might be more productive.

Endnotes

1 Rothwell, W. J. and H. C. Kazanas, *The Complete AMA Guide to Management Development*, New York: AMACOM, 1993, p. 265.

2 Cited in Kirkpatrick, Donald L., *Evaluating Training Programs: The Four Levels*, San Francisco: Berrett-Koehler Publishers, Inc., 1994, p. 17.

3 Adapted from Yelon, S. "Classroom Instruction," in Stolovitch, H. and E. Keeps (eds.), *Handbook for Human Performance Technology*, Washington: The National Society For Performance and Instruction, 1992, p. 385.

4 Fitz-Enz, J. *Benchmarking Staff Performance*, San Francisco: Jossey-Bass, 1993.

5 See Murphy, J., "Westinghouse Benchmarking Study," *efmd Forum*, 3, 1994, p. 17.

6 Ibid.

7 See Kirkpatrick, Donald L., *A Practical Guide for Supervisory Training and Development*, 2nd Edition, Reading, MA, Addison-Wesley, 1983 and 1994. See also Robinson, Dana Gaines and James C. Robinson, *Training for*

Impact, San Francisco: Jossey-Bass Publishers, 1989, pp. 164–279. See also Kirkpatrick, Donald L., *Evaluating Training Programs*, Alexandria, VA, American Society for Training and Development, 1975.

8   Kirkpatrick, 1994, op.cit., preface.

9   Rae, L., *How To Measure Training Effectiveness*, Brookfield, VT: Gower, 1991.

10 Kirkpatrick, 1994, op.cit., p. 42.

11 Personal correspondence dated May 2, 1995.

12 Robinson, Dana Gains and James C. Robinson, op. cit., 1989, p. 196.

13 O'Reilly, Brian, *Fortune*, October 17, 1994, p. 93.

14 Goldsmith, Marshall, *The Impact of Feedback and Follow-up on Leadership Development*, San Diego: Kielty Goldsmith & Company, 1994, pp. 1–6.

15 Ibid.

16 O'Bannon, Michael, *Topology of Top Management Skill Profiles*, unpublished January 17, 1995.

17 Rothwell and Kazanas, 1993, op.cit., p. 273.

18 Phillips, Jack J., "Measuring Training's ROI: It Can Be Done", *William and Mary Business Review*, Summer, 1995, p. 6.

19 Rothwell and Kazanas, 1993, op.cit., p. 273.

20 Wiggenhorn, William, "Motorola University: When Training Becomes an Education," *Harvard Business Review*, July–August, 1994, p. 72. On August 6, 1995, during an Academy of Management Meeting presentation in Vancouver, Wiggenhorn indicated this return on investment information had been so widely quoted that Motorola was trying to downplay the standard. He pointed out, however, that the company remains committed to measurement and expects leadership development and training initiatives to be profitable.

21 Reported in Kirkpatrick, 1994, op.cit., pp. 182–187.

SECTION III

THE FUTURE

9

THE LEADING EDGE

In this chapter, we present five leading edge examples of new paradigm leadership development. Although we cannot claim to have benchmarked every best practice organization in the field of executive education/leadership development, we do believe that these five exemplar initiatives are among the most innovative approaches we have found. We offer them as an opportunity for readers to do their own benchmarking, and to provide detailed examples of how prominent organizations are responding to the challenge of the new world for strategic leadership development.

Although each of the five exemplar initiatives is grounded in well-conceived, systemic approaches to the process, each addresses a particular dimension of strategic leadership development.

1 The Center for Creative Leadership's LeaderLab Program exemplifies innovative program design.

2 AT&T's Leadership Development Program For Middle Managers exemplifies innovative development of key middle management talent.

3 ARAMARK's Executive Leadership Institute exemplifies comprehensive, action-learning based approaches to leadership development.

4 The new leadership development initiatives at Johnson & Johnson exemplify emerging strategic approaches to the process.

5 MIT's Center For Organizational Learning exemplifies the emerging university/corporate collaboration in leadership and organizational development.

Innovation in Program Design:
The Center for Creative Leadership's LeaderLab Program[1]

The Center For Creative Leadership's LeaderLab program was launched in 1991. Since its inception it has run over 30 times and well over 500 participants have completed the program. According to program designers Victoria Guthrie and Bob Burnside, the stated purpose of LeaderLab is, "to encourage and enable leaders to take more effective actions in their leadership situations, actions which develop themselves and others in pursuit of goals that benefit all." This statement embodies a belief that leaders will in future need the resources to act, and not just to reflect, to effectively confront the serious challenges that await them.

LeaderLab's content falls into three basic categories:

1   Review of the significant generic challenges faced by leaders today
2   Development of the competencies necessary to deal with these challenges, and
3   Assessment and development of skills and knowledge to help participants understand their specific leadership situation and take action.

A fourth category – the information and personal awareness each participant generates through the specific assessment in category 3 – is developed during the course of the program and is unique for each individual.

LeaderLab expands on the Center's traditional model of a self-awareness program by providing mechanisms for support and accountability over an extended period (six months) to help participants transmit course learning back to the workplace. Extensive pre-course preparation is required, including qualitative analyses of the individual's personal and work situations, as well as a variety of feedback instruments that are thoroughly debriefed during the program to help the individual gain a deeper understanding of him or herself. Participants spend time at the Center learning ways to lead in a variety of situations and developing the processes and tools to achieve lasting behavioral change. They create an action plan to implement in their own work environment with the help of a Center staff person called a *process advisor* (PA), a "coach" who maintains frequent contact with the participant via telephone. During the program itself, and back in the workplace, the participant is supported by several "change partners." These are fellow program participants, or individuals personally selected by the participant back in the workplace, who act as resources to encourage, coach, and give honest feedback to participants on their work.

Unique, Action-Based Program Methods

Several unique, action-oriented techniques created for LeaderLab are used in concert with more conventional training methods like discussion, exercise, simulations, and use of learning journals to achieve the program's objectives. Two of the guiding principles of the program are that learning should be connected to the back-home leadership situation and that it should occur over time. LeaderLab makes this happen through two time-phased training sessions, implementation of action plans back in the workplace, and continuous work with the process advisor and change partners. The program features and rationale are summarized as follows.

Method	Rationale
Action learning over time	Intervening and learning over time leads to change; addressing real issues helps transfer learning to leadership situation
Developmental relationships: process advisor (PA), change partner	Support for change–feedback–challenges; provides wisdom/advice
Reflective learning journals	Connects participant to program over 6 months – distill patterns, key lessons; encourages self-analysis; provides content for process advisor phone calls
Visioning and action planning	Provide process and structure for targeting changes and improvements – emphasizes positives or "ideals" to guide change process
Non-traditional activities Acting Artistic activities 3-D problem solving (group sculpting)	Tap creative, emotional sides of learning – help get outside the box of linear thinking; also emphasizes importance of of using effective and behavioral domains as well as cognitive

The program begins with a six-day classroom session culminating in each participant's development of an action plan for improving their leadership. Participants then return to their jobs for three months during which time they work to carry out the plan. Following that intervening period, a second classroom session of four days takes place. At that time, participants review how their action plan progressed and modify it based on their experiences of the first three months. A revised action plan, established at the end of the second classroom session, is then implemented over the remaining three months.

The entire intervention lasts six months. The process advisor and change partners within the participant group provide support and help to process learning. Work site change partners provide feedback, support and advice on behavioral, organizational and technical goals. This approach closely parallels action learning which posits real-world action as a valuable source of knowledge about self, and, conversely, views organizational change as a manifestation of individual growth and development. LeaderLab embraces the fundamentals of action learning in that the problems participants address are real; they are addressed over time; and they are addressed with the support and confrontation of change partners and process advisors.

Program Process

Based on the program's objectives, different elements of instruction are combined in a unique and potentially powerful experience. The basic components of the program are outlined below.

Intervention over time   LeaderLab begins with a six-day session where, among other things, an action-plan is developed by each participant to improve his or her leadership, followed by a three-month interval during which the participant carries out the plan, continuing with a second four-day session, during which time the action-plan is reviewed and another three-month interval is set up. This type of intervention over time is a critical factor in the program's ambition to create lasting behavioral change. It is structured to accommodate the full adult learning cycle to operate (planning, doing and reflecting).

Program activities in an action-oriented format   The focus on learning to learn and relating learning to the individual participant's unique leadership situation call for classroom activities in addition to traditional lectures. These include discussion, exercises, simulations, use of a learning journal, and non-traditional activities. Discussions promote cross-fertilization of ideas among participants, allowing them to bring their experience and expertise to each other. Exercises serve as the first safe place that new ideas and behaviors can be put into practice. The simulation is an extended exercise (known as a "simmercize" in LeaderLab) which puts participants into the organizational roles of a fictional company, dealing with rapid change and difficult issues while wrestling with seemingly conflicting individual and divisional values. The daily learning journal provides a vehicle for reflection on learning and provides the individual with themes or patterns of behavior that can be useful in taking more effective action.

Process advisor   This staff person meets with the participant during both weeks of training and helps in the construction of his or her action-plan. The advisor also contacts the participant monthly by phone during the three-month intervals. The advisor's purpose is to continually prod and encourage the participant to address issues and blocks in their development.

Change partners   The main task for each participant in this program is to create and follow through on an action-plan for his or her leadership situation. A system of support, both in the program (change partners), and in the workplace (back-home change partners) is set up to support the participant in this goal. In LeaderLab, a diverse, three-person, in-course work group collaborates to encourage the individual. At home, each participant must also establish a group of change partners in the organization to help him or her with leadership improvement.

Diversity of participants and trainers   The LeaderLab classroom composition is a mix of gender, ethnic groups, and work situations, since diversity is one of the challenges of the future. A working actor and artist facilitator serving as trainers have added an important element of experiential diversity.

Non-traditional learning activities: art, acting and sculpting A number of additional components which have not been traditionally part of a leadership development program are presented in LeaderLab. Frequently, being in a management position develops one's abilities to intellectualize and verbalize, but the not the use of other methods of expression. Art is used to address this issue. In one segment, the participant draws with pastel chalks to communicate a particular situation in his or her life. In another, participants create a *touchstone* sculpture that communicates a metaphor for their approach to leadership. They are asked to think back on their experiences of the week and put on the touchstone whatever they want most to remind themselves of back in the daily chaos of their work environment. They may select from a pool of materials that includes leaves, wood, stones, string, and numerous other materials. One participant, explained his touchstone as follows:

> ❝ *This piece of plywood is me. See, it's right angled at one end, that's where I'm coming from, very analytic and hard edged. This big, open shell is my analytic side. No problem with that, it's well developed and I rely on it a lot. But here, next to it is my emotional side. It's a lot smaller, only open a little way, and it's pretty well covered up. These other two shells here at this end are more equal in size. They represent my analytic side and my emotional side more in balance. That's where I want to go. But how am I going to get from here to there? There's a straight path here at the right-angled end. It's fast and smooth, but if you notice, it doesn't get me all the way to the other end. The other path, the twisty, turning one, does go all the way. It'll take me longer. It's winding and rough, but it will get me there.* ❞

The acting component has been designed and is implemented by a working actor and incorporates methods used in acting instruction. Its focus is on awareness of the participant's physical self-presentation (tone of voice, body posture, gesture) and its effect on others. The "acting leader" is the first of the non-traditional segments to be presented in the program. It comprises two classroom sessions in week one of the program, plus a personal assessment provided by the trainer of each participant's behaviors as observed during the opening "simmercize." In a brief individual session, each participant is given a "suggesture" (from suggested gesture), based on what he or she typically tends to do, that would make the participant more effective. Two more sessions take place in week two which focus more on group interaction based on the same principles.

The body sculpting component was designed by a practicing family therapist and makes use of the pioneering work of Virginia Satir in identifying and working with family dynamics issues non-verbally. This session occurs on the second day of week one. In its adaptation to the leadership development context, participants work with an issue or situation that has caused difficulties at work, using classmates to stage a scenario, representing first a problem situation, then creating a scenario representing a possible solution. The scenarios are verbally debriefed in depth. A second session occurs during week two, during which time participants form groups to create scenarios representing problems they have faced in meeting their action-plans, and then creating scenarios representing resolution of these difficulties. Because the participants are using their bodies as "clay" to construct their own unscripted scenarios, these exercises are relatively unstructured. They require skilled facilitation, both in the process and in the debrief which involves being able to translate a non-verbal experience into terms relevant to the participants' work environment.

Impact of the Experience

Participant comments from the final essay prepared at the conclusion of LeaderLab provide insight on the unique nature of the experience:

> 66 *LeaderLab provided me with a more clear sense of purpose and a plan for moving forward. The competencies and holistic model provided context within which to identify options and develop strategies. Conversations with my process advisor, coupled with the journaling process, helped me stay focused on that sense of purpose and start to find a balance between short and long-term issues and goals.* 99

> 66 *LeaderLab reinforced the importance of continuing my team leadership approach while thoroughly assessing situations and developing very specific and measurable action plans. The most significant impact of my LeaderLab experience is the importance of viewing results as learning events and to reflect on the experiences.* 99

Dianne Young at the Center recently completed a rigorous follow-up study of 37 LeaderLab participants from three different programs to assess the impact of the experience nine to twelve months after attendance.[2] Although the participants were very high on the experience, perhaps the most telling finding was that individuals who worked with the participants noted substantial (statistically significant) positive change in them. In particular, participants were found to have made tangible progress in coping with difficult, stressful situations; developing and maintaining personal relationships; and perhaps most impressively, initiating changes in organizational practices. The participants themselves cited as the most helpful aspects of the course the extended time interval (six months), coupled with the emphasis on action planning. In addition, the coaching aspects of the program received high praise as a mechanism for focusing on development and ensuring follow-up. Perhaps most interestingly, although the artistic aspects of the content were often evaluated more critically by participants during the program, they actually received much higher praise in the follow-up research. This may reflect the longer term value of a "stretch" or personal awareness exercise for participants when that exercise is linked with an action plan for personal growth.

Summary

LeaderLab is a unique experience that combines aspects of conceptual, feedback, and personal growth approaches to leadership development with coaching and action learning to create a process for individual learning and knowledge creation. By drawing from several steps of the Knowledge Creation Cycle (Chapter 5), the program appears to be a more holistic, well-rounded approach to individual development. Based on the follow-up research, the program seems to have a powerful, positive impact on the personal development of participants.

Building Leadership Depth:
The AT&T Leadership Development Program for Middle Managers[3]

In Chapter 1, we discussed the critical role of middle managers in today's flatter, more networked organizations and the importance of targeting leadership development initiatives at this group. We stated our belief that the battered and bruised middle managers of today's organizations may just hold the key to future competitiveness of the firm. In the aftermath of significant downsizing and restructuring, the importance of middle management in creating competitive advantage is being rediscovered. AT&T's Leadership Development Program For Middle Managers (LDP), a two-week, residential program delivered five to six times each year to groups of approximately 45 high-potential middle managers from throughout the company, is a benchmark attempt to deal with that challenge. Program director Deepak (Dick) Sethi helped design the experience, which is delivered by external experts at the new learning center at company headquarters in Basking Ridge, New Jersey.

Always noted for its commitment to executive education and leadership development, AT&T launched LDP in 1988 in a format that might best be described as a traditional, mini-MBA executive education experience. The company took a radically different approach to the program when they redesigned it in 1992. The redesign was driven by the vision of CEO Bob Allen, who had just dramatically reorganized the company into strategic business units and committed it to a core set of strategic imperatives, including emphases on customer focus, globalization, diversity, total quality, and innovation. The goal was to make AT&T into a fleet-footed world leader in the telecommunications industry or, in AT&T terminology, the world's best at bringing people together. Allen and the AT&T HRD staff realized that this new way of operating, far removed from the traditional perspective of a huge regulated monopoly, would require a new style of leader, one who would combine strong general management skills with the drive of a change agent (see Figure 9.1). The Leadership Development Program For Middle Managers was recreated to help meet this requirement.

The core objectives for the redesigned LDP are to transform middle managers into general managers and leaders, and to create agents of change who can transform AT&T's culture, starting with themselves. The program relies heavily on experiential and action learning techniques to address the critical dimensions of leadership in the new AT&T environment. Although classroom discussion sessions are used to present concepts and ideas which are important to the direction of the program, these discussions are intended to add dimension and perspective to its real thrust, that of learning through dialogue, networking, and action planning. The program takes a holistic approach to leadership

From		To
Functional	→	General manager perspective
Risk averse	→	Innovative
Responsive	→	Takes charge/responsible/accountable
Internal/individual	→	Customer/market/team collaboration
Upward/transactional	→	Relationships
Domestic	→	Global
Power over	→	Power with/Power under
Controls	→	Coaches
Manager	→	Leader/manager
Reacts to change	→	Leads change

Figure 9.1   Leadership Transformation at AT&T

development, addressing hard and soft business issues, as well as issues in wellness, fitness, and work/family balance.

Program process

LDP is rooted in two basic philosophies:

1   *Unlearning* is a prelude to new learning, and
2   Learning has not taken place if behavior has not changed.

The program is designed to create a climate of safety, trust, and learning where participants learn from and with each other in a manner that imparts both knowledge and performance enhancement. Risk taking, entrepreneurship, and influence skills are emphasized, and even making a mistake is championed, as long as someone learns from it. During the program, participants are encouraged to speak their minds and get involved. Nothing is reported back to their supervisors.

Pre-course work   About eight weeks prior to the start of a session, the 45 managers who will be attending it are asked to document the key business challenges they face. As the participants will learn, these business challenges then become a key focal point of the program. In a recent enhancement of the program, each participant discusses the issues with a coach prior to attending the program in preparation for the experience, as well as after the program in an effort to reinforce the learning that has taken place. Furthermore, participants are expected to meet with their supervisors prior to attending the program to discuss the experience and their joint expectations for it, and again after the program to debrief the experience.

"Gap" group process   At the outset of the program, participants are assigned to "gap" groups of six or seven people, "gap" being the difference between where they currently are and where they need to be in relation to their pre-defined business challenges. Each day, a different participant discusses his or her challenge with the gap group for approximately 30 minutes. Group members offer ideas, advice, and support for their colleague. Program director Sethi and an outside consultant act as group facilitators when needed. Sethi refers to the outcomes of this approach as "compound organizational learning" in that each individual can use group feedback to better frame personal issues and generate creative solutions to problems, while at the same time, each gap group member learns from the experience of their colleagues. The gap group participants often maintain their network following the program.

Classroom discussion   In addition to the gap group process, participants engage in discussion and dialogue with leading business school professors and consultants who discuss issues identified as critical for the company. These sessions address issues like industry trends, change management, financial management, and global business development. Rather than focusing solely on lectures and case studies, however, the experts facilitate discussion and dialogue around the actual issues of concern to the group and the company. These sessions help promote a greater awareness of the general management challenge among the participants, as well as a deeper understanding of the key roles of leaders in a changing organization. Discussions with senior AT&T executives and major customers also take place during the program, giving participants an opportunity to further broaden their perspectives on the company and its business. CEO Bob Allen typically joins each of the groups for a discussion session.

Learning circles   At the end of each day, participants engage in "learning circles," small groups, different from the gap groups, that discuss what happened during the day and what learning actually occurred. These debriefings help participants clarify what they have learned and how applicable it is to the work situation they face.

Leadership laboratories   Another feature of the program is the "leadership laboratory," experiential exercises in which participants have a chance to work in teams to solve unique problems. For one assignment, the group simulates a "production process" by tossing tennis balls within and between three circles of people. The object is to place a tennis ball in a basket after everyone in all three groups has touched it. The group gets $1 million for each ball it successfully places in the basket, but loses $3 million for each ball dropped. Teams representing investors, customers, marketing, and management are selected to help coordinate the process, with all other participants being designated as production workers. Typically, after 30 minutes of activity verging on total chaos, the exercise ends with skeptical investors, enthusiastic customers, worried management, unhappy workers, and a bunch of dropped balls. At their conclusion, exercises like this are thoroughly debriefed to help participants gain greater insight into the leadership process. In the instance above, management has usually crafted a well-developed plan for completing the exercise, but often has failed to communicate the plan to production workers. The result are disastrous, just as in the real world. These experiences help to bring the basic principles of leadership to life, and facilitate feedback and dialogue around critical leadership skills.

Holistic activities   In addition to business issues and leadership dimensions, the program endeavors to address "mind and body" issues. Activities such as daily hour-long exercise periods, mild aerobics, and discussions on personal well-being and work/family balance are built into the program to complete its holistic approach.

Action plans   Participants leave with a documented action plan at the conclusion of the course in addition to having addressed their business challenges in the gap group process.

Impacts and Implications

Participant reactions to the experience tend to praise its highly engaging, interactive approach and its action orientation. The program is consistently seen by participants as having made a difference in their approach to both leadership and their jobs. In addition, the peer coaching and learning laboratory aspects of the program are viewed very positively, as is the opportunity for cross-business unit networking. The comments below are typical:

> ❝ *Excellent group process. Allowed members to not only learn/relearn skills, but to put them immediately into action.*
>
> *The gap process touched and taught me one of the most important learnings of the course: everyone brings value and a great perspective to any task, everyone should be heard.*
>
> *There was more interaction ... and respect shown for the intelligence and talent of participants. [It provided] real insight into leadership skills.*
>
> *The program brought together some of AT&T's sharpest minds ... the intellectual stimulation was a sheer delight.*
>
> *In that room I had to force myself to articulate my problem to folks who don't know anything about it. I came back with such solid ideas.* ❞

AT&T has built several reinforcement elements into the program to ensure its transfer to the workplace. They include post-program meetings with participant supervisors to discuss transfer, and follow-up calls to participants from program staff and coaches following completion of the program to discuss the experience and the individual's ongoing development. One of the most lasting benefits of the program may be that the gap groups continue to meet long after the program ends. In addition, the documented action plan prepared during the course provides an opportunity for immediate implementation of ideas generated. Taken together, this hands-on, holistic approach does seem to have the potential to make a real impact on both the participants and the organization.

Although AT&T believes that such positive impacts actually result from the program, the company is seeking hard data to verify their perceptions. In a study completed in 1993, appropriately referred to within AT&T as "Beyond the Smiles," over 70 participants on previous programs were interviewed along with a their superiors and a group of peers and subordinates. The study found that over 75 percent of the participants had followed through on their action plans, most quite successfully. It also included an in-depth analysis of which elements of the program had the most impact on the participant in both their professional and personal lives.[4] These data were then used to further refine and enhance the experience. A similar study is currently underway in which participants' supervisors, colleagues, subordinates, and customers will again be surveyed in an effort to determine what impact the program had on individual participant's performance as a leader. AT&T believes if it can verify whether individual leadership behavior has been positively affected by the program, and also verify whether the program has met one of its core objectives, creating change agents who can transform AT&T's culture, starting with themselves.

Action Learning Based Leadership Development:
The ARAMARK Executive Leadership Institute[5]

In Chapter 3, we discussed the ARAMARK Executive Leadership Institute (ELI), a strategic leadership development initiative targeted at the most senior leaders of the company. ELI was designed to help the company's senior leaders address the organization's core strategic imperatives: achieving a high level of profitable growth by becoming the world leader in managed services. Thus far, over 150 senior executives have completed a version of ELI, including CEO Joe Neubauer and his fellow corporate officers.

ELI is a unique, nine-month leadership development experience consisting of four program "modules" and an action learning experience. In addition, an accompanying 360-degree assessment process using the Center For Creative Leadership's *Benchmarks* instrument is conducted over the duration of the program by RHR Associates of New York. The end product of this assessment is a personal development plan for each participant jointly agreed upon by the individual and his or her boss. The database developed through the 360-degree assessment process also has become the basis for the development of an ARAMARK leadership competency model that has guided the redesign of selection and appraisal systems in the company.

Program Process

The overall structure for the program is presented in figure 9.2. The first module of ELI is a one-week, classroom-based program that features a specially designed series of discussions on the critical issues and core analytical frameworks that ARAMARK has deemed essential to its future success. These discussions make extensive use of ARAMARK case studies and hands-on application exercises, including an outdoor leadership development experience. Participants also are introduced to the 360-degree assessment process on the final day of the module. Faculty for the week include professors from major universities, includ-

Figure 9.2 ARAMARK Executive Leadership Institute

Module One					
Introduction Leadership through teamwork	Managing the cycles of change The challenge of service excellence	Market analysis Improved decision-making – when judgement isn't enough Dialogue with chairman	Business development plans and programs	Systems thinking: The core of fact-based analysis	Summary Introduction to the executive leadership plan Action project implement-ation

Module Two			Module Three		
Organizational alignment: a force for competitive-ness	Financial management: Analysis for growth	Action project discussions	Finalization action project presentations	Action project presentation to business unit presidents and liaisons	Strategic Leadership II Module Four planning

Module Four	
Action project update presentations	Exploiting changes for market leadership

ing people who are well-versed in the history of ARAMARK and its current strategic objectives.

The ideas, techniques, and skills learnt during the first module make up the basic tool kit for the use in an action learning assignment called an "Action Project." The objectives for ELI's Action Project process are:

- To give participants the opportunity to apply the concepts of the Executive Leadership Institute to real-world situations.
- To give participants the opportunity to work with individuals from other business units and to build internal networks.
- To share *best practices* across business units.
- To have *fresh eyes* with which to investigate and analyze opportunities for business development and revenue growth.
- To institutionalize the practice of *fact-based analysis* among ARAMARK senior managers.

At the end of module one, participants are assigned to an action project team. The teams then engage in an experiential exercise in which they address the above objectives by analyzing and resolving a critical company concern. Those concerns have been identified and submitted to the ELI staff by ARAMARK's business unit presidents and approved by CEO Joe Neubauer to ensure they are important and relevant. The only stipulation with regard to the action project teams themselves is that no participant can work on a problem from within his or her own business unit. This helps in achieving ARAMARK's objectives for the initiative, particularly with regard to enabling the organization to get a fresh-eyes perspective on difficult organizational problems. It also provides powerful opportunities for internal networking, an additional objective of the institute.

For the next six to eight weeks, participants work on their projects, balancing the demands of their regular jobs with the challenge of the action projects. Although the time commitment involved can pose a problem for some participants, for most it does not. During this interval, the groups have frequent contact with a "coach", an external resource who serves as a consultant and sounding board to the team. Although the coach plays a critical role in the process as a facilitator, he or she does not do any of the work on the project.

At the end of this interval, the entire class gets back together for module two, a three-day classroom-based program. Two days of that program involve additional presentations on critical skills and concepts that ARAMARK leaders will need to be successful in the future. Not coincidentally, those same skills and concepts are also becoming more critical to the completion of the action projects. The final day of this module is spent in project team meetings with the coach present.

A second six- to eight-week interval ensues in which the action project teams, working with their coaches, finalize their analysis and presentations. The presentations themselves are delivered during module three of the program. During the first day of this two and a half-day module, teams have an opportunity to polish their presentations and brief project sponsors on their final analysis. On the second day, the presentations are made to the entire ELI class as well as project sponsors. ARAMARK senior officers attend the presentations, and are actively involved in the question and answer process.

On the final morning of module three, participants are given an opportunity to suggest ideas for module four, the final component of the program. During this concluding two-day module, typically conducted three to four months following module three, project sponsors are given an opportunity to meet with the action project teams to debrief the project and update the team on what has been done with their recommendations. Although action project sponsors are not required to conduct a debriefing session, few have refused to do so. In addition to the debriefing session, the class participates in one final classroom session to cap their experience, and they engage in a well-deserved celebration of their achievements.

Action Project Roles

ELI designers have delineated the following set of critical roles in the action project process, several of which have been mentioned in this discussion.[6]

Action project sponsor   Generally, this role is filled by each project's sponsoring business unit President. Its purpose is to demonstrate support of the action project team and provide sufficient preliminary information for the team to begin meaningful work on the project. The sponsor receives periodic progress reports from the team, and attends the team's formal presentation during module three.

Business unit liaison   This role is the critical link between the action project team and the sponsoring business unit. The liaison's role is to provide the team with access to "inside" information that they need to complete their project work. The liaison is also responsible for keeping the action project sponsor apprised of the team's work on the project. Like the sponsor, the liaison receives periodic progress reports from the team, and attends the team's formal presentation during module three.

Coach   The coach is an external resource who acts as a process consultant for the action project team. This role includes serving as a "sounding board", questioning and critiquing the team's assumptions, and providing analytical guidance. The coach is a facilitator only, and does not do any of the actual project work.

Corporate support   The individuals in this role provide direction and assistance for teams seeking access to critical information such as financial or market data.

Executive Leadership Institute staff   These individuals oversee and monitor the entire program, including the action project process, ensuring the entire initiative stays on track. In addition, they provide special assistance when needed by the teams.

The Action Project Process

Teams, typically comprised of six individuals, each representing a different business unit or department of the company and all from units other than the one sponsoring the project, are given their assignment on the final day of module one. The team has some time that day to begin to structure its work, but the bulk of its effort is put in between the formal sessions. Ultimately, the teams make fact-based presentations to their business unit sponsors and liaisons during module three.

The sponsoring business unit president is asked to compose a memo to the action project team explaining his or her view of the project. The purpose of this memo is to provide the team with a framework from which to work, demonstrate that the sponsoring business unit is in support of the team and their efforts, and to identify the action project liaison. The sponsoring business unit is also asked to provide essential background information to the team: history of the issue, courses of action taken on this issue in the past and their outcomes; information regarding marketplace trends; relevant financial information; and any other pertinent material. The basic guideline is anything that the organization would supply to an external consulting firm hired to work on the project should be supplied to the action project teams before they commence work.

Milestones/progress reports   The first task of the teams is to select a contact person and formulate milestones for the completion of their projects. The contact person maintains responsibility for providing the coach, the liaison, and the sponsor with periodic progress reports. Those reports can be one-page summaries, but should provide specific information, including an update on the group's progress, details on things on/off track, reasons for variations, milestones achieved, and any revisions to the group's work structure.

Process suggestions   In an introductory session at the end of module one, team members are provided with a short (90-minute) orientation to the action project process by the coaches, and given a three-page set of guidelines for organizing themselves and moving forward with their analysis. This includes a set of initial considerations for addressing their project, and a brief set of expectations for the kinds of analysis they are expected to perform. Beyond this brief orientation to the process, the teams are on their own to structure themselves and move forward.

Fact-based presentations   Teams deliver their final analysis and recommendations during module three. They are allotted approximately 20–30 minutes for their formal presentation, with an additional 20- to 30-minute period for questions. The presentations should include commentary on all pertinent issues, including personal benefits attained from project work. A final written report must also be provided to the sponsor, liaison, and the ELI staff. This report should include copies of overheads or slides used in the final presentation, an outline of recommendations, and all supporting analytical information.

Follow-up Opportunity for debriefing, updates on progress, and follow-up on team recommendations is provided during module four. As mentioned above, project sponsors are not required to conduct a debriefing session, although most are quite willing to do so.

Impacts and Implications

The success of ELI can be measured in a number of ways. On their evaluations at the end of module four, a full 100 per cent of the ELI participants felt that overall the program met or exceeded their expectations. Additionally, nearly 95 percent of the participants felt the action projects were a meaningful process for their own development as well as the development of ARAMARK. In follow-up interviews, ELI participants indicated that the program had a very positive impact on promoting self- and company awareness, facilitating internal networking, promoting a more collaborative leadership style, and encouraging risk taking and "out of the box" thinking. Typical comments on the impact of the experience were:

> ❝ One of the truly valuable outcomes of ELI is that you see a shift from resistance to change to desire to change... A willingness to change only comes about when the culture fosters risk taking and allows you to take risks in order to improve... I think ELI did a very good job fostering that willingness to take risks which allows us to make change.
>
> The action project gives you new ideas. In fact, we started an action project within our division ... using the format we learned in ELI. It was very beneficial with regard to the specific action project as well as a way to use it in my own business.
>
> Interaction/networking was a big plus for me. It's increased my understanding of our business and our people, and also given me personally more confidence in how I fit into the organization. ❞

In addition to participant reactions to the program, CEO Neubauer is even more specific in his critique of ELI:

❝ *We could not even dream of Mission 10–5 [the company's five-year growth plan] without the foundation of the Executive Leadership Institute. The market focus and organizational momentum we gained from the education and action projects has been the basis of conceiving that we actually could grow the company 10 percent for each of the next five years.* ❞

Finally, ARAMARK has an additional tool for assessing the impact of ELI, the results of the action projects. Although, as is to be expected, some projects had more impact than others, the company can point to several examples where an action project team's recommendations had a significant impact on the company. This includes a role in the decision to merge two business units to gain operating efficiencies and leverage customer relationships, the identification of opportunities for better utilization of information technology in another business unit, and a decision *not* to engage in a particular plan for cross-selling initiatives across business units. In all these instances, the company has generated clear results that demonstrate the positive impact of ELI.

Summary

ELI has played an enormous role in the revitalization of ARAMARK. ARAMARK was already a successful, profitable company, but ELI seems to have added an additional spark to the organization. The initiative itself was so meaningful to the 150 senior level participants, that they have commissioned the design of a version of the program for the next 400 to 500 managers in the company.

Strategies for Leadership and Organizational Development:
From Programs to Systems at Johnson & Johnson

The key to understanding leadership development (and almost everything) at Johnson & Johnson lies in the commitment to its Credo and its philosophy of decentralization. In 1886, when Robert W. Johnson founded the firm, his aim was "to alleviate pain and disease."[7] Shortly after the turn of the century, he expanded this view into a business

234 • The Future

ideology rooted in the belief that service to customers and concern for employees should be ranked ahead of returns to shareholders. This philosophy was articulated in a number of ways throughout the history of the company until, in 1943, Robert W. Johnson, Jr., codified the ideology in a document entitled *Our Credo*. The article has been periodically reviewed, challenged and slightly revised, although the hierarchy of responsibility from customers to employees to shareholders, along with the concept of *fair* return rather than maximum profitability, has remained constant throughout the firm's history.[8] There is an interesting Harvard Business School case study on how J&J puts its Credo into action, including how the Credo affects organizational structure, internal planning processes, leadership development, compensation systems, and strategic business decisions. The case also discusses how the Credo serves as a tangible guide for action in critical times such as the 1982 Tylenol crisis.[9]

J&J believes a total commitment to and universal familiarity with the Credo is the key to successful implementation of a decentralization philosophy that is also sacrosanct for the company. Its structure, with approximately 168 separate companies with their own president, management boards, financial statements, brand names, and corporate logos sends a clear signal:

> ❝ *J&J wants leaders to operate the autonomous, entrepreneurial business units with total commitment to the company's core values.* ❞

Commitment to decentralization, allowing leading units tremendous autonomy beneath the umbrella of the Credo, explains why the J&J leadership development initiatives previously discussed in this book were not undertaken with more direction from top corporate management. J&J is constantly looking for ways to add value at the corporate level without diminishing the autonomy of managers throughout its family of companies.

In 1993, partially because of input from the *Creating Our Future Program* (Executive Conference II discussed in Chapter 6) and with direction from McKinsey & Co., the Johnson & Johnson Executive Committee began a process called *FrameworkS* to examine and clarify key issues facing the firm. FrameworkS initiatives were created that focused on matters like US healthcare reform, global consumer healthcare opportunities, organizational changes, as well as specific opportunities in Europe and China. A 1995 FrameworkS initiative (FrameworkS VI) was specifically targeted at "Leadership, People and Team Work." As one might expect at Johnson & Johnson, a mix of Executive Committee members and senior managers from a range of J&J companies were involved as participants in this project. Through this initiative, in the midst of widespread recognition of its business successes in 1995, Johnson & Johnson began the process of reinventing its approach to leadership development both in response to feedback on its current initiatives, and in anticipation of challenges expected to emerge over the coming decade.

FrameworkS VI began with a short but intensive research effort which included an executive-level survey of needs and activities in the field, an analysis of information generated from the 360-degree feedback data-base, highlights of previous Credo Survey results, and a 1994 study, *Views On Leadership*, which reported on interviews with thirty-five top J&J executives. An executive report based on this analysis revealed that the company saw education as a strategic lever to "increase the capability of leaders as well as a method to solve immediate organizational issues through action learning or combining classroom education with focus on business problems." The report further indicated that while J&J viewed learning as a core competence, its career planning, evaluation and succession planning systems could be improved. The FrameworkS group used this information to debate the challenge of developing leadership talent in a company expected to triple in size within a decade, and committed itself to making continuous learning and knowledge creation a core competence.

Leadership development had always been viewed as an important contributor to Johnson & Johnson's ability to create a talent pool of leaders throughout the organization. Still, there was concern that anticipated levels of growth would strain its capacity to develop leaders who would be able to staff, energize and manage a $50 billion organization by the year 2005. To help focus leadership development on this important challenge, and to align the overall HRD system, the firm began the process of auditing, coordinating, and revising its HRD efforts to practice the best tenets of anticipatory learning.

If It's Not Broke, Fix It Anyway!   As we have suggested, leadership development at Johnson & Johnson would have been viewed by almost anyone as a tremendous success. The Executive Conference series was drawing rave reviews from participants and had been publicly recognized by the Chairman as being instrumental in shifting the thinking of the executive team and in providing a stimulus for new business development. Successful "Advanced Management Programs" were being conducted for middle-level managers throughout the world at such prestigious academic institutions as IMD in Switzerland, Northwestern University, University of California at Berkeley, and Duke University. Supervisory training was conducted on a decentralized basis, but built upon a competency study conducted in the late 1980s to "identify specific characteristics that affect Johnson & Johnson supervisors and to develop a behavior model of the effective supervisor." The Key Attribute Model (KAM) which grew out of this effort was the foundation for very successful supervisory training that was offered by internal trainers as well as external providers. To gain some economies of shared services while maintaining the rights and initiatives associated with decentralization, a "Learning Services Consortium" had been created to pull together a catalogue of courses offered by outside vendors who had been certified to meet J&J standards. A total of 82 courses in six major locations were available for a variety of skills and managerial training ranging from "Active Listening" to "Writing for Impact."

To create the future rather than react to it, reexamination of the existing successful base began in 1995. Ongoing programs such as the Advanced Management Program were put on hold and a new concept of "core" educational strategy began to evolve. It was understood that the Credo along with its attendant J&J values would be the single greatest differentiator for the company and, with leadership issues, should provide the foundation for the majority of any core program. It was further recognized that some core programs would probably need to be designed specifically for individuals as they first became managers, as they became managers of managers, and as they became board members of operating companies and moved into their first executive-level responsibility.

As a result of its debates, the FrameworkS group came up with a set of recommendations for a new approach to leadership development at J&J. For first-level managers, one module would focus on the Credo and what it means to individuals in basic management jobs. Because of the large numbers of people involved in this constituency, delivery would be by line executives and advanced technology to minimize time away from the job. While content would be "suggested" for the regions, local autonomy would be preserved. For middle-management programs, it was determined that line managers would deliver with assistance from appropriate technology such as CD-ROM or interactive video programs. These would gradually replace classroom education in the 21st century. For managers of managers, the program will focus on Credo issues and their impact on regional leadership challenges. These would be delivered on a regional basis around the world.

Because of the corporate level responsibilities associated with executive roles, the core program for new board members would focus on how the Credo of Leadership Values played out within the J&J organization. To provide direct contact with executives throughout the world and to provide exposure for high-potential individuals in this category, this level initiative would take place in New Brunswick with some traditional classroom sessions involving global leadership issues and 360-degree feedback relative to the Credo and key leadership competencies.

Summary

Johnson & Johnson recognized the evolution of leadership development in a world where leaders, and therefore organizations, are expected to be continuous learners. Their approach to leadership development has become an ongoing process which involves leaders from throughout a highly decentralized company in the creation of successive, successful initiatives that constantly reflect and address the firm's changing environment. In this manner, leadership development at Johnson & Johnson is conducted in a manner consistent with the values and strategy of the total organization.

The current redesign of leadership development is based on a view of where the organization wishes to be in ten years. Because of this, the company is committed to utilizing emerging technologies and addressing evolving issues that are crucial to long-term competitiveness. And, by involving line executives in various regions of the world, Johnson & Johnson is creating a cadre of "partners" with whom the challenge of leadership development will be shared. The company exemplifies the move toward creating processes that blend experience, training, education and other forms of development into a knowledge creation cycle that is tied into an aligned and integrated HRD system.

University Approaches to Corporate Partnerships:
The MIT Center for Organizational Learning

Throughout this book, we have commented on the challenge facing university business schools in the field of executive education/leadership development. Although some institutions are struggling, others are moving to provide a bridge between the creative thinking done in academic institutions and its application in the business world. The Organizational Learning Center at MIT provides a striking example of how one university reaches out to various corporate partners to bridge the gap between research and practice while enriching the competencies of all participants.

For years, Peter Senge labored in relative obscurity as a research director of the New Management Project at MIT's Sloan School of Management. A protege of Jay Forrester (the inventor of core memory and the father of systems dynamics), Senge was attempting to bring some of the rigor of systems dynamics to the softer areas of leadership and organizational behavior. The tremendous success of Senge's best-selling book *The Fifth Discipline*[10] in 1990 moved him and his work into the forefront of American thought. As a result, the New Management Project has evolved into the Center for Organizational Learning, and today it is one of the best examples of a partnership between talented researchers and leading business practitioners.

The Center officially began in 1991 and grew rapidly to its self-imposed limit of 20 company sponsors. In January, 1996, another 20 firms were on a waiting list to become members. Approximately 1000 had attended the five-day Core Competencies program. The Center was in the process of assessing its organization and mission. The statement of purpose was evolving but seemed to include the following:

> *To encourage a global community of people and organizations working together to develop, test, disseminate, and implement theory and method for more effective systems of:*

> – *organizing work*
> – *organizational learning, and*
> – *leadership*[11]

The Center for Organizational Learning describes itself as *a consortium of innovative organizations working with MIT researchers to advance the state-of-the-art in building learning organizations through collaborative research and practice.* One major premise underlying the Center's work is that individuals and organizations must fundamentally alter both thinking and management practices in order to thrive in an increasingly dynamic and interdependent world. A second premise is that these essential fundamental changes, because they *are* so fundamental, are difficult to achieve while working in isolation. While individual companies have different purposes and businesses, the core processes and systems that define their work have a great deal in common. To explore and test the hypothesis, the COL was formed as a research consortium focused on developing new learning tools. COL's goal is to achieve a "significant impact on management practice and on management education."

Partners in Building Learning Organizations

According to Senge, "the center is designed to spread ideas, to create a few successful models of the learning organization that cannot be ignored."[12] Recently, the following organizations were involved in various aspects of the Center: Amoco Production Company, AT&T, EDS, Federal Express, Ford Motor Company, GS Technologies, Harley Davidson, Herman Miller, Hewlett Packard, Intel Corporation, Merck & Co., Motorola, National Semiconductor, Pacific Bell, Philips Display, Quality Management Network, Shell Oil Company and US West.

The Structure of the COL The research agenda of the center is determined by representatives of sponsoring organizations, working with faculty and research staff at MIT. Together, they select and research areas of common interest. Most projects entail designing learning processes within an organization and studying their effectiveness. Typically, during their first year of involvement, sponsoring organizations participate and focus on a variety of core *foundation-building* activities. These activities establish a base of experience and understanding upon which more specific learning capabilities can be developed. Essentially, the first year of membership is spent gaining an understanding of center language, tools and perspectives so as to build a foundation for creating a project specifically tailored to the sponsor's needs and interests. This involves sending a cadre of managers to various Center programs and activities to gain an understanding of COL's work and its philosophies. In addition, sponsoring organizations have opportunities to participate in a variety of *capacity-building* activities. These activities are designed to develop a core group of people inside the organization with the requisite skills, knowledge, and commitment required to support pilot projects and additional organization change efforts.

Sponsoring organizations make a substantial annual contribution that enables them to participate in the foundation-building activities of the Center. These include a five-day core course, semi-annual meetings, seminars, advanced courses, dialogue courses, and opportunities for networking with researchers and other sponsors. Organizations may also participate in optional capacity-building activities which are research focused and involve additional costs depending on the level of MIT resources required. While some potential members wince at the high membership fee, COL provides three major benefits to sponsoring organizations:

1 Sponsors are guaranteed several places in Center seminars and workshops are guaranteed. In many instances, the tuition for these programs would cost as much as the membership fee.
2 Membership provides an unparalleled opportunity to network with highly involved (and evolved) managers who are wrestling with some of the most significant issues of the day in innovative ways. Membership meetings provide detailed insight into the successes (and set-backs) of cutting-edge projects.
3 Project formulation and execution are often handled by MIT faculty and staff whose time is billed at a fraction of their usual consulting rates.

Research and Learning Agenda

COL's current research agenda and member projects can be grouped into the following four major areas.

1. Learning Laboratory Projects These efforts focus on particular areas where teams are attempting to build in-depth knowledge of generic management issues. The learning laboratories may help managers understand how to reduce the time of new product development, examine the effects of service quality and value-added services and streamline the supply.

In these projects, COL staffers work in partnership with companies to develop, implement, and assess ongoing learning processes that can be integrated with how people actually do their work. For example, a learning laboratory for surfacing, testing, and improving mental models may become part of a company's product development process, or customers and sales people may be combined to build a joint knowledge of complex global logistics issues. Current learning laboratory projects are underway at Ford, Federal Express, Harley Davidson and National Semiconductor. These projects are likely to utilize some of the tools and concepts associated with the discipline of system dynamics, the original thrust of the center.

2. Dialogue Projects These activities focus on enhancing the depth and generative nature of conversation in diverse working teams. Teams are defined as groups of people who need one another to take action. First-generation dialogue projects have been conducted in different types of organizational settings and have been characterized by embedded sources of conflict. Examples of current dialogue projects include union–management relations at GS Technologies (formally ARMCO Steel), healthcare organization stakeholders in the community of Grand Junction, Colorado, and urban leaders in Boston, Massachusetts.

A recent issue of *Organizational Dynamics* was focused on the practice of dialogue.[13] The process appears to be powerful in breaking down some of the barriers that affect some attempts at communication. Despite the praise of its advocates, and most participants in this process, the concept of openness and honesty is frightening to many. The Ford Project was viewed by everyone involved as a great success. A new model Lincoln Continental was ahead of schedule with record lows in defects, yet the project manager was asked to take early retirement. He feels, and others agree, this may have been precipitated by the fact that many managers were uncomfortable with the new environment being created through the work with COL.

GS Technologies makes steel for mining machinery and mattress coils. In 1990 when it joined the COL, markets were eroding, labor relations were hostile (almost 500 grievances were on file), and employment had been reduced from 5000 to 1000 in just a decade. Three years later, the firm had successfully skirted bankruptcy and had seen sales and profits increase dramatically. Unfortunately, workers who were not involved in the dialogue process grew suspicious and voted out the union leader who had championed learning-organization ideas at GST. The new union leadership passed a motion banning dialogue from the shop floor. In retrospect, management realizes that it made the mistake of not spreading the program fast and deep enough. Company CEO, Robert Cushman remains committed to the ideas of the learning organization, but realizes that his vision will now take longer to achieve.[14]

As new dialogue sites are being initiated, the Center expects to begin to distinguish between different types of dialogues such as *generative* dialogue, which is a sustained inquiry into the deepest assumptions and habits underlying everyday experience, and *strategic* dialogue, which focuses on particular questions critical to the success and effectiveness of the organization.

3. CEO Leadership Project   This initiative involves an inquiry into the evolving nature of leadership required to build and sustain learning organizations and the particular issues which must be addressed by top management, such as the evolution of corporate governance and the moral foundation of senior managers. Current participants in the project include CEO- or president-level executives from Harley Davidson, Herman Miller, GS Technologies, Philips Display Components, Shell Oil and Analog Devices.

4. Learning Organization Curriculum   These projects currently involve implementing and assessing the effectiveness of a five-day learning organization core curriculum. This curriculum is intended to provide an experiential introduction to the core concepts and disciplines required to build learning organizations. Also, there is a pilot project underway at EDS aimed at developing, implementing and assessing an extended learning experience involving classwork, business projects and ongoing coaching. The target audience for this effort is a group of 40 EDS managers all of whom are committing about half their time over the year to the project. Current plans include making a similar project available to other COL sponsoring organizations.

In addition to the four major research areas, the learning center itself is a conscious experiment in building a learning organization at MIT. Staff members at the center attempt to actively practice the principles associated with the "five disciplines." Regular staff meetings make use of the dialogue process. Support staff, as well as researchers, are highly conversant with the tools of system dynamics and practiced systems thinking. There is general agreement as to the vision of how the learning center could "make a difference in the world." This is not simply a grandiose statement. People at the learning center are committed to creating a better vision of organizational life than most of them have known in any other setting. Each person at the center seems committed to improving his or her "personal mastery."

A Win-Win Partnership

The center is built on a model of partnership between academic researchers and business practitioners. Research is focused on areas that are of strategic importance to business, as well as interesting and relevant from an academic research perspective. Such a partnership will only be viable if it leads to mutual benefits that are both significant and unique.

Sponsors of the center's research can expect the following more specific benefits:

- Develop internal capacity in the form of individuals and groups with competence in basic learning disciplines, including systems thinking, working with mental models, dialogue and personal mastery.
- Gain access to leading-edge learning tools under development at the center.
- Build knowledge of what is being learned about building learning organizations, for example, new roles for leaders, innovations in organizational structures and processes, and dilemmas in moving from traditional authoritarian cultures.

- Work with and learn from other companies committed to developing new learning capabilities.
- Gain assistance from MIT staff with in-house learning projects.

In turn, MIT benefits from the partnership through access to research funding that enables them to develop better theories of generic organizational systems and processes, new tools which embody these theories, and practical knowledge of the barriers to organizational learning and the capabilities needed to overcome these barriers. Specifically, the organizations participating in the learning center enrich the research process through:

- Focusing research on critical management issues
- Providing field research sites
- Bringing the practical know-how of leading organizations
- Establishing credibility, based on field testing, for innovative tools and methods, and
- Creating internship opportunities for MIT students.

Everyone associated with the COL seems to be committed to creating win-win situations. Sponsoring organizations do make a significant financial contribution. In return for this commitment, however, they are involved with some of the best minds in contemporary business thinking. MIT benefits because some of its faculty get a unique exposure to real-life business laboratories, graduate students who receive internships have a wonderful blend of theory and practice, and new learning tools are developed and refined in such a way as to benefit the practice of management far beyond the limits of COL sponsors.

Endnotes

1 This description was based on personal correspondence with Victoria Guthrie and Bob Burnside of CCL. Also, see Burnside, R. and V. Guthrie, *Training for Action: A New Approach to Executive Development* (Report N. 153), Greensboro, NC: Center For Creative Leadership, 1992; also Conger, J., *Learning To Lead*, San Francisco: Jossey-Bass, 1992, pp. 192–198.

2 See Young, D.A. and N. M. Dixon, *Getting Results from an Action Based Leadership Development Program*, unpublished manuscript.

3 This description was based on personal correspondence with Deepak (Dick) Sethi, LDP program director. Also see "AT&T Grooms Middle Managers With New-Look Leadership Program," *Training Director's Forum*, **11**, 6, 1995; Moore, M.T., "AT&T Prepares Managers For Change," *USA Today*, August 14, 1995, p. 7B; Lancaster, H., "The Right Training Helps Even Dinosaurs Adapt To Change," *Wall Street Journal*, March 28, 1995, p. B1; Gatewood, D., "AT&T Managers Play a New Game," *New York Newsday*, October 23, 1994, p. 7.

4 This information was taken from an unpublished presentation prepared by the AT&T School of Business entitled, "Beyond the Smiles Test."

5 This description is based on personal correspondence with Chris Giangrasso, director of ELI, as well as first-hand experience with the institute.

6 The ELI Action Project process and roles were developed by Maria Taylor, Virginia Freeman Tucker, and Albert A. Vicere at Penn State.

7 Foster, Lawrence G., *A Company That Cares*, New Brunswick, N.J.: Johnson & Johnson, 1986, p. 17.

8 Aguilar, Francis J. and Arvin D. Bhambri, *Johnson & Johnson (A)*, Harvard Business School Case No. 384–053, 3.

9 Collins, James C., and Jerry I. Porras, *Build to Last: Success Habits of Visionary Companies*, New York: Harper Business, 1994, p. 80.

10 Senge, Peter M., *The Fifth Discipline*, New York: Doubleday, 1990.

11 Clanon, Jeff and Peter Senge, Correspondence dated January 5, 1996.

12 Dumaine, Brian, "Mister Learning Organization," *Fortune*, October 17, 1994, p. 148.

13 *Organizational Dynamics*, Autumn, 1993, **19**, 2.

14 Dumaine, 1994, op cit.

10

MEETING THE
CHALLENGE

In the Introduction, we discussed the analogy between the discovery of a New World in 1492 and the contemporary discovery of a new world for leadership development. In a new world, old maps are no longer appropriate. No matter how thoroughly he looked, Columbus could not find the Ganges River in his Caribbean new world. The maps which showed that river were accurate in a totally different environment but irrelevant to his new surroundings. It was necessary for Columbus to create new maps for a new reality. These maps were quite primitive at the beginning. The map maker could see only what was in the immediate vicinity but had no idea what might be over the next horizon. Yet, these crude maps made life easier for the next adventurers, despite being far from a finished product.

As we ponder today's changing business environment, and as we review the exemplars presented in Chapter 9, it appears that our old maps for leadership development no longer accurately reflect contemporary reality. At the same time, it also seems that where we stand today is simply a temporary stage. Throughout this book, we have presented a perspective on the field of executive education/ leadership development – where it was in the past, where it is at present, and where it appears the field is headed. The map in Figure 10.1 illustrates what we call the "Seven Ps" – the seven key elements of the leadership development process. The map follows the evolution of these key elements from the past, through today's transition state, to a view of the future. In presenting this map, we are both summarizing the discussions in this book, and also proposing a preliminary prescription for enhancing the impact of future strategic leadership development initiatives.

Participants

Participating in a leadership development program today is a very different experience than it was a generation ago. Many of our readers will recall programs for which participants arrived with little understanding of the curriculum that lay before them. At check-in, they were usually given a series of books and an agenda that outlined how each hour was to be spent for the duration of the program. Extensive amounts of blank paper were provided in the notebook since the major role of the participant was to be a listener. He (only occasionally was it a she) was expected to take voluminous notes from the assembled presenters who would share their insights and knowledge, often in discrete 90-minute segments.

That model has evolved dramatically over the past few years. Today, participants expect not just to listen to information presented by experts, but also to put that information to work by engaging in case discussions, debating recommendations or alternatives, and sometimes making presentations based on their conclusions regarding class assignments. During the transitionary period, these assignments frequently were related to a business case that had little direct relevance to participants' situations back at the office; however, it was hoped that the participants

Figure 10.1   The Evolution of Leadership Development

Key elements	Past	Transition	Future
Participants	Listener	Student	Learner
Program design	Event	Curriculum	Ongoing process
Purpose	Knowledge	Wisdom	Action
Period focus	Past	Present	Future
Players	Specialists	Generalists	Partners
Presentation focus	Style	Content	Process/outcome
Place	University campus	Corporate facility	Anywhere

would be able to make applications when and if similar situations presented themselves.

In the evolving new world of leadership development, participants will listen occasionally, interact frequently in simulated situations to test their skills or understanding, and devote a significant portion of time to demonstrating their ability to apply concepts to real challenges through some form of action learning as described in Chapter 9. In those examples and others throughout this book, we have discussed the value of hands-on, real-world leadership development initiatives. These efforts are paving a path toward a new world for leadership development, one that blends work experience, classroom instruction, and teamwork into a powerful process for change and development.

We now know participants generally take learning to the level most relevant to their immediate needs or level of motivation. With action learning, some participants may make minimal effort and learn relatively little. However, our experience is that most individuals rise to demanding challenges, expand their knowledge base, and make significant contributions to organizational goals when learning takes place through a hands-on approach. Participants who take the experience seriously usually find themselves rewarded both personally and professionally. Organizations that take the experience seriously usually find their investments in leadership development have a true payoff. By making learning actionable, interest and motivation tend to increase. What's more, as we saw in the examples presented in Chapter 9, the end results of participation in a program are more observable and measurable.

Program Design

As we noted in the Introduction and Chapter 1, most organizations traditionally viewed participation in an executive or leadership development program as a once or twice in a lifetime event. A person viewed as having the potential to become a CEO might be sent to the one-year Sloan Program at MIT or the thirteen-week Harvard Advanced Management Program. Individuals who were viewed as having significant potential but not a probable future as a CEO, might be sent to a four-week program at another leading business school. Attendance was always an important rite of passage, but it often had little relationship to other developmental activities taking place in a progressive career. As we reported earlier, current research suggests that participants in executive/leadership development programs no longer are specially targeted individuals who have been "anointed" by senior management for future promotion.[1] At General Electric, the "Work-Out" program has involved a total of 220,000 people, and on any given week 20,000 GE employees will be participating in some stage of a Work-Out effort.

It appears that during the transition period, leading companies evolved beyond the "programs as an isolated event" mentality toward a focus on preparing leaders for key career transitions by designing somewhat lock-step, career-long corporate curricula.[2] One successful corporate practitioner described his firm's approach as a "slalom course."

Figure 10.2 illustrates the approach used by one of the leading corporate educational programs of the 1980s. Every manager was expected to engage in at least 40 hours of management education each year. At each stage of an individual's career, he or she was expected to attend a program appropriate for that stage of development. Individuals promoted to a management job were expected to attend a "new manager program" within 30 days of receiving their new position. This would take place at a corporate facility where a carefully defined curriculum was presented to new managers from throughout the company. The next one or two development events were expected to take place in individual business units.

Once managers achieved middle management status, they were expected to again make the pilgrimage to corporate headquarters where they would receive training that was appropriate for their new responsibilities. After having satisfied this corporate requirement, future events would be scheduled on a regional or divisional basis until executive rank was achieved. At that point they were invited to attend the top-level corporate program focused on general management issues. There, they would probably have a chance to interact with the CEO or key members of the executive committee. This particular firm was often cited as an industry leader because it had evolved development to an organized set of events that were planned over a person's entire career. Figure 10.3 reveals that most leading corporations were utilizing this approach by the early 1990s.

This growing commitment to continuous learning as a source of

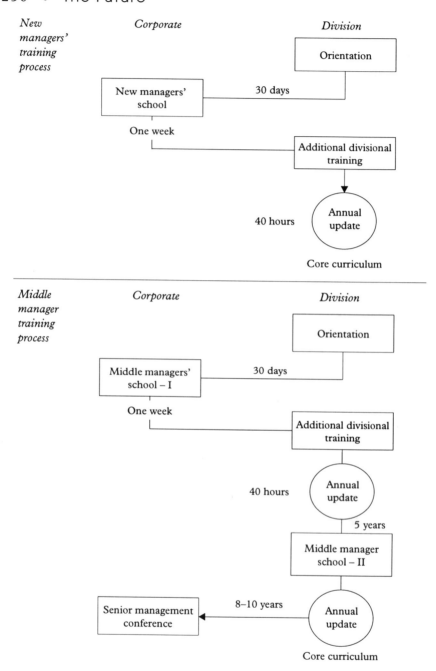

Figure 10.2 Training processes
Source: Robert M. Fulmer and Ken Graham "A New Era of Management Education"
Journal of Management Development, **12**, 1993, p. 37.

Figure 10.3 Management Education Program Coverage

Company	Pre-management	Supervisory	Manager level	Director level	Officer level	Internal executive program senior executive
GE	Yes, 6–12 months	Yes, New appointment 90 days	Yes, New appointment 90 days	Yes, New appointment 90 days	Yes, New appointment 90 days	Yes
HP	None, –	Yes, New appointment 90 days	Yes, New appointment 90 days	Yes, New appointment 90 days	Yes, New appointment 90 days	Yes
IBM	Yes, 6–12 months	Yes, New appointment 90 days	Yes, New appointment 90 days	Yes, New appointment 90 days	Yes, New appointment 90 days	Yes, New appointment 90 days
Tenneco	None, –	Company selects, Yes	Company selects, Yes	Company selects, Yes	Company selects, Yes	None
UTC	Yes, –	Yes, New appointment 90 days	Company selects, Yes	Company selects, Yes	Company selects, Yes	–
Xerox	Yes, 6–12 months	Yes, New appointment 90 days	Yes, New appointment 90 days	Yes, New appointment 90 days	Yes, New appointment 90 days	Yes
Allied Signal	None, –	Yes, Sector selects	Yes, Sector selects	Yes, –	In progress	Yes
Lockheed	Yes, 12–18 months	Yes, Branch selects	Yes, Branch selects	Yes, Company selects	Corporation selects	Corporation selects
Bell	Yes, –	Yes, New appointment 90 days	Yes, New appointment 6 months	Yes, –	Yes	None
Coca-Cola	None, –	Yes, Division selects (develops and conducts)	Yes, Division selects	Yes, Company division selects	Yes, Company division selects	None
Federated	None, –	Yes, New appointment	Yes, New appointment	Yes, On-going	Yes, On-going	Yes, Corporate

Source: Robert M. Fulmer and Ken Graham "A New Era of Management Education," *Journal of Management Development,* **12**, 1993, p. 35.

competitive advantage has led to college-sized organizations being created to help their firms become "learning organizations."[3] Jeanne C. Meister identified 30 companies which share the common goal of seeing "training as a process of life-long learning rather than a place to get trained." As Meister pointed out in her book, *Corporate Quality Universities*[4]

> ❝ *successful firms – those who will be prominent players in the 21st century – must do more than commit to training their work force. Truly dominant players understand the need to organize themselves as learning systems, where every part of the system – hiring, training, and recognition of employees – promotes both individual and collective learning.* ❞

In March 1996, Meister updated her original research and suggested that almost 1000 firms had or were actively investigating the formation of a corporate university with particular emphasis on financial services, health care, utilities and telecommunications. While the average operating budgets for corporate universities had grown to $12.4 million, 60 percent of the groups reported budgets of $5 million or less. Of course, the budgets of giants like Motorola, GE, and Anderson significantly increased the average figure. Perhaps more significantly, organizations with corporate universities reported spending 2.5 percent of their payroll on learning, almost twice the national average.[5]

In a recent study, Bob Miles analyzed four leading corporate universities sponsored by Motorola, GE, Arthur Andersen, and Apple Computer. He observed that all four were part of organizations that shared similar strategic orientations – a focus on aggressive growth and continuous innovation. However, while some placed more emphasis on supporting employee career development through their corporate universities, others were tilted in the direction of addressing key business issues.[6] For example, Arthur Andersen has a carefully designed career ladder with courses required at each stage in a person's career. The company is developing a career tracking system that includes every employee throughout the world. On the other hand, GE has organized its Crotonville facility around particular "moments of opportunity" when leadership development can make a major impact on individual and organizational performance. These "moments" occur when an individual moves into a position of expanded scope and responsibility, and is therefore struggling to make the transition to a new level of management thinking. Regardless of which of these directions a corporate university takes, it tends to share a major focus on linking the development of leadership competencies, skills, and perspectives with the strategic imperatives of the sponsoring firm.

While the corporate university movement has be viewed as a positive affirmation of an organization's commitment to life-long learning, a slight danger looms on the horizon. Traditional universities typically are not viewed as the most flexible, progressive and change-oriented institutions. Practices which date back several centuries are still embraced because of tradition rather than contemporary appropriateness.[7] Any strength, if carried to excess, will become a weakness. The commitment to learning which leads an organization to establish a corporate university must be carefully monitored, kept flexible, and focused on the strategic imperatives of the sponsoring organization if maximum benefit from the investment is to be reaped. To add real value, a corporate university must maintain its focus as a means to corporate success, and avoid the pitfalls of becoming a storehouse of programs and courses.

As we look toward the future, the pace of change and competition have caused the stakes for leadership and organizational development to increase significantly. This pace is so relentless that the need for life-long education is now a given. Just as professionals in other disciplines must commit to a life-long process of learning and updating their knowledge, so too must leaders and their respective organizations. In this environment, organizations are looking for approaches to development and learning that make a real difference. The following section describes one of the most dramatic examples of current approaches to organizational learning.

Work-Out at GE

General Electric's "Work-Out" is not a typical leadership development program. Rather,

> ❝ *It is a process of concentrated decision making and empowerment to resolve issues. A team of experienced, knowledgeable people with a stake in the issue is charged to develop solutions and action plans. They are*

sanctioned by the key stakeholder to proceed with implementation (or given clear reasons why not to proceed, or specify direction for further study). There is follow-up to ensure completion of the action plans.[8] **"**

The Work-Out initiative is part of GE's effort to create a culture of speed, simplicity, and self-confidence in a manner consistent with continuous improvement. Expected results of work-out activities include:

- Boundaryless, cross-functional teamwork
- Empowered employees
- Building of trust
- Focus on customers
- Focus on greater use of process thinking
- Improvement of business process.

The term "work-out" refers to the company's efforts to reduce the amount of work people have to do by getting rid of bureaucratic red tape and minutia ... As a result of these sessions, GE was able to downsize and increase productivity at the same time.

Steve Kerr, Chief Learning Officer
General Electric

Key Roles in Work-Out   *Business leaders* within a particular GE organization will define the issues to be addressed in Work-Out sessions, select team members and approve recommendations made by the initiative. They also have responsibility for removing barriers that might exist to the implementation of an approved recommendation.

While originally facilitated by an elite team of university-based professors, GE now has several hundred trained Work-Out *facilitators* whose job it is to sense problems in the organization, facilitate team building and problem solving, and provide support for follow-up actions to ensure that implementation of recommendations actually takes place.

The heart of Work-Out is a team of *employees* who are sometimes joined by customers and/or suppliers. They are asked to articulate problems, develop recommendations to address these problems, and then get whatever help is needed to implement the recommendations when they have been approved.

Typically, 60 to 100 people meet for an open agenda event aimed at *reducing work*. These are Phase I Town Meetings. Smaller groups (20 to 60 people) become involved in Phase II meetings which focus on *problem solving*. Phase III sessions typically involve *process mapping* and may involve sub-groups of 10 to 20 people who focus on a process rather than a problem. In Phase IV, natural work teams facilitate the *implementation* of their own recommendations.

Key elements of the Work-Out process are shown in Figure 10.4. But what about Work-Out's effectiveness – has it made a difference at GE? In *Control Your Own Destiny Or Someone Else Will*, Noel Tichy noted:

> ❝ *Work-Out has made believers of GE's top 1,000 or 2,000 executives. I've been inside scores of the world's best and biggest companies, and I can't think of another where intellectual freedom and like-mindedness coexist to an equal degree... As a formal mechanism for sustaining a revolutionary process – and for transferring real power to employees – Work-Out is unsurpassed so far.*[9] ❞

Purpose

In a simpler era it was assumed that specific types of new knowledge were required at different stages of a person's career,. Consequently, it was possible to design programs that would provide this knowledge in advance of when it would be needed. This was particularly true as a person approached the general management stage. As functional specialists began to be considered for additional promotion, or sometimes immediately before becoming a general manager, they would be sent to a general management program at a leading university. These programs were often referred to as a mini-MBA. They provided fundamental knowledge of the tools and techniques of the core functional disciplines. This knowledge was viewed as critical to broadening the arsenal of management tools and techniques in an executive's repertoire.

During the transition period, more sophisticated programs provided opportunities for executives in training to practice using those tools in complex simulations (often computerized business games). These sophisticated simulations were used to help participants apply the knowledge they had acquired to solving problems in a simulated world. Although simulations offer a good opportunity for informal practice,

Figure 10.4 Elements of an Effective Work-Out Process

(1) Issue:	The issue or topic of the Work-Out session is selected by the Sponsor(s). The issue is linked to the key business initiatives.
(2) Sponsor(s):	The key stakeholder(s) who will benefit from the workout process charters a Champion to form a Work-Out team. Sponsors communicate the Work-Out plan and objectives.
(3) Champions:	A Champion frames the issue, clarifies the topics to address and selects participants for the Work-Out team. (A planning committee and support resources may be needed to plan and conduct the more complex Work-Out sessions.)
(4) Participants:	The participants are chosen to represent a broad cross-section of people who have the knowledge and skill to resolve the issue and (given that they are empowered) can implement action plans to permanently fix the issue.
(5) Planning/Data:	The Champion and/or planning committee plans the Work-Out session, assembles background information and makes expert help available to the Work-Out team so that action plans are data-based.
(6) Facilitators:	People experienced in building teams and capable of coaching groups through the process are made available to the Work-Out team.
(7) Empowerment/ accountability	The Work-Out team is given time to resolve the issue, develop action plans, and present them to business leaders. It is empowered and held accountable for implementing the action plan.
(8) Follow-up	The Champion is responsible for following up to ensure that the team has the resources and help to implement the action plan on a timely basis. A reunion is scheduled to ensure follow-up.

Source: "Work-Out Continuous Improvement," unpublished GE document, March 15, 1995, p. 10.

contemporary approaches to leadership development are addressing this issue by emphasizing, through action learning, the solution of actual business problems in a real-world setting. Similarly, Peter Senge of the MIT Center for Organizational Learning has written eloquently about the importance of "practice fields" or "micro-worlds" in which managers have an opportunity to practice some of the concepts they are learning in real time.[10] Unlike professional athletes or symphony orchestra musicians, leaders seldom have an opportunity to practice their skills and receive feedback outside the real world. The growing interest in action learning techniques, as well as anticipatory learning techniques such as those taught by COL, reflects the intention to address this critical problem.

At Motorola University, an Application Consulting Team (ACT) was created in the late 1980s to help facilitate workplace application of knowledge gained from Motorola courses. The ACT is staffed by managers with twenty or more years of experience who prefer to mentor, coach and assist in the transfer of learning in their organizations rather than continuing with traditional management responsibilities. Another approach to action learning at Motorola University involves a number of corporate partnerships that focus on developing knowledge in a mutually important arena with a series of other leading firms. One illustration of this approach is the *Six Sigma Institute*. In 1990, Motorola joined with ABB, Digital Equipment, Eastman Kodak and IBM to accelerate the development of *Six Sigma Quality* and to transfer this knowledge in the most effective manner.

Another key illustration of action learning was a workshop sponsored by Bob Galvin, former Chairman of Motorola, for over 100 Motorola Senior Executives to help them understand the market potential of selected Asian countries. Rather than bringing in experts to talk about the subject, participants were asked to analyze the existing competition and to determine how Motorola could compete in those markets. After doing their homework, teams of these executives traveled to Asia to analyze local market opportunities first-hand. They were then asked to teach what they had learned to the next 3000 Motorola managers. They first studied the issue, then they verified their impressions with first-hand observations, and finally they solidified their learnings, and contributed to the company's knowledge base, by teaching what they had learned to others.[11] This approach is a good example of the Knowledge Creation Cycle (Chapter 5) in action.

Period Focus

Because of its real-world orientation, the case method has had a tremendous impact on business education. Long associated with Harvard Business School, it is utilized in the majority of executive development programs both within companies and in many other business schools. Despite the many positive aspects of the case method, the system has an inherent drawback in that a case is almost always a historical document. It reflects what could have been done, given a particular set of circumstances that existed in the past.

Many readers will recall attending programs in which 10- to 20-year-old cases were used to illustrate classic concepts. The "Chain Saw Industry In 1974"[12] is still used in many business policy programs because it does such a superb job of illustrating the difficulty of forecasting demand in the face of various environmental constraints and the impact of interacting strategies that actually play out in the competitive marketplace. While participant feedback has encouraged most instructors to use more contemporary cases, historicity is still an inherent problem.

The current focus on best practices has changed the time horizon of leadership development. Companies now want to know who is doing the best job in a particular area even if that firm is not a direct competitor of theirs. Firms in a variety of industries may look to WalMart to understand its excellence in logistics management or the extent to which ABB is able to manage the paradox of being a global company with 1300 local operating business units in 140 countries.

As we move into the new world of the future, organizations are beginning to use techniques like "future-oriented cases" or scenario development as a means of coping with this challenge. In perhaps the most comprehensive treatment of this subject, to date, John Gutman concludes that future-oriented cases can bring projections and future issues to life by encouraging problem solvers to consider the issues they will be addressing.[13] In a future-oriented case, participants are asked to develop scenarios of what the business environment will be like some time in the future.

The J&J 2000 case used in the Johnson & Johnson "Creating Our Future" program is a good example. Using this technique, participants can challenge conventional wisdom about how their industry will evolve.

Discussion, background research, and expert advice can dramatize the trends that are beginning to shape industry practices and forecast important ways that business might be different in the future. In addition, participants can focus on how actions in their own organization may help to create or mold the future. This helps them to realize that it is within their capability to influence the external environment. Finally, future-oriented cases can, under the tutelage of good case leaders, begin to explore the assumptions that undergird various participant views about the future. Awareness of a common "mental model" that can impede creative thinking is the starting point for effectively creating a new future for an organization.

This level of sophistication appears to be part of a conscious attempt on the part of firms to anticipate where opportunities are going to lie rather than where they are currently. Gary Hamel and C.K. Prahalad have alerted large numbers of managers to the importance of *Competing for the Future*."[14] They continually emphasize that the best way for an organization to deal with continuous change is for it to extend its "opportunity horizon." The Johnson & Johnson FrameworkS process for revitalizing its leadership development strategy, discussed in Chapter 9, is a good example of this kind of thinking. We believe a similar *future-focus* will dominate all aspects of the field in the years ahead.

Players

In a more comfortable and predictable world, the major players in the field of leadership development were specialists who became proficient in their roles and in managements' expectations. Professors developed teaching modules that could be inserted in a variety of program contexts. Executive program administrators in universities were expected to know the various areas of expertise that existed among their faculty and how this expertise could be combined and packaged into a program. Corporate human resource specialists became adept at knowing which university programs seemed to offer the best fit for the needs of their managers. Going to professional meetings of groups such as UNICON (The International University Consortium for Executive Education) was a pleasant, predictable event because people stayed in their appropriate roles.

During the transition period, roles began to blur. Universities began to do customized programs. Open enrollment programs offered by consulting firms proliferated. Companies began to conduct more and more programs themselves. Even individuals began to change roles, with corporate HRD managers moving to leadership positions within universities and university professors going to work in corporate HRD units. Interestingly, individuals who often top today's lists of leading practitioners in leadership development often have experience across two or three of the sectors mentioned above. Noel Tichy of the University of Michigan not only has served as a professor at several major business schools, but he worked for several years at GE while on a sabbatical, in addition to running his own successful consulting firm. Steve Kerr at GE was formerly Dean of the University of Southern California Business School and a successful consultant in his own right. Todd Jick, managing partner at the Center for Executive Development in Cambridge, Massachusetts, a very successful consulting firm, is a former faculty member at both Harvard and INSEAD.

This cross-fertilization of perspectives has contributed to the professionalization of the field and set new standards of performance for leadership development professionals.[15] Senior practitioners across all sectors are expected to be generalists, capable of designing initiatives that contribute to the strategic development of the firm, but with the professional networks needed to bring these designs to a rapid reality. In effect, they are expected to be experts at establishing partnerships. University-based program experience provides an individual with exposure to cutting-edge thinking in a variety of disciplines. It promotes commitment to honest inquiry and a willingness to seek new answers. Corporate experience adds the dimension of relevance. In a corporate setting, ideas have little currency unless they can be applied and related to corporate performance. Since most corporate executive educators operate without line authority, their success depends on their ability to build relationships, engender trust, and demonstrate the added-value of the function. These abilities are critical to the partnership-building process. Consultants must develop a broad set of analytical skills and must learn to listen more acutely than most other people. Because their own resources are often quite limited, they tend to become very good at networking and supplementing their own capabilities.

In the new world, leading practitioners build partnerships and networks that blend the above skills to enhance both organizational learning and personal/professional development. A number of firms are developing partnerships with key academics or consultants who become a semi-permanent part of the organization. This may be seen as part of a "Shadow Pyramid" as discussed in Chapter 3, or part of what Charles Handy called the *Shamrock Organization*.[16] Handy argued that like the leaves of a shamrock, today's business organization is made up of three very different groups of people. Each group is managed, paid, and organized differently, and each has quite different expectations for work. The first leaf in the shamrock organization is comprised of core employees. These are permanent employees who are viewed as essential for the ongoing business of the firm. They are expensive and their numbers are shrinking. The next leaf of Handy's shamrock consists of part-time and temporary workers, the contingency workforce. The third shamrock leaf is comprised of organizations and professionals to whom jobs are farmed out. These may be specialist sub-contractors who can do certain jobs better and cheaper. Or, as in our illustration, they may be highly trained professionals who are too expensive and too opposed to constraints to work for a single organization. Yet, by spending a significant numbers of days per year with a single organization, those "contract" employees tend to invest both time and intellectual capital to become more productive partners with that organization, leverage their skills within and have a much more visible, often dramatic impact on its performance. When, for example, Philips asked a number of academics to invest 90 days per year in the Centurion Project, it was making a major commitment to these individuals in terms of learning and income. On the other hand, the individuals who were given this opportunity brought with them high-level experience with a variety of other organizations. The same is true of many of the major corporate initiatives mentioned throughout this book.

Presentations

In assessing presenters within a traditional executive program, style often seemed to count more than content. For example, certain presenters were known to be good "closers." They left an audience with a feeling of excitement and enthusiasm that often carried through to the overall program evaluations. For program managers, these individuals provided a sure fire wrap to the experience that virtually guaranteed its success. Upon hearing about an academic study being conducted to determine what elevated certain presenters to superstars status in executive education, one seasoned human resource vice president exclaimed, *why does anybody need a study to determine that? The answer is simple. It's entertainment!* Neither the executive nor his comment was as naive as might first appear.

> Content must be packaged and presented in a way that is well-received and understood. For individuals unaccustomed to sitting in classrooms for days on end, a presenter's ability to deliver information in a timely and engaging way is an important attribute.

During today's transition period, while entertainment value is still important, the corresponding demand for content relevance has increased significantly. The message not only must be presented well, but it must also be an important message. There is little tolerance for sessions that might be described as "fluff," despite their ability to entertain. As we move through the 1990s, the challenge for presenters is developing the ability to process as well as present applicable, relevant information. The most noted executive educators are becoming those who are able to involve participants in application processes that often result in the resolution of real business issues. This kind of processing is at the heart of action learning.

There is a Chinese proverbs that says "A good leader is one whom the people respect, the poor leader is the one who people hate, but the great leader is one who, when the people have finished, they say, *we did it ourselves.*" This sentiment is very appropriate for future leadership development initiatives. In many ways, the future is calling for a difficult adjustment by traditional presenters. No longer revered simply for what they know, success for presenters is equally related to what they are able to stimulate others to accomplish. This shift toward a more process-oriented delivery mode requires new approaches to program design such that when a program is completed, participants believe that "they have done it themselves."

Place

As we have suggested, executive education was traditionally reserved for a select handful of future senior leaders and delivered primarily by business schools. As recently as 1988, a report prepared for the American Assembly of Collegiate Schools of Business reported that two business schools, Harvard and Stanford, had one-third of the total market for executive education programs in general management.[17] Corporate HRD directors, university program managers and participants agreed with the importance of avoiding traditional surroundings in order to contemplate, listen, and learn. Location even played a part in some peoples' decision making. Some executives, not unreasonably, would prefer to go to Sea Island, Georgia, in February rather than Chicago. One British participant in our research commented, "Management development's greatest contribution in the UK has been to the restoration of country houses." (Although he was referring to the recent tendency for both users and providers to make massive investments in training centers as evidence of their commitment to executive education/leadership development, careful readers might detect an ironical sideswipe at the UK's management development industry.) However, commitment to learning and leadership development can be measured in many other ways.

University campuses are still important settings for leadership development. Participants often report that it is easier to change their own paradigms and see things from a different perspective when they are "on sabbatical" in the midst of a bustling, academic environment. Nevertheless, more and more leaders are participating in leadership development programs that are conducted in their own facilities. Many companies now boast campuses that compete with those at major colleges and universities. Arthur Andersen purchased a former college campus outside Chicago and has satellite educational facilities in Europe and Asia. Andersen's worldwide investment in education exceeds $300 million dollars, or more than seven percent of its total revenues. The Andersen Center at St. Charles, Illinois, operates with a staff of 200 educational specialists. Over 60,000 trainees come to the St. Charles campus each year to study accounting practices, gain industry knowledge, or study fundamental business skills such as business ethics, negotiation, presentation skills, and so on. Slightly more than half of them work for Andersen. The remaining trainees are clients or outside customers.

Andersen has invested almost $150 million in the 645-acre St. Charles campus which it purchased from Saint Dominic College in 1971. The facility can accommodate 1700 overnight students. It boasts 130 classrooms, six auditoriums, two amphitheaters, five large conference centers, 1000 computer work stations, a staff complex, several restaurants, a barber shop, a shoe repair shop, a book store, a discotheque and a nine-hole golf course. In addition to the professional staff of 200, the Center employs 200 support personnel and a comparable number of operations people.[18]

Organizations such as Andersen, General Electric, and Motorola can justify their large commitment to such facilities because of their tremendous throughput of participants. Most companies, however, are finding it more efficient to make a commitment to what we might call "learning space" rather than to hotel operations or conference centers. For example, rather than making an investment in major conference and lodging facilities, Johnson & Johnson conducts its Executive Conference on approximately half a floor of a New Brunswick, New Jersey office building. Participants stay at negotiated rates at a nearby Hyatt Hotel. Rather than a dedicated "case room," the Executive Conference series uses portable risers that create a tiered room and provide space to run wiring for individual computers that tie into the company's LAN system. Breakout rooms for small group discussions are available on the same floor. Meals are served buffet style in a room adjacent to the company cafeteria on a different floor. Since the Executive Conference runs approximately ten times per year, the flexibility provided by this arrangement is a more cost-effective alternative than going off site to a specialized conference center or making the commitment to the high fixed costs associated with a full-time corporate conference facility.

CSX Corporation, a $10 billion international transportation company offering a variety of transportation, intermodal logistics, and related services, announced in 1995 its commitment to create a "State of the Art CSX Learning Center" that will "provide a learning environment for present and future CSX leaders that fosters efficient individual growth and promotes effective inter-unit collaborative learning." Their commitment includes a plan for effective physical space and for the best use of technology as a learning tool. While this is to be a world-class facility, it will be located in one of their division headquarters buildings. The Center will include two large classrooms, an auditorium, breakout rooms, networking areas and support services. Again, CSX concluded that this type of facility would be the most-effective solution to its needs rather than the creation of a separate campus. Regardless of which alternative an organization chooses, it is clear that the caliber of ideas discussed is more important than the quality of the facilities.

Despite this focus on facilities, as we move toward the future learning is far *less* likely to be associated with a particular place. As we saw at Johnson & Johnson, participants increasingly will log onto interactive learning experiences via networked computers. They will participate in video-conferencing involving colleagues from around the world without the requirement for extensive travel time. They will also go physically to a variety of places where people are brought together for some form of "distributed" learning, whether that be through simultaneous broadcast of presentations and discussions, some other form of electronic multi-media learning experience, or, rather than bringing people to massive training centers with all the time and expense involved, through more traditional programs delivered at numerous sites around the world that could include a hotel conference room in Singapore, a public conference center in Brussels, or a corporate meeting facility in New Jersey. In fact, research sponsored by UNICON and Quality Dynamics, Inc. reported that respondents from corporate universities predicted that 50 percent of all their training would be delivered via technology by the year 2000.[19]

Federal Express provides a dramatic illustration of education that is not restricted by place. The company has spent almost $70 million to create an automated educational system. Annually, it spends almost five percent of payroll to enhance learning among its 40,000 couriers and customer service agents through the use of interactive video disks (IVD). Federal Express owns 1225 IVD units in 700 locations. Each has a 20–25 video disk (equivalent to 37,500 floppy disks) curriculum that is updated on a monthly basis. Each employee receives four hours of company-paid study and preparation in addition to two hours of self-administered tests semi-annually.[20] The FedEx example has a substantial training focus and a better illustration of this movement might be MIT's effort to deliver distance learning to China by satellite. Given the size of China's managerial population and the travel distances and time commitments involved for US-based faculty to go there for developmental programs,

MIT has decided that the use of new telecommunications technology is essential if MIT really wishes to serve this expanding market.

An example of face-to-face distributed learning can be found at Sterling Winthrop, which offered a series of senior and middle management programs on six continents during a three-year period. Put most simply, the company found it was easier and far more cost-effective to transport three to five instructors/facilitators to distant locations than it was to bring people from every corner of the world to a central location.

The best way to predict the future is to create it.

Peter Drucker

Any Time, Any Place, Gray Matter

Since the days of Albert Einstein, we have generally recognized that the workings of the universe involve time, place, and matter. Yet, perspectives on all three of these elements are being subjected to reexamination and redefinition within today's new physics paradigm. Similarly, new paradigms for business development are causing HRD professionals to reexamine and redefine processes for leadership development. In his book *Future Perfect*, Stan Davis suggested that in the evolving age of information, the rules of competition will be "any time, any place, no matter."[21] Davis made the point that customers will favor the organization that is able to provide goods or service *whenever and wherever* the consumer wants, *any time, any place*. Those demands pose a significant enough challenge, but the challenge of Davis' third rule, *no matter*, is perhaps even more profound. The world of "matter" as has traditionally been defined in "products" is being more and more defined by information that is collected from or about the consumer or organization for whom a *value* is being provided. The most effective competitors feed this information back to customers along with their products and services, further enhancing the value of the product or service and enabling the customer to leverage their investment. Clearly, this accurately describes the current trend in leadership development.

Assessing Your Own Situation

There is little in the way of bricks or mortar (matter) that can compete with the caliber of good ideas that are discussed and applied to address emerging opportunities for leadership and organizational development. As organizations attempt to map their leadership and organizational development processes against the companies and programs discussed throughout this book, they may wish to ask themselves the following questions.

- Do you recognize leadership development as a competitive capability that can assist in the development, implementation and revitalization of organizational strategy?
- Have you made continuous learning and knowledge creation a core competence?
- Do your leadership development efforts focus on building both the individual talents of leaders and the collective knowledge base of the organization?
- Do you view leadership development as a tool for creating a talent pool of leaders at all levels of the organization?
- Do you view leadership development as a system?
- Do you focus on the leadership development process and not on programs?
- Does your leadership development process blend experience, training, education, and other forms of development into a Knowledge Creation Cycle?
- Do you utilize the real-time solving of real-life business problems as part of your leadership development process?
- Do you make the leadership development part of a consistent HR strategy that blends the processes of recruitment, selection, development, and appraisal into an integrated system for talent pool management?
- Do you view leadership development as a process for the continuous revitalization of your organization?

When an organization can answer "yes" to all of these questions, it is well on its way to joining the ranks of the new paradigm companies that are creating the future for strategic leadership development, companies that are mastering the challenge of crafting competitiveness in a world of change.

Endnotes

1 Vicere, Albert, Maria Taylor, and Virginia Freeman, *Executive Education Major Corporations: An International Study of Executive Development Trends*, Penn State University, 1993, p. 7.

2 See Fulmer, Robert M. and Ken Graham "A New Era of Management Education," *Journal of Management Development*, **12** (3), 1993; also, Vicere Albert A. and Kenneth R. Graham, "Crafting Competitiveness: Toward a New Paradigm For Executive Development," *Human Resource Planning*, **13** (4), 1990, pp. 281–295.

3 See Fulmer, Robert M., "Executive Learning as a Strategic Weapon," *Executive Development*, **3** (3), 1990.

4 Meister, Jeanne C., *Corporate Quality Universities*, New York: Richard D. Irwin, Inc., 1994.

5 Meister, Jeanne C., *Future Directions of Corporate Universities*, UNICON Conference, March 17, 1996, p. 2–5.

6 Miles, Robert H., *Corporate Universities: Some Design Choices and Leading Practices*, Atlanta: Emory Business School, 1993.

7 Vicere, A.A., "A Little Something To Think About," *Journal of Continuing Higher Education*, Fall, 1992, pp. 52–57.

8 "Work-Out Continuous Improvement," unpublished GE document, March 15, 1995.

9 Tichy, N. and S. Sherman, *Control Your Own Destiny Or Someone Else Will*, New York: Currency Doubleday, 1993, pp. 212–213.

10 Senge, Peter M., *et al., The Fifth Discipline Fieldbook*; New York: Doubleday, 1994, pp. 30–37. See also Senge, Peter M., and Robert M. Fulmer, "Simulations, Systems Thinking and Anticipatory Learning," *Journal of Management Development*, **12** (6), 1993.

11 Based on Miles, Robert H., op. cit, pp. 19–22.

12 Harvard Business School Case No. 379–157.

13 Gutman, John A., "Developing Cases and Scenario's for Anticipatory Learning," *Journal of Management Development*, **12**, November 6, 1993, pp. 52–59. See also Gutman, John A., "Creating Scenario's and Cases for Global Anticipatory Learning," *American Journal of Management Development*, **1** (3), 1995.

14 Hamel, G. and C.K. Prahalad, *Competing for the Future*, Boston: *Harvard Business School Press*, 1994.

15 See Ready, D., A. Vicere, and A. White, "Executive Education: Can Universities Deliver? *Human Resource Planning*, **16** (4) 1994, pp. 1–11.

16 See Handy, Charles, *The Age of Unreason*, Boston: Harvard Business School Press, 1990.

17 Porter, Lyman, and Larry McKibbon, *Management Development: Drift or Thrust Into the 21st Century*, McGraw-Hill, 1988.

18 Miles, Robert H., 1993, op. cit., pp. 37–41.

19 Meister, op. cit., p. 7.

20 Davis, Stan and Jim Botkin, *The Monster Under the Bed*, New York; Simon & Schuster, 1994, p. 96.

21 Davis, S., *Future Perfect*, Reading, MA: Addison-Wesley, 1987.

APPENDIX

THE STATE OF THE PRACTICE:
OUR RESEARCH BASE*

In what might be called "The Age of the Learning Organization," the major challenge facing leadership development practitioners may well be coping with closed minds in a world of constant change.[1] Arie de Geus, former head of strategic planning at Royal Dutch Shell, summarized this challenge very well: "Over the long term, the only sustainable competitive advantage may be a corporation's ability to learn faster than its competition. The purpose of planning (at least at Shell) is not to create plans, but to change the way managers see the world."[2]

If de Geus and Shell are right, creating leaders who can build learning-oriented competitive advantage should be a big business. Nohria and Berkley estimated that corporate expenditures for employee education and training have grown from $10 billion to $45 billion during the past decade.[3] In 1996, Jeanne Meister of Quality Dynamics reported that this had grown to over $50 billion.[4] *Business Week*[5] estimated that approximately $12 billion of this amount was devoted to executive education, the traditional vehicle for leadership development. This included corporate investment in university-based open enrollment

* The research effort upon which this appendix is based was partially sponsored by the International University Consortium For Executive Education (UNICON) and the Penn State Institute For the Study of Organizational Effectiveness. It involved a comprehensive review of the literature as well as the collection of interview and/or survey data from an international group of 78 executives from 47 companies, 48 consultants, and 52 university leaders representing 35 business schools throughout the world.

programs, executive MBA programs, company designed and delivered programs, and customized courses developed and taught by business schools and consultants.

Approximately 25 percent of the $12 billion investment in executive education is directed through business schools. University-based executive education at both degree and non-degree levels has become a major source of income for these institutions. In 1994, *Bricker's International Directory* listed 472 executive education programs offered by business schools throughout the world. The price range was from $695 for a three-day course at George Washington University to $50,500 for a nine-month program at Stanford University. A *Wall Street Journal/Bricker* survey in 1994 revealed that costs in general average more than $3700 per week for each participant.[6] In 1992, research at Penn State found that annual corporate executive education expenditures had grown to an average of $2 million per year and the pool of potential attendees within each firm had grown to over 1000. These same firms projected even more dramatic growth in the executive education efforts in the future.[7]

A Big Business That is Good for Business

When asked by *Business Week* in 1991 to rate the return on time and money invested in executive education programs, former program graduates estimated an average return of 81 percent on the cost of attending an executive education session.[8] Motorola reports even more dramatic results. From a forecast budget of $35 million over a five-year period, a sum which Bill Wiggenhorn, President of Motorola University, reported that many people felt excessive, Motorola now spends over $60 million annually for programs, plus an additional $60 million in time spent away from the job.[9] Motorola's emphasis ranges from an intensive program designed to give 400 executives a four-week "MBA" to a $50 million annual commitment to address literacy problems. Perhaps the most dramatic lesson of the Motorola experience is their often quoted statistic that a dollar invested in education and training can yield a return of $33. The details are as follows:

❝ *In those few plants where the work force absorbed the whole curriculum of quality tools and process skills and where senior managers reinforced the training we were getting a $33 return for every dollar spent, including the cost of wages paid while people sat in class.*

Plants that made use of either the quality tools or the process skills but not both, and then reinforced what they taught, broke even.

Finally, plants that taught all or part of the curriculum but failed to reinforce with follow-up meetings and a new, genuine emphasis on quality had a negative return on investment. [10] ❞

Executive education and leadership development can also be good business for organizations and individuals that provide high-quality executive programs. Although few institutions are willing to divulge their profit margins, several leading business schools report that executive education efforts generate from $1 million to $10 million a year in discretionary income for their schools. Professors who excel in executive education may double or triple their teaching income.

However, not everyone is impressed. Jim Baughman, a former Harvard professor, who headed the executive development function at General Electric before assuming responsibility for this function at Morgan Guaranty in 1994, believes that "[University] programs are too long. They're not flexible enough. They're too expensive, and they lack action learning [situations where executives work on real problems to come up with actual solutions which companies can implement]." [11] But while Baughman may be opposed to university-based education as it is traditionally practiced, he has nevertheless utilized many leading faculty members from various business schools around the world in his programs, a fact not lost on today's resource-constrained business school deans.

Business schools have unparalleled access to the basic raw materials for excellence in executive education. Their challenge seems to be managing these materials in a more innovative, flexible manner.

The Current State of the Practice

A recent study documented the fact that total budgets for executive education are growing significantly (see Figure A.1).[12] Most of this growth is for in-company programs that are aimed at a relatively large number of executives. The size of corporate budgets and the number of people who are participating in executive education are indicators of its growing role in helping implement strategic initiatives. Interestingly, the "averages" reported in that study reflect a distribution that is bi-modal. Firms that are typically viewed as being among the best managed, as well as those undergoing major change efforts, often report budgets that are two or three times higher than the average. Conversely, many other firms report relatively small budgets for formal executive education or leadership development.

Over 75 percent of all executive education dollars now go to customized programs, rather than to traditional public or open-enrollment courses offered by business schools and marketed to individuals from a wide variety of companies and countries. Most companies indicate plans to focus even more on customized programs in the future. Firms such as Motorola, Xerox, and General Electric have set up corporate universities to develop and run internal educational programs on a huge scale. ADL (formerly Arthur D. Little Co.), based in Cambridge, Massachusetts, offers an MBA program which is accredited on a regional basis. Coopers & Lybrand has indicated that learning capability is one of the core competencies it wants to develop for internal purposes as well as to deliver to its external clients. A number of other leading firms, including Coca-Cola, British Airways, Digital, and AT&T, either have established or are seriously exploring the possibility of establishing a corporate university.

Since 1982, Jim Bolt of Executive Development Associates (EDA) has conducted a bi-annual survey of the field of management education. In 1993, he reported that the most frequently mentioned core objectives for executive education/leadership development initiatives were to:[13]

- *Address the key business issues/challenges* facing the company (i.e., help to equip leaders with the capabilities needed to address those issues/challenges).

Figure A.1 Analysis of Budget and Eligible Pool for Executive Education

Total Executive Education			
Average total budget $2,058,295			
Median total budget $1,000,000			
In-Company Programs		**University Programs**	
Average in-company budget	$1,439,220	Average university budget	$486,640
Median in-company budget	$571,500	Median university budget	$250,000
Average in-company pool size	1,088	Average university pool	590
Median in-company pool size	700	Median university pool	300
Average budget per person in pool	$2,783	Average budget per person in pool	$2,377
Median budget per person in pool	£1,250	Median budget per person in pool	$756
Average number attending	344	Average number attending	24
Median number attending	200	Median number attending	10
Average budget per participant	$9,146	Average budget per participant	$35,311
Median budget per participant	$5,000	Median budget per participant	$20,000

Source: Vicere, A.A., M. Taylor and V. Freeman, *Executive Education in Major Corporations: An International Study of Executive Development Trends*, Penn State University, 1993, p. 7.

- *Develop shared vision/unity of purpose.* This is a common theme in the survey and also illustrates an important trend. Traditionally executive education was nice to do, but not linked to business strategies and challenges. In the last five to ten years, it has been focused more on helping companies achieve their strategic objectives. What we now see is leadership development being used as a forum to reexamine and/or create vision and strategy.

- *Communicate/implement strategy.* Linked to the above item, we see executive education being used to help create strategic unity, i.e.:
  (1) Create a compelling vision and clear strategies
  (2) Build understanding and commitment to the vision, strategy and values
  (3) Deploy the strategy, resulting in aligned goals and actions throughout the business, and
  (4) Equip leaders with the capabilities designed to achieve the vision, live the values and successfully implement the strategies.
- *Build teamwork and networks.* This objective is becoming more explicit; in the past it was just a welcome side benefit. Now the design of executive education programs often includes elements aimed directly at achieving this objective rather than simply hoping it happens during the breaks and social events.

Development and Delivery Cost

Figure A.2 presents our analysis of reported budgets for development and delivery of one-week executive education/leadership development programs from the standpoint of corporate users as well as responding consulting firm and university providers. The average figures are somewhat distorted because of the inclusion of low priced, packaged programs offered by some consulting firms. In general, for programs that are clearly executive in level and scope, numbers at the top end of the reported ranges are more typical.

Figure A.2 Program Development and Delivery Costs

	Development	*Delivery**
Corporations	$89,000 (75,000–242,000)	$32,880 (20,000–100,000+)
Consulting firms	$33,050 (3,000–129,000)	$34,000 (3,000–70,000+)
Universities	$19,000 (5,000–32,000)	$61,000 (18,000–120,000)

* Average costs followed by range of survey responses

The relatively low figures for development costs reported by consulting firms and universities are surprising but can be explained by the fact that many, perhaps most, organizations have standard programs that they offer as "open-enrollment" programs but which may be "customized" and offered to individual clients with a minimum amount of modification. Customized versions of existing courses can be developed less expensively than courses specifically designed to drive a corporate initiative. True custom programs frequently require a minimum of $100,000 to develop, and often cost significantly more.

Myron Goff, Director of Executive Conference at Johnson & Johnson, makes an important point when he states that:

> ❝ *We [Johnson & Johnson] do not want customized programs; we want custom programs. That basically means we want the program consultant to start from scratch.* ❞

To establish a custom program, consultants start with a series of interviews to collect information about the company and its needs. One recent Johnson & Johnson initiative involved interviews with over a hundred executives in six countries. Original cases and exercises were then developed from that information. In Johnson & Johnson's most recent Executive Conference, ten computerized exercises using *Lotus Notes* and an extensive scenario called "J&J 2002," and a future-oriented, integrative exercise were central to the process.

Our figures suggest that universities tend to be more expensive in delivering a one-week program. However, it is important to look behind the figures. If consulting firms use their own salaried staff to deliver a packaged program on a regular basis, the daily rate for instruction tends to drop significantly. If consulting firms use presenters/facilitators with a world class reputation and ability, their costs are closer to those of business schools. High-visibility consultants or well-known business school professors tend to charge prices that are at least comparable to those charged by universities. In other words, professors may be paid $2500 per day to deliver a program for their university, but charge $5000 or more to do the same kind of program for a company-specific seminar whether they are working directly for the company or for a consulting firm that has put the entire program together for the corporate client.

Principals of consulting firms suggest that their major competitive advantage is not cost but the ability to listen to and respond directly to client requests. Consultants see themselves as being more flexible in drawing resources from a variety of sources and even in their ability to motivate professors to be more adaptive to client requests. For example, corporations offer a typical program twice as often as universities. Several university respondents talked about not wanting to repeat programs several times a year because it would "make undue demands" on their faculty. They also reported that faculty members tend to "get bored if they repeat the same program too many times." Our conclusion is that such boredom occurs only when a business school pays its faculty below-normal market rates. Off-campus, some professors are delivering the same or similar programs between 10 and 50 times per year.

Even though custom/customized programs sound more expensive, it does not necessarily work out that way, especially if an organization plans to send a significant number of executives through a program. For example, the University of Pennsylvania's Wharton School reports that it charges companies an average development fee of $20,000–$25,000 per one-week session. There is no development fee for an established program, but the weekly tuition may run to $4350 per person as opposed to $2500 a week per person for a customized program. Simple arithmetic shows that if a company sends 30 executives to a public program, the total cost for this off-the-shelf initiative is $130,500 compared to a total of $100,000 for a customized program, even with the development costs. That may be why some 60 percent of the 4500–5000 professionals attending executive education courses at Wharton are enrolled in programs sponsored by specific clients.[14]

Some corporations attempt to reduce the cost of a program by contracting directly with individual faculty members rather than engaging a consulting firm or university to coordinate the details of program design and delivery. Of course, the actual savings may be distorted because the figures reported may not include the time of corporate staff which must be allocated to the various aspects of a program.

One final note regarding cost. While it is possible to pay too much for the development and delivery of an executive-level program, our experience indicates that price is seldom the deciding factor – more often, it is the *perceived quality* of the experience, which is often related to the perceived quality of the developers and presenters involved.

Figure A.3 Who Delivers Executive Education/Leadership Development?

	Internal staff/faculty	*Other university professors*	*Non-university presenters*
Consulting firms	81%	8%	11%
Universities	79%	12%	9%

Who Delivers Executive Education/Leadership Development?

Figure A.3 compares the use of faculty/facilitators for executive programs by consulting firms and universities. Surprisingly, the survey indicated that there was little difference in the composition of program faculty. Both groups tended to use their own staff in the programs they deliver.

Although a relatively minor development at this point, there seems to be an increasing number of consulting organizations that have a very small internal staff but a large network of faculty from business schools around the globe who deliver their programs. Executive Development Associates (La Jolla, California) operates with a staff of two but uses faculty and independent consultants from a wide variety of sources. Global Access Learning, Inc. (Atlanta, Georgia) uses a cadre of current and former university professors to design a program, provide course management and deliver some of the content. The firm reports having employed 60 professors from 24 business schools along with 14 independent consultants in a variety of programs during the past decade. In its promotional literature, the firm describes itself as a "virtual business school."

Such access to a wide variety of intellectual resources may emerge as one of the important sources of competitive advantage in the emerging environment.

How Revenues Are Allocated

Figure A.4 compares how consulting firms and universities allocate revenues received from their executive education/leadership develop-

Figure A.4 Allocation of Revenues

	Marketing	Overhead	Delivery by staff	Account mgt.	Course mgt.	Delivery by outsiders	Other
Consultants	9%	16%	34%	10%	8%	15%	8%
Universities	14%	28%	29%	7%	12%	7%	3%

ment activities. Perhaps the most important distinction is that 42 percent of revenues received by universities are allocated to internal activities (marketing and overhead) while only 25 percent of consulting firms' revenues are used for this purpose. This also means that 67 percent of revenues received by consulting firms go into program delivery while only 55 percent of university revenues are allocated to program delivery.

This may be because university executive program operations typically have extensive overhead commitments for residential facilities, classrooms, and related expenses. In addition, the open-enrollment programs they frequently offer as part of their portfolio require an extensive marketing investment. On the other hand, since most consulting firms do not have these overheads, and since the principals of consulting firms are very likely to be involved in the delivery process, they can allocate a greater portion of total revenues to the delivery of the program. This frequently includes paying business school professors more than they receive from their home institution to teach on a program.

One leading corporate practitioner helped put the above comparison into perspective. He noted that the $67,000 consulting fee for a recent senior-level executive/leadership development initiative represented only 65 percent of out-of-pocket costs. That proportion dropped to 50 percent if classroom rental charges were included, and dropped further to 35 percent if hotel costs were included.

Industry Dynamics

The emergence of executive education and leadership development as a lever for strategic change is one of the most significant trends in the field, and we can use industry analysis to look at ways the competitive

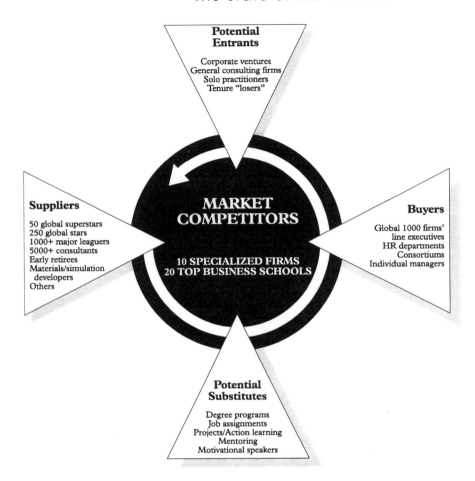

Figure A.5 Forces Driving Competition

environment is changing. As Michael Porter points out in his classic work on competitive forces, "The essence of strategy formulation is coping with competition."[15] Figure A.5 applies Porter's "Forces of Competitive Analysis" to the field of executive education/leadership development.

Competitors

At the present time, the field is dominated by approximately 20 leading business schools and a handful of specialized consulting firms ("new entrants"). These business schools comprise the traditional competitive

Figure A.6 Leading Business Schools in Executive Education

Schools (alphabetical) *	Annual revenue ($ millions)	Five-year growth (%)	Customized programs (%) **	Programs offered
Ashridge Management College	16.1	8	47	110
Columbia	7.0	0	25	39
Cranfield	12.9	105	41	152
Duke (Fuqua)	9.1	44	60	76
Havard	30.1***	20***	5***	28
IMD	23.5	2	44	25
INSEAD	37.0	42	39	124
London Business School	9.9	34	50	13
Michigan	21.5	53	10	63
MIT (Sloan)	8.3	–7***	20	42
Northwestern (Kellogg)	14.0	75	35	42
Pennsylvania (Wharton)	25.0	257	55	100
Penn State (Smeal)	4.2	17	40	38
Southern California	4.4	75	39	35
Stanford	6.9	103	2	10
Thunderbird	6.0	900	55	28
UCLA (Anderson)	8.0	186	29	26
Wisconsin	4.5	72	11	130
Virginia (Darden)	10.5	40	29	454

* *Business Week* lists the Center for Creative Leadership on this list. However, since it is not a business school, we discuss it in our section on "potential entrants."
** Percent of revenues from programs designed specifically for client companies
*** *Business Week* estimates   Source: *Business Week*, October 23, 1995

cohort. Excellence in executive education/leadership development often creates a virtuous cycle for business schools. Corporations typically look to the "best" business schools for assistance with their needs for leadership development. Ambitious business schools often find that a commitment to high-quality executive programs helps build the reputation of their MBA program and its graduates. Several surveys have attempted to establish which schools are the real leaders in the field. A list compiled by *Business Week* appears in Figure A.6.

Figure A.7 Individual Suppliers of Executive Education/Leadership Development

Classification	World total	Daily rates	Days per year
Global superstars	50	$10,000	100+
Global stars	250	$5,000–10,000	75+
Major leaguers	1,000–1,500	$2,500–5,000	50+
Professionals	2,500–5,000	$1,000–2,500	50
Semi-pro	5,000–25,000	Under £1,000	10+

There is intense competition among the major players in this arena. Several less-renowned business schools have dropped programs or have suffered major setbacks in recent years. Emory University, for instance, has dropped its 25-year-old Advanced Management Program. MIT has taken a "hiatus" from general management programs. Most business school programs, even the venerable Harvard AMP, have been shortened in length. As the field of leadership development changes, the university business school cohort is finding itself challenged by a new set of competitive dynamics.

Global dynamics also are playing a part in the emerging competitive environment. While US providers dominate the *Business Week* list, five European institutions are already significant players. In addition, strong new competitors are emerging in Spain and the Scandinavian countries, and significant players are beginning to emerge in the developing nations of the world. The Asian Institute of Management conducts programs throughout the Pacific Rim. INCAE (Costa Rica) offers courses and programs in seven Latin American countries, and has executive education revenues of nearly $10 million per year.

Suppliers

From our standpoint, the major suppliers of executive education/leadership development are the individuals who deliver programs for corporate customers, whether they be university professors or consultants. Figure A.7 summarizes our analysis of this key group.

While exact figures are difficult to develop, our best estimate is that there are about 50 people in the world who are "global superstars." Many are riding the crest of a very successful book and are able to charge prices that range from $20,000 to $50,000 per session for 100+ teaching and/or consulting days per year, working throughout the world. Tom Peters, Ken Blanchard, Steve Covey, and Mike Hammer probably fall into this category. Others, such as Ram Charan or Maurice Saias, bill an incredible number of days each year. A few, including John Kotter of the Harvard Business School and Peter Senge of MIT, charge extremely high rates to limit the number of days they spend on the road. Most academic institutions limit the amount of time that professors are able to spend away from campus. High demand and limited availability can result in daily billing rates of $20,000 or more for the *crème de la crème* of individual faculty suppliers.

There are probably another 250 "global stars" who charge $5000 or more per day and bill at least 75 days per year for a variety of companies around the world. These individuals tend to be as effective as the "superstars" in terms of dealing with clients, but they frequently have done less visible research or lack the popular book which can catapult an author into superstardom.

It appears that $2500 per day or more is the mark of a "major leaguer," especially if the individual is able to generate 50 or more days per year. We believe there are a thousand of these individuals around the world. They will often work a significant number of days for a limited number of clients. In return for guaranteeing a "major leaguer" 20 to 50 days per year, a client gets the services of the individual on a retainer arrangement. These individuals may become a semi-permanent part of their client's staff and have genuine understanding of the corporate strategy, culture and challenges.

Then there are probably another 2500 to 5000 "professionals" that charge between $1000 and $2500 per day and generate $50,000 per year or more as a full-time occupation to supplement their university incomes, or to supplement early retirement pensions. Often, these are former professors who have decided to become independent consultants or individuals who have taken early retirement but maintain a working relationship with their former employer.

Finally, there is a large number of individuals, perhaps 25,000 in total, who tend to work at relatively low rates either to supplement faculty employment or to provide a career that offers a degree of flexibility and independence. These "semi-pros" typically are platform presenters who utilize materials developed by others, but are capable in delivering material to specific audiences.

One of the key challenges to providers of executive education/leadership development is the ability to identify facilitators/educators who have not yet become stars but have the potential to develop this capability. Motorola has done an exceptional job of identifying individuals who have not hit the big time but are very effective teachers and facilitators.

A major new source of potential suppliers is the pool of early retirees from leading business firms. As corporations encourage early retirement to reduce census count and streamline operations, talented, experienced executives are leaving organizations and beginning second careers as independent consultants. To ease the transition into actual retirement, many are able to negotiate consulting contracts with their former employers to provide a few days per month consulting, often in the area of management development or executive education. Hoechst Celanese and General Electric have been quite successful with this concept. As these individuals begin to network more efficiently, they may become significant players in the field.

Another category of suppliers to the executive education/leadership development market are firms that develop, package, and market the materials used in programs, including questionnaires that provide insight into managerial style, organizational culture, or competitive orientation. These materials often are used by consultants and professors as part of standard programs, or by corporate trainers or other managers as an alternative to more traditional programs. Firms that design these materials, like Harbridge House (Boston), Zenger-Miller (San Jose) or Forum (Boston), also put together entire programs on themes such as team effectiveness, quality, customer service, or diversity. These programs may be delivered by consultants associated with the firm that developed the package, or may be sold/licensed to corporations for use in internal programs delivered by company-selected personnel. Frequently, a large-scale, corporate-wide initiative may start with senior-level consultants delivering programs to top executives. As the program cascades throughout the organization, "graduates" of the program may be trained to deliver many of the modules to reduce the cost and to increase the cadre of qualified instructors.

Computerized and non-computerized simulations can be powerful components of a corporate learning experience. Generic simulations often are used to illustrate various aspects of competitive strategy, financial analysis, or leadership styles. Customized simulations can give managers low-risk experience in making decisions that reflect current challenges in the organization's operating environment. If fact, skillfully customized simulations can actually reflect the industry that a participant may be operating within. These kinds of vicarious learning experiences are called "Managerial Practice Fields" by Peter Senge.[16] Senge and the Center for Organizational Learning at MIT are perhaps the best-known academic source of managerial practice fields. The Center for Managerial Learning and Business Simulation at Georgia Southern University also has gained international recognition through the contributions of Bernard Keys who also leads the Association for Business Simulation and Experiential Learning (ABSEL). INSEAD, a leading European business school, has also done an excellent job developing and using simulations for executive education/leadership development. The Strategic Management Group in Philadelphia, Executive Perspectives in Boston, Interpretive Software in Charlottesville, VA, and the Burgundy Group in Colorado Springs are other corporate leaders in the creation of computerized business and management simulations.

Potential Entrants

While there are relatively few firms that actually specialize in customized, high-level executive education/leadership development programs, this is clearly a significant growth area. A list of the non-university providers we studied and their specialties appears in Figure A.8. Revenue assumptions are based on the authors' estimates and have not been verified by every firm.

Recent entrants may illustrate how other non-university competitors may emerge. One of the most successful ventures of this sort, the Center for Executive Development based in Cambridge, Massachusetts is a firm whose partners exclusively are former Harvard Business School professors whose teaching excellence was not rewarded with tenure. During the past five years, CED has probably become a leader in the development and delivery of top-level executive education/leadership development programs. Another emerging player, Global Access Learning Inc., an Atlanta-based firm, has among its principals former professors who gave up tenure, others who decided that academia had

Figure A.8 Key Non-university providers of Executive/Leadership Development

Firm	Location	Speciality	Estimated revenue ($ millions)
Center for Creative Leadership	Greensboro, NC	Leadership, 360-degree feedback	30*
Center for Executive Development	Cambridge, MA	Strategy, leadership and change	10
Covey Leadership Institute	Provo, UT	Leadership/values	90
Executive Development Associates	La Jolla, CA	Global strategy	1.5
Global Access Learning	Atlanta, GA	Leadership development	2.5
Keilty Goldsmith & Company	San Diego, CA	360-degree feedback	11
Pecos River Learning Center	Santa Fe, NM	Outdoor action learning	25
Institute of Mgt. Studies (IMS)	Reno, NV	One-day seminars	5.5
Forum Corporation	Boston, MA	Customer service teams	39.5
Personnel Decisions, Inc.	Minneapolis, MN	Skill development	36.8
Blessing/White Inc.	Princeton, NJ	Personal growth	20.5
Westcott Communications	Carrollton, TX	Distance learning	95
Wilson Learning	Minneapolis, MN	Training	40
Strategic Mgt. Group, Inc.	Philadelphia, PA	Simulations	12
Executrain Corp.	Alpharetta, GA	Computer training	110
Blanchard Training & Development	San Diego, CA	Training	15

* Approximately one-third of CCL's revenue is from customized programs

become "more and more about less and less" and resigned from the tenure race, as well as other professors who continue to maintain academic affiliations.

In conducting interviews throughout the world, we were amazed at how many universities had stories about the "best teacher award curse." Significant numbers of "best teachers" wind up failing to generate the publication record required for tenure. Consequently, universities sometimes launch talented competitors by denying tenure to their best executive educators. Hence, they retain excellent researchers but have relatively few individuals who are able to meet the special challenges of the executive-level classroom.

Traditional views on research and tenure seem to be shifting, however, as leading business schools such as Northwestern, Michigan, Duke, Cornell, and the University of Southern California experiment with a category of faculty members often called *clinical* appointments. Sometimes these individuals have been given five-year contracts without tenure. They may have regular academic teaching assignments, but more typically have a specific level of responsibility for executive education and occasionally MBA teaching. They may have little other involvement with the university other than participating in executive education. For example, before joining GE on a full-time basis in 1994, Steve Kerr lived in Los Angeles, had a contract to spend 10 weeks each year at the University of Michigan doing executive education, and still did a number of consulting days with GE through his private practice. Kerr exemplifies a new breed of practitioner/academic who partners with a university and with a series of clients to extend the capabilities of each.

In the UK, several schools, such as Manchester and Ashridge employ a core faculty that is widely supplemented with a variety of associate faculty or visiting professors who may teach in several executive programs or merely serve as an occasional guest lecturer. With the advent of the virtual corporation, consultants and professors are in the process of creating "virtual business schools." Without bricks, mortar, or significant capital investment, some firms are able to call upon exceptionally talented resources throughout the world. Keilty, Goldsmith & Company describes itself as a firm of 17 principals and approximately 50 associates with absolutely no overhead. While various partners and associates have overhead expenses with their individual practice, the firm itself operates with zero commitment to support staff and other administrative overhead. As mentioned previously, one firm uses the term "virtual business school" in its promotional literature.

General consulting firms seem to be busy enough dealing with strategic management issues and have yet to make a major move into the executive education/leadership development field.[17] As the lines between consulting and education continue to blur, this could change. JMW Consultants (Stamford, CT) have identified leadership development as a means of enhancing relationships developed through consulting, and plan to leverage educational activities to expand their consulting practice. Other firms like Arthur Andersen and McKinsey have the resources to become significant players in executive education and leadership development. To date, however, they have not judged these activities to be as profitable as their traditional consulting practice. That may be due to the fact that it is nearly impossible to hire freshly minted MBAs who can manage the demands of the corporate learning laboratory. As discussed previously, individuals who are skilled in this area command much higher levels of compensation than do new MBAs. As a result, many general consulting firms do not see the potential margins they seek in the field. Nevertheless, firms that specialize in the executive/leadership development arena often talk, off the record, of margins that exceed 40 percent.

Some corporations have become so proficient at their own internal education programs that they have begun to market them to suppliers and to the public. After receiving favorable coverage in *In Search of Excellence*,[18] Walt Disney University opened its doors to firms of all types, and Disney is actively investigating further opportunities in the field. IBM's Skill Dynamics at one time planned to utilize experienced IBM educators in a separate business unit providing educational services to other corporations, but the project was cancelled in 1994.

Potential Substitutes

The advent of the Executive MBA program – wherein mid-career individuals, usually with ten years' experience, complete a regular MBA curriculum while maintaining a full-time job – provides another rapidly growing area of the field that is supplanting more traditional methods. Pioneered by the University of Chicago and Wharton, these programs are now offered in most schools accredited by the American Assembly of Collegiate Schools of Business (AACSB). The concept of Executive MBA programs is now spreading throughout Europe and Latin America.

In April, 1996, one US consulting firm was conducting a feasibility study to determine the potential of creating an independent business school that offered, on a for-profit basis, an Executive MBA program. The firm was considering the use of an international faculty from a variety of institutions, interactive technology and action learning components. A measure of whether or not this particular project has been successful will probably be a future growth in the number of business schools that are not affiliated with any traditional universities. Already such major players as IMD, INSEAD, INCAE, Ashridge and Thunderbird operate without university ties. Some UK schools, such as London Business School and Manchester, already operate with considerably more independence than their US counterparts. As business schools are asked to enter into more "partnership" arrangements with their corporate clients, the lines between business schools will continue to become more blurred.

Another area where business schools are offering competition to their own traditional executive education program is through the creation of university research centers. The Center for Effective Organization (CEO) at the University of Southern California led by Ed Lawler, a recognized leader in the area of participative management, conducts courses and programs for its members that could just as well be offered by the executive education arm of the University. MIT's official Office of Executive Education does not offer customized programs, yet, the Organizational Learning Center at MIT offers a series of courses on the "Core Competencies of the Learning Organization" for its members. It also designs comprehensive programs in systems thinking, dialogue, mental models and other aspects of the five disciplines articulated by Peter Senge in his landmark book, *The Fifth Discipline*.[19] Reportedly, Electronic Data Systems (EDS) recently invested $740,000 on a seven-month program for 35 people who are pioneers in changing the company's culture. The extent of these types of activities is such that one university-based executive program director commented, "Our dean would be amazed at how much executive education is being done on this campus that he is not receiving his percentage on."

Executive education itself is a relatively small part of the leadership development process. Most organizations recognize that only 10 to 20 percent of a person's preparation for top management will come through educational activities. The overall objective of the varied activities associated with leadership development is to "grow" individuals who have the experience, wisdom and insight to move their organizations successfully into the future. Consequently, job assignments and mentoring are key elements of the process but are seldom discussed in an analysis of the subject. Formal budgets are seldom directed to these activities. Yet, they are probably the most significant part of the overall development process. As the emphasis on real-time, hands-on leadership development initiatives continues to grow, these areas may well receive more attention within the corporate community.

As firms look for more efficient ways to achieve objectives, action-learning projects can be used to replace consulting assignments traditionally given to outside individuals and firms. Naturally, it is not in consulting firms' short-term interest to emphasize this trend. However, when this practice becomes more widespread and more widely recognized, we believe corporations will question the decision to spend several million dollars for outsiders to do work that could be performed by high-potential executives from within the organization who have been given appropriate coaching and direction. At that point, the impact on both the executive/leadership development and traditional consulting markets will be significant.

Customers

Most of the corporate buyers for custom or customized executive/leadership development programs are among the Global 1000 firms. The costs of developing and delivering a custom program makes the ticket for admission too high for many smaller firms. At the same time, executives from medium-sized firms and from emerging companies and countries are rapidly becoming a core source of enrollment for the public programs offered by university business schools.

In many instances, a strategic initiative championed by a corporate executive is the impetus for a customized program. In fact, consultants and university executive education directors agree that the chances for significant impact are much greater if they are able to have an initiative sponsored by the CEO or by senior line executives within a firm. On the other hand, provider selection is typically handled by human resource executives. As one consultant described it,

" I want to get to the top person in the organization, but I don't want to upset the HR executive in that process. The HR person may not be able to make a major initiative happen, but he or she has the ability to shoot me out of the saddle if I haven't played the game appropriately. "

A new approach to the buying process, pioneered by Babson College, is the "consortium." This new model typically features a team of consultants, usually university-based faculty, who link together with several non-competing corporations. These corporate "members" have agreed to work over an extended period of time to create executive/leadership development initiatives that specifically address the collective objectives of the corporate membership. Although universities have been slow to embrace this concept, a few schools have been successful with consortia. The University of Indiana, for example, has focused its efforts on this distinctive niche. According to Cam Danielson, Director of the Indiana program, most of these projects have led to more detailed involvement in consulting or ongoing coaching for the faculty members who participated in the on-campus sessions. Atlanta's Emory University has just inaugurated a consortium program that was put together through the initiative of Ed Adison, CEO of the Southern Company, but involving several other leading Atlanta firms.

The Strategic Transnational Executive Programme (STEP), coordinated by Olle Bovin of International Leadership (Switzerland) and Maurice Saias, Institut d'Administration des Enterprises, Aix-en-Provence (France), is perhaps the most successful consortium program for Senior Executives in Europe. It has been running since 1983 and has included such members as Volvo/Renault, Wartsila, Midland Bank, Alcatel, Hewlett-Packard, Shell, ABB and Tetra-Laval. Each initiative is viewed as a joint venture of five or six non-competing member firms. Each firm nominates four or five participants per year, appoints a senior executive to serve as sponsor, and identifies "challenge work" projects for their participants to address during the program. The programs consist of three modules of five days each conducted over a full year. Historically, the three modules have been offered in Europe, however, plans call for expanding the programs to include at least one module in North America.

The corporate community also seems to be embracing the idea of collaboration among executive development providers. In planning an initiative for 800 mid-level managers at Hoechst Celanese, one of the key requirements for identifying contractors was a "willingness to partner." One of the potential suppliers being interviewed mentioned that the project's scope was beyond their capacity and recommended partnering with another firm based in a different city. The term "partnering" excited the evaluation committee, since most of the universities and firms they had talked with seemed to be focused only on pushing their own ideas and resources. The willingness of two potential competitors to collaborate became the key point in the selection decision.

Open-enrollment programs will continue to serve the specific career development needs of individual managers. While public programs offered by universities are the largest source of these individual initiatives, organizations such as the American Management Association (AMA), the Young Presidents Organization (YPO), and Management Centre Europe provide many programs for their members. Additionally, the Institute for Management Studies (IMS), headquartered in Reno, Nevada, offers programs in 25 North American and European cities for managers who work for any of their 454 corporate members. A number of the leading individual suppliers of executive education/leadership development offer one-day programs through IMS on a variety of subjects. Trade and professional associations also tend to provide various firms of executive education/leadership development. Because of their involvement with an industry or profession, they often are able to focus effectively on the special needs of their members.

The American Society of Association Executives (ASAE) offers a wide range of programs to increase the proficiency and professionalism of the professional staff that manage trade, professional and individual membership organizations. The management development programs offered by the Atlanta-based Life Office Management Association (LOMA) are another example of how industry associations provide executive/leadership development opportunities.

What's Ahead?

We now describe the trends we observed in our research and make a number of predictions about the immediate future of executive and leadership development. One of the early reviewers of this manuscript reminded us of the Chinese proverb, "it is very difficult to make predictions … especially about the future." In reality, it is very easy to make predictions about the future, it's just difficult to be right with any degree of consistency. We look forward to the challenge of reviewing these predictions when the 20th century comes to a close, in just a few short years.

Trend 1: More Customized, Strategic Programs

As executive/leadership development comes of age, it is increasingly viewed as a key lever for strategic change rather than a series of disconnected programs and initiatives. As such, generic programs are becoming less and less appropriate. Consequently, corporations are demanding programs that support their specific strategic objectives, reflect their vision or values, and involve a critical mass of key players.

As previously stated, over 75 percent of all executive-education dollars go toward custom or customized programs rather than to public or open-enrollment courses. To provide examples of the scale and scope of custom/customized initiatives, two mammoth projects and two significant, but smaller, initiatives are summarized in the following paragraphs.

Work-Out at General Electric   In their *Handbook for Corporate Revolutionaries*, Tichy and Sherman suggested that in a country or company, revolution requires control of the police, the schools, and the media.[20] The key to "organizational revolution" is not simply structural change, but *cultural* change as well. To successfully complete a revolution in a corporate setting, "revolutionaries" must shrewdly use rewards and punishment (the police) to shape behavior. Instigators of change also need to maintain control over the educational system (the schools) and the media (corporate communications) to drive and institutionalize strategic change initiatives. In an increasingly competitive global environment, contemporary corporations are using all three levers to try to make their organizations become faster, leaner, smarter, and more innovative.

At GE, Tichy's leadership of the Crotonville Executive Education operation was critical to CEO Jack Welch's corporate revitalization effort. Welch, upon taking the reigns at GE, recognized that despite being one of the world's most successful organizations, GE had to make dramatic changes if it was to remain competitive in the global marketplace. He recruited approximately 20 business school professors and top-flight consultants to initiate the highly lauded "Work-Out" effort. Work-Out is a forum in which "participants get a mental workout. They take unnecessary work out of their jobs, and they work out problems together."[21]

One report on how the Work-Out name was generated suggests that Professor Kirby Warren of Columbia University jokingly asked Welch after a breakfast meeting, "Now that you have gotten so many people out of the organization [at this point over 100,000 workers had been cut], when are you going to get some of the work out?" The creative Welch picked up on the phrase because it not only suggested the possibility of eliminating work but also suggested the imagery of a physical workout whereby a flabby organization might become more fit. Work-Out became a transformational initiative at GE and the concept has been widely emulated elsewhere.

First announced in early 1989, the program involved town meetings of 40 to 100 employees picked by management from all ranks and functions. As a first step in the three-day sessions, a member of the management team set up the agenda, which could be summarized as "the challenge of eliminating unnecessary work." In the next step, after the "boss" disappeared, the participants worked in smaller groups to tackle different parts of the agenda. For a day and a half, the groups discussed complaints, debated solutions, and eventually prepared presentations. On the third day they presented their proposals to management who were held accountable for responding to and acting on the participants' recommendations.[22]

The Work-Out process has been very successful. Not only has it contributed to GE's competitiveness but, more importantly, it has also fostered a sense of trust between the rank and file and management by providing all employees with an avenue to raise their concerns and voice their suggestions on improving the company's performance.

Philips' Centurion Project   Executive and leadership development were also recognized as powerful levers for change by another corporate giant. At troubled Philips International N.V., CEO Jan Timmer recognized the potential of using the function as a catalyst for a massive turnaround effort called "Operation Centurion."

In early 1990, after several years of losing money and market share, Philips went through the greatest crisis in its existence. Its share price dropped to an all-time low and within several months Timmer had been named the company's new chief executive officer.[23] By this time, external and internal factors had led to such deterioration of the company's financial and competitive positions that a detailed investigation concluded the organization's future was "hopeless." Confronted with Philips' dire situation, the newly-appointed CEO developed a dramatic plan, Operation Centurion, to engage the organization in a drastic change process including both cost-cutting and building internal capabilities. The key threads of the effort were restructuring and revitalization through cascading initiatives that generated consensus and commitment to an urgently felt agenda for change.[24]

The Operation Centurion communication process involved top-down Centurion Sessions and bottom-up Town Meetings. The former consisted of three-day meetings of 30 to 70 individuals from the top levels of the company. The first step was to familiarize the group with the real state of the business. Subsequently, participants were encouraged to list the most important issues facing the company. The next phase was to present the group with approaches for "building a winning organization." This was designed to help them formulate and build commitment to "stretch targets" for improving the business. The last step involved project formulation and action planning.

In the first top-level sessions, a decision and commitment to cut the workforce by some 45,000 people was reached collectively by 120 people, rather than being dictated by the board. This communication process was then "cascaded downward" in similar three-day sessions with large groups at lower levels, where specific targets were discussed to help generate acceptance throughout the organization. The three-day sessions were followed up by meetings four to six months later to review the implementation of change projects and to plan the next stages.

Town Meetings, the second part of the communications process, involved much larger groups – up to 400 employees – from operator level to senior management. These meetings provided a forum for discussions on how to improve business performance and led to a significant number of practical suggestions for positive organizational change.

Timmer's Centurion project has been quite successful. Philips' financial performance has improved steadily and significantly despite a recession-plagued industry. As Sumantra Ghoshal and Christopher Bartlett pointed out in *Linking Organizational Context and Managerial Action*,[25] the specific decisions to dramatically cut employee headcount and working capital were key; however, these business actions worked in conjunction with "deeper, less visible" changes in the internal environment. Many of the people involved in the turnaround effort emphasized that the cultural changes were at least as important. As a junior employee explained: "What matters most is that the smell of the place has changed. I now enjoy coming to work. It's not one thing, but overall it's become a very different company."[26]

Smaller Projects With Impact   Although not as dramatic as in the two cases mentioned above, a significant cultural shift was precipitated at Bertlesmann Music Group, a privately owned division of the German media powerhouse, when it acquired RCA and Arista Records from GE in 1986. A clash of cultures seemed unavoidable. To prevent this from materializing, CEO Michael Dornemann, International President Rudi Gasner, and Joe Isenstein, Senior Vice President of Human Resources, created a one-week leadership development program for key executives. The program reinforced Bertlesmann's corporate philosophy of teamwork and partnership. It combined the efforts of four senior corporate executive speakers and business school professors from Columbia, William & Mary, UCLA, Emory, and Aix-en-Provence. Over the past six years, program offerings have alternated between Europe and the US, and now are part of the corporate enculturation process as new executives are brought into the growing concern.

At Johnson & Johnson, Chairman Ralph Larsen became concerned that the world's largest and most diverse healthcare products company might become complacent because of its past successes. Previously, the company had conducted "Executive Conference," a very successful, three-year executive education initiative focused on competitive analysis. To build on this success, Larsen created a high-level working committee to create a new Executive Conference program designed to challenge complacency and to stretch the thinking horizons of his top 700 executives. The consulting team responsible for this project interviewed over 100 executives in six countries. Eventually the Corporate Working Committee identified the theme as "Creating Our Future."

Part of this program involved groups of executives from around the world working together for one week under the guidance of outside consultants to create or invent a future to which they could feel committed. The program concluded with presentations of the team's recommendations to a member of the Executive Committee. These presentations were transcribed and circulated, along with the presentation overheads, to all the members of the corporate Executive Committee on a regular basis. Within the first year, company executives could identify multiple business initiatives that had begun as a result of suggestions made during the program and from a top-level effort that parallelled the program.

Trend 2: Shorter, More Focused, Large-Scale, Cascaded Programs

With almost universal corporate pressure to do more with less, executive educational/leadership development initiatives are being designed to reduce their major cost, that is, managers' time away from their jobs. This is especially essential as larger numbers of people are involved in programs in order to have company-wide impact in shifting strategic directions or changing corporate cultures. There appears to be widespread recognition that many vertical slices rather than one thin horizontal slice of the organization must be involved in executive/leadership development efforts to have significant impact.

A leader in developing shorter, more focused programs is Keilty, Goldsmith & Company. Since 1981, KGC has served a variety of companies by specializing in helping "organizations achieve their vision and live their values by developing leaders in a manner that meets their organizations' unique needs."[27] KGC clients include BellSouth, General Electric, McKinsey and Company, and Texaco. At BellSouth they were responsible for developing the "Leadership Inventory Process," a mechanism for leaders to receive feedback on their perceived effectiveness in living BellSouth's vision and values. The program was delivered to the top 1500 executives in the organization. At General Electric, KGC was responsible for a part of four different leadership programs at Crotonville. They have developed leadership inventories for General Electric and have trained 2000 of GE's leaders throughout the US. At the premier management consulting firm, McKinsey and Company,

KGC developed a feedback process that is currently being used on an ongoing basis by McKinsey Partners and Directors around the world.[28]

A typical format for KGC is to begin an initiative with a two-day orientation and a customized 360-degree feedback exercise. Participants receive evaluative reports based on questionnaires completed by their boss, their peers, and their subordinates. In other words, participants get a picture of how they are perceived by individuals above, below and around them in terms of how well they demonstrate the values and competencies sought by their company. Six months after the initial two-day program, the group reassembles for another one-day session designed to reinforce action plans that participants developed based on their initial feedback. One year after the initial session, participants return for a second dose of 360-degree feedback, hoping to have made progress in at least two or three of the major variables identified as areas for improvement during the initial session.

The Center for Creative Leadership in Greensboro, NC, is probably the world leader in the use of 360-degree feedback for executives, and its "Benchmarks" may be the most widely used profile. The Center's strength is its tremendous database compiled from information provided by managers around the world. However, a negative aspect of this strength is the fact that programs built around this profile are not as customized as those from some other providers like KGC.

An even more dramatic example of scope is offered by the Pecos River Learning Center, founded by Larry Wilson, the dynamic entrepreneur who recently sold his Wilson Learning Corporation. While the Pecos River group can bring their unique business enhancement programs to almost any city in North America, Europe, or Asia, PRLC encourages clients to visit the "largest permanent training site in the enchanting state of New Mexico," some 30 miles north of Santa Fe. The land surrounding this site often served as a gathering place where Native American tribes met to make agreements. PRLC attempts to carry this tradition forward by "helping companies to reach agreements, take action, and move into a successful future."

A typical Pecos River Learning Center program is three days long and covers the following areas:

1 Team building and strategic planning for small companies or individual departments.

2 Experiential outdoor adventure program for individuals and teams who want to discover their potential.
3 A taste of the PRLC curriculum and teaching techniques which can be customized to meet specific corporate needs.

During the startup phase of Saturn, General Motors believed that success depended on retraining tradition-bound GM employees to work as teams, to solve problems creatively, to master quality principles and to bridge the traditional chasm between union and management. As part of the effort to achieve this transformation, Saturn partnered with Pecos River Learning Center to build a training facility near their Tennessee complex and design a curriculum for all employees. Over 2500 manufacturing team members attended the three-day "Playing to Win" course. Additionally, a two-day program was designed for marketing and retail managers, and a five-day introduction was created for Saturn's five hundred dealers.

Many business schools and other consulting firms use similar "adventure learning programs," but no one seems to approach the same level of volume as the Pecos River Learning Center.

Trend 3: More Action-Learning Projects with Measurable Results

The ultimate test of relevance is the ability to observe and measure significant change. As we have seen, Motorola has led the way with its research indicating that targeted educational efforts can generate better than a 30:1 return within three years.[29] Moreover, the Work-Out program at General Electric and the Centurion Project at Philips are examples of efforts that were designed to apply concepts introduced in the corporate classroom to real-life situations in measurable ways.

Obviously, this trend calls for a totally new outlook on executive education/leadership development. Professors are less able to rely on notes developed several years ago. The analysis of cases originally written in the 1970s, even though classic, becomes much less relevant than the application of concepts to contemporary issues. History is not likely to maintain the interest of today's executive-level audiences who are much more interested in thinking about how to shape the future. These executives are much more driven by *action*, which is why action-learning approaches are gaining such widespread interest. Action learning is a hands-on, applications-driven, real-world approach to executive/leadership development in which participants actively diagnosis, discuss, and resolve actual business challenges as part of the developmental initiative.[30]

Corporate, university, and consultant respondents to our survey agreed the majority of their new initiatives were relying less on classroom time led by a professor and more on facilitated, small group, action-learning applications. This is not just a question of how time is divided between lecture, discussion, and case analysis. Rather, classroom time increasingly is being seen as a way of illustrating a concept, or developing tools, which then must be applied to a current challenge or issue on a real-time basis as part of the developmental experience. In fact, several firms, such as the Swedish MiL Institute, view the action-learning approach as their specialty.

In this arena, corporations such as General Electric and Philip Morris have emerged as leaders in making executive education and leadership development a hands-on process. British business schools have been much more innovative than their American counterparts in designing programs that take the learner out of the classroom and into the real world, often the corporate sponsor of the program. In fact, MBA programs in several British institutions have strong action-learning components. Manchester, Oxford, Cambridge, Ashridge, and Henley programs all utilize classroom sessions interspersed with application projects. This means that an executive-level student will spend more time learning on the job than on the university campus.

Conclusions

We can see, then, that executive education and leadership development are evolving towards a systems perspective, a recognition that training or education alone cannot develop a leader, nor can assignments without adequate coaching and career plans, nor can experiences that are unrelated to corporate strategic objectives. Having the right people ready to assume new responsibilities at the right time requires the integration of *all* of the above activities into a leadership development system that provides momentum for the overall growth and development of the entire organization.

> Corporations are recognizing the power of executive education and leadership development initiatives as part of a system that can help align managers, workers, and organizational processes in pursuit of strategic objectives.

This means the field is changing. The traditional objectives of improving the knowledge and broadening the perspectives of participants are disappearing and contemporary leadership development initiatives are more likely to focus on "improving customer satisfaction ratings by 20 percent" and "opening up new markets among emerging economies." Measurement has long been the most difficult and challenging aspect of the field since traditional programs were primarily knowledge based. Contemporary programs tend to be more activity- or challenge-oriented. As a result, outcomes are easier to measure. As a further result, future initiatives are likely to be even more focused on real-world, hands-on learning and measurable output.

Endnotes

1 Fulmer, R.M. "Executive Learning As A Strategic Weapon," *Executive Development*, **3** (3), 1990, p. 23. See also Senge, P. and R.M. Fulmer, "Simulations, Systems Thinking, and Anticipatory Learning," *Journal of Management Development*, **12** (6), 1993, p. 21.
2 de Geus, A. "Planning as Learning," *Harvard Business Review*, March–April, 1988, pp. 70–74.
3 Nohria, Nitin and J.D. Berkley "Whatever Happened To The Take-Charge Manager?" *Harvard Business Review*, January–February, 1994, p. 130.
4 Meister, Jeanne, "Future Directions of Corporate Universities," March 17, 1996, presentation to the International University Consortium for Executive Education.
5 Bongiorno, Lori "Corporate America's New Lesson Plan," *Business Week*, October 25, 1993, p. R4.

6 Fuchsberg, G. "Taking Control," *Wall Street Journal*, September 10, 1993, p. R4.

7 Vicere, A.A., M. Taylor, and V. Freeman, *Executive Education in Major Corporations: An International Study of Executive Development Trends*, Penn State University, 1993, p. 7.

8 Bongiorno, op. cit.

9 Wiggenhorn, W. "Motorola University: When Training Becomes an Education," *Harvard Business Review*, July–August, 1994, p. 72.

10 Ibid., pp. 75–76.

11 Quoted in Bongiorno, op. cit.

12 Vicere, *et al.*, op. cit.

13 Bolt, J. *1993 Survey of Executive Education Trends*, La Jolla, CA: Executive Development Associates, 1993, pp. 7–8.

14 Tichy, N.M. and S. Sherman, *Control Your Destiny Or Someone Else Will*, New York: Doubleday, 1993.

15 Porter, M. "How Competitive Forces Shape Strategy, *Harvard Business Review*, March–April 1979, pp. 137–145.

16 Senge, P. *The Fifth Discipline*, New York: Doubleday, 1990.

17 See Byrne, J. "The Craze for Consultants," *BusinessWeek*, July 25, 1994, pp. 60–66.

18 Peters, T. and R. Waterman, *In Search of Excellence*, New York: Harper & Row, 1982, pp. 167–168.

19 Senge, P., op. cit., pp. 40–45.

20 Tichy, N.M. and S. Sherman, *Handbook for Corporate Revolutionaries*.

21 Stewart, T.A. "GE Keeps Those Ideas Coming," *Fortune*, 12, 1991, p. 42.

22 Ibid., pp. 42–43.

23 The following section is largely based on: Freedman, N.J. "The Transformation of Philips: What Have We Learned About Learning," unpublished manuscript, Philips International N.V., 1994, p. 3.

24 Ibid., p. 4.

25 Ghoshal, S. and C. Bartlett, *Linking Organizational Context and Managerial Action*, Fountainebleau, France: INSEAD Working Paper, 1994, p. 6.

26 Ibid.

27 Keilty, Goldsmith & Company, *Keilty, Goldsmith & Company and the Leadership Excellence Process*, San Diego, CA: KGC, 1994.

28 Ibid.

29 *BusinessWeek*, March 28, 1994, p. 158.

30 See *The Journal of Management Development*, **12** (2), 1993, a special issue focused on action-learning techniques.

INDEX